ENGLAND & WALES
ISLAND
BAGGING

ENGLAND & WALES
ISLAND
BAGGING

A GUIDE TO ADVENTURES ON THE ISLANDS OF ENGLAND,
WALES, THE CHANNEL ISLANDS & THE ISLE OF MAN

LISA DREWE

Vertebrate Publishing, Sheffield
www.v-publishing.co.uk

ENGLAND & WALES
ISLAND
BAGGING

A GUIDE TO ADVENTURES ON THE ISLANDS OF ENGLAND,
WALES, THE CHANNEL ISLANDS & THE ISLE OF MAN

First published in 2021 by Vertebrate Publishing.

VERTEBRATE PUBLISHING
Omega Court, 352 Cemetery Road, Sheffield S11 8FT, United Kingdom.
www.v-publishing.co.uk

A CIP catalogue record for this book is available from the British Library.

ISBN 978-1-83981-090-9 (Paperback)
ISBN 978-1-83981-091-6 (Ebook)

Front cover: Porth Twr Bach (Ynys Llanddwyn / Llanddwyn Island).
Back cover: L–R: La Coupée (Sark); Ynys Llanddwyn / Llanddwyn Island; barn owl (Havergate Island); gig races (St Mary's);
Old Harry Rocks; tombolo (Burgh Island); view of Mumbles Head from Middle Head; Hilbre Island.
Photography by Lisa Drewe except where otherwise credited.

Mapping contains OS data © Crown copyright and database right (2021)
and Openstreetmap.org data © OpenStreetMap contributors.
Cartography by Richard Ross, Active Maps Ltd. *www.activemaps.co.uk*

Design by Jane Beagley, production by Cameron Bonser, Vertebrate Publishing.

Printed and bound in Europe by Latitude Press.

Vertebrate Publishing is committed to printing on paper from sustainable sources.

Every effort has been made to achieve accuracy of the information in this guidebook. The authors, publishers and
copyright owners can take no responsibility for: loss or injury (including fatal) to persons; loss or damage to property
or equipment; trespass, irresponsible behaviour or any other mishap that may be suffered as a result of following the
route descriptions or advice offered in this guidebook. The inclusion of a track or path as part of a route, or otherwise
recommended, in this guidebook does not guarantee that the track or path will remain a right of way. If conflict with
landowners arises we advise that you act politely and leave by the shortest route available. If the matter needs to be
taken further then please take it up with the relevant authority. **Landing is not permitted on some of the islands;** they can
only be viewed from paths on the mainland or from other islands. There may also be restrictions at certain times of the
year due to wildlife. See access details for the islands for further information.

Opposite Teän, view from the high point

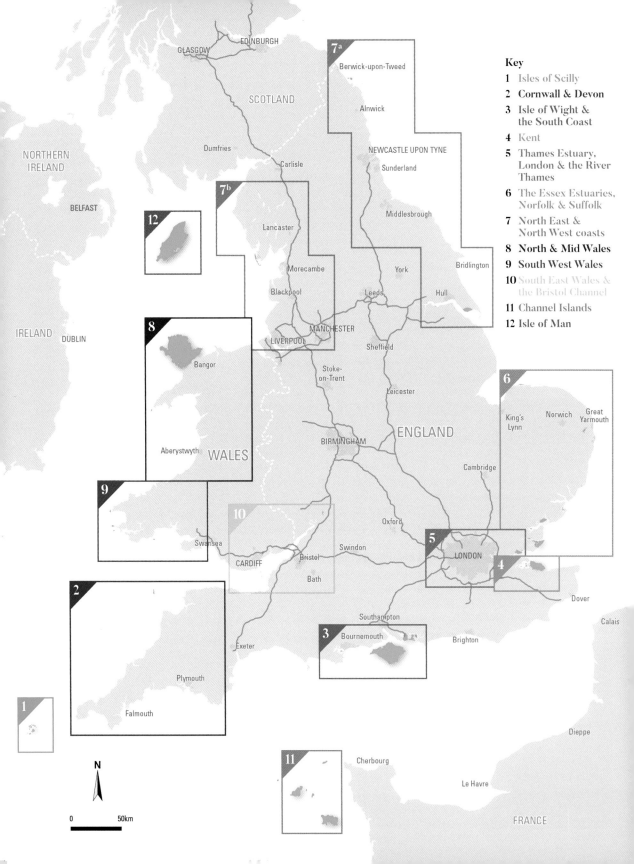

Key

1 Isles of Scilly
2 **Cornwall & Devon**
3 **Isle of Wight & the South Coast**
4 Kent
5 **Thames Estuary, London & the River Thames**
6 **The Essex Estuaries, Norfolk & Suffolk**
7 **North East & North West coasts**
8 **North & Mid Wales**
9 **South West Wales**
10 South East Wales & the Bristol Channel
11 **Channel Islands**
12 **Isle of Man**

Introduction

The magic of islands

Close your eyes and imagine an island. What do you see? Maybe a sweep of dazzling white sand, fringed by palms, and a hammock swaying gently in the breeze, surrounded by clear, warm seas. Vibrant communities and smiling locals with an enviably slow pace of life. An adventure set in a far-flung place. Enjoying wonderful seafood under starlit skies, with a Milky Way so vast that you feel a part of it. One thing is for sure – just thinking about an island will bring a smile to your face.

Now how many of those islands of your imagination do you think could be in England, Wales, the Channel Islands and the Isle of Man? You may be surprised to know that almost all of your imaginary places are. Yes, even if you were thinking sun-warmed pools, subtropical plants, hammocks on deserted beaches, tales of pirates, exotic wildlife, the friendliest of welcomes and adventure like no other. I have explored nearly 500 islands of the British Isles over the last twelve years. I find them completely irresistible. I spend my time poring over Ordnance Survey maps and scouring coastlines to find new ones to visit. Believe me, these are special and wild places and they sit just off our shores, just waiting to be discovered by those seeking new possibilities for beauty, nature and culture. This book has been written as a guide for you to visit and experience the best of them. They are waiting to share their magic.

The islands of England, Wales, the Channel Islands and the Isle of Man

Many authors have used different definitions of what an island is. For inclusion in this book an island is defined as: land of any nature that is touched by salt water and surrounded by water at high tide. This means that around 300 islands are included (approximately 200 in England, 70 in Wales and 40 in the Crown Dependencies of the Channel Islands and the Isle of Man).

They vary from larger, populated islands like Anglesey, Portsea, Jersey and the Isle of Man to islands with smaller tight-knit communities and remote, uninhabited rocky islets. Some are in the large river estuaries of the Thames, Severn and Humber and close to great cities; others are in stunning natural harbours including Poole Harbour, the largest in Europe. Many are on the coastal fringes of England and Wales where the full effects of the mighty Atlantic Ocean are strikingly evident in their landscapes. Wherever these islands are, one thing is for certain; each and every one of them is unique and special, crafted from geology, oceans, tides and human inhabitation since the dawn of time.

Geologically, our islands are some of the most fascinating places to visit in the world. Some offer the globe's most ancient rocks exposed on their coastlines; on others you can place each foot on separate tectonic plates, see cooled lava that originated from underwater vents or hunt fossils and jet (a rare gemstone derived from wood) along the shoreline. Sea erosion and geology together have created the fabulous sea caves of Sark, their walls resplendent with marine life, as well as the iconic chalk stacks of The Needles and Old Harry Rocks and the bird-filled sea stacks of Holy Island, off Anglesey. Cei Ballast, in North Wales, is made from rocks from across the globe which have been deposited over time to create a man-made island.

The oceans themselves have shaped islands by playing with the underlying rock over millennia. The Isles of Scilly and Burry Holms, in South West Wales, give an impactful insight into the effects of rising sea levels. Once high points amid vast grass plains, and used by ancient man as burial grounds, their peaks are now islands surrounded by the ocean, their ancient stories told through archaeological finds of Bronze Age graves and Iron Age homes. Sea levels affect other islands in different ways too; without human intervention many islands in the estuaries of Essex and Kent would be underwater, lost to the oceans years ago. Today, man wages a constant battle to keep water ingress at bay. All except Wallasea Island, that is, where sea walls have been removed and the land flooded to create new habitats in the hope that lost and dwindling species of bird will revive. It's not just the sea levels that have shaped the islands, though. The ocean's explosive power has carved out new islands within the timeline of humans living on earth, as evidenced by the many promontory forts in Wales, once part of the mainland and now tiny rocky islands. Oceans continue to reclaim and create new land. Spurn Head, for example, only became an island in 2013 and is the newest island in this book.

Tides shape these special places too. The waters of the Humber, Thames and Essex estuaries continue a process of building, eroding and redefining the boundaries of their islands. The Bristol Channel, with the second largest tidal rage in the world, creates the extraordinary natural spectacle of the tidal bore at Alney Island. Tides are an adventurer's friend, offering a huge variety of challenges in a good way, while to the unwary they are an ever-present danger. Almost 80 of the islands in this book are tidal and most of these can be walked to via beaches and causeways. Others can only be walked to on low spring tides, when it is possible to stay dry while walking along the seabed between islands in the Isles of Scilly, or reach islands along vast tracts of drying reef in Jersey. One route, alongside Foulness Island, is known as The Doomway by virtue of the number of poor souls who misjudged the tides and perished.

There are plenty of other ways of getting to these islands, though. There are large ferries to the Channel Islands and Holy Island, smaller ferries to the Isle of Man and even smaller ferries between islands. There are wildlife watching boat trips, fishing boats and sea tractors or, if you prefer, you can swim, paddleboard or kayak under your own steam. If none of these are possible, then many of the islands can be easily viewed from one of our great network of paths, including the Isle of Anglesey Coastal Path, Pembrokeshire Coast Path, South West Coast Path and the England Coast Path, which are all a joy to walk in themselves.

Our islands showcase the timeline of the human history of Britain. They tell us about how Neolithic, Bronze Age and Iron Age peoples lived and the successive occupations by Romans, Vikings, Normans and Germans. For over five hundred years they formed the front line in the defence against invasion by the French, Spanish, Dutch and Germans, their castles and forts updated again and again to face successive foes, each time with stronger fortifications and increasingly sophisticated weapons ranging from early cannon to World War II anti-aircraft guns. In between wars, they have been used to house prisoners, isolate disease, conceal illicit activities and test military hardware – all making the most of their open spaces away from civilisation. Conversely, islands have also been places of pilgrimage and spiritual retreat with modern-day pilgrims still making their way to Lindisfarne, Bardsey and Anglesey with St Michael's Mount the end of a British leg of the Camino de Santiago.

The birds, animals and plants of these islands are extraordinary too, both in rarity and spectacle of numbers. Skomer and Skokholm are home to half the world's population of Manx shearwaters, while the Isle of Wight has recently re-introduced white-tailed eagles. The waters around the Isle of Man are a nursery for basking sharks; the puffins on Coquet, Farne and Lundy islands are loved by all; and Sheppey Island has an extraordinary National Nature Reserve – the only one you can legally spend a night on. That's not to mention the bizarre or rare island species such as the Walney geranium and one of Britain's scarcest bumblebees on Canvey Island to name a few.

As an island's surface and its surrounding ocean brims with life, the skies above burst with stars and planets. Many islands are Dark Sky Discovery Sites offering the best views of our home galaxy, the Milky Way. With the lack of light pollution, it is even sometimes possible to see the ethereal lights of the aurora borealis

1 Asparagus Island, view from the high point   **2** Stone Marsh, oyster shells on the beach   **3** Spike Island, views at western point

streaming above many of the northern islands such as the Isle of Man, Lindisfarne, St Mary's and Anglesey.

Aside from the natural and historical wonders, islands are also the destination for adventures. They are places for fun, to relax and restore. The very nature of islands means that fewer people tend to venture out to them, so their sublime beaches are generally rarely busy and you are likely to have many to yourself. They offer every type of water sport from swimming and snorkelling to kayaking, paddleboarding, kitesurfing and more. There is plenty of walking too, some with distinct coastal circumnavigations and others with easy scrambles around the perimeter. There are beachside campsites and glamping sites, top-end hotels, great B&Bs and group accommodation. With the freshest of seafood, breweries, home-made ice cream, great cafes, coffee roasteries and quirky island pubs,

any stay on an island will also be a foray into the best of local food. For those seeking to dispense with modern-day life, there are the wild islands too. They are guaranteed to add new meaning to the term 'off-grid'. One thing is for certain; no two islands are the same and each and every one will delight, whichever coast you find it on and whatever season you visit in.

How to 'bag' an island

Unlike mountains where 'bagging' means reaching the summit, bagging an island is more about exploration and not just setting foot on an island and rushing on to the next. It's about meeting the islanders, tasting the food or staying a night or two to enjoy the night skies. It's about experiencing the island at low and high water, leaving footprints on its beaches, getting up close to its wildlife, playing in its waters and walking its coastlines. In short, 'island bagging'

Key

- ⛺ Campsite
- 🏕 Other accommodation
- ☕ Food and drink
- 🎣 Activity
- ⭐ Attraction
- 👥 Families
- 🦋 Nature and natural features
- 🌊 Beach
- 🏛 History

1 Herm, Shell Beach   **2** Ynys Môn / Anglesey, Porth Wen Brickworks   **3** Black Nab   **4** Burgh Island, coast path

means whatever you want it to mean, just so long as you don't rush it. If you do, you'll miss that very thing that makes it so special.

How to use this book

Each chapter groups islands together in a region and the individual entries detail how to access the islands (if possible; some can only be viewed from a mainland path) and the best activities to do once there. It is not exhaustive in all island highlights, and focuses more on the wild spaces, nature and outdoor activities than the more commercial offerings which have details on their own websites. Many of the routes and further information can be found at *www.islandeering.com*

Tides

Nearly 80 islands can only be accessed at low tide, with most accessed via a tidal crossing, causeway, path or road. Some can only be accessed on the lowest of spring tides. It is therefore important

that tide timetables are consulted and any trip planned around the low tide.
www.bbc.co.uk/weather/coast_and_sea/tide_tables

Most islands have a high and low tide every twelve hours and twenty-five minutes. The extra twenty-five minutes per tide is why a high or low tide does not occur at the same time and place each day but constantly shifts by fifty minutes per day.

Every day the position of the moon has an impact on the height, as well as time, of tides. So low tide on different days will mean different depths of water and possibly the difference between a walk and a swim. The lowest of low water is on a spring tide, during the full and new moon phases. Here, at low tide, the water goes out a bit further and, at high tide, it comes in further up the beach. Neap tides, when the moon is at first or third quarter, lead to low tides that are higher than average, and high tides that are lower – or in essence the tide goes out

less and comes in less. This all means that on the day of a tidal crossing, the height of the low tide needs to be checked in addition to the time of the low tide. Some islands remain underwater even at low tide for most of a lunar month, with water levels only dropping sufficiently to walk across the causeway on the lowest of spring tides.

The depth of water at low tide can also be affected by unusually high and low pressure systems, or prolonged periods of strong winds and larger swells, which can all mean that an incoming tide can reach you before the predicted time. The height of water in tidal estuaries fed by mountain rivers may also vary depending on the amount of rainfall that the higher ground upriver has recently received.

If you are swimming or paddling to islands, knowing the state of the tide will be key to having a safe adventure. If you imagine splitting the time between a high tide and low tide into six one-hour periods, slack tide, where water flows are the slowest, will often be found in the first and last hour period. The fastest flows of the ebbing tide will generally be experienced during the third and fourth hours which might be great if they are going in the same direction as you, but might make travel impossible if they are against you.

Finally, the speed of the incoming tide can be faster than you can walk. Over shallow beaches, the incoming tide (the flood) can race in extremely quickly and sometimes fill in around you, especially if there are deeper channels on your crossing, so it is essential to give yourself plenty of time. If, for example, access is stated as three hours either side of low tide, you must aim to complete your crossing within the three hours after low water rather than start it.

Weather

The main thing to remember is that once you leave the mainland and head out to sea, the weather generally gets breezier and cooler. Always look at the forecast but bear in mind that things can change more rapidly on an island and can be very different between the leeward and windward coasts.

Fog is the biggest challenge, particularly if you are on a tidal crossing with no markers and you are relying on your navigation skills. Always check the forecast before you head out. *www.metoffice.gov.uk*

Exploring respectfully

Islands are special places and if we all follow some basic guidelines they will remain so for longer.

Stating the obvious: don't start fires, leave litter, pick flowers, remove shells, remove fossils, harass the wildlife or visit areas where restrictions have been imposed due to wildlife.

Dogs are generally welcome but always check first, particularly if you are entering a known wildlife area. Always follow the Countryside Code *www.gov.uk/government/publications/the-countryside-code*

Wild camping is not permitted in the areas covered by this book unless you have the permission of the landowner. Many islands do have fantastically located commercial campsites.

Rats: some bird-friendly islands are very keen to keep rats out, after they have previously devastated wildlife, some of which has never returned. Be friendly if the boat crew need to check inside your bag

Nature: there are many special places for nesting and migrating birds on islands. Please be sensitive about walking, swimming and kayaking along cliffs and ground nesting sites. Once disturbed, many birds will not return to the nest. Similarly, many plants are rare and damage must be avoided. Grey seals pup between October and January and common (harbour) seals pup in June and July. In general, seals should not be approached closer than twenty metres; dogs should always be controlled near them.

Dubbed 'England's Enchanted Archipelago', this outstandingly beautiful, uncrowded and unspoilt group of islands are a world apart in every way. Lying just off the coast of Cornwall, there are some 140 islands here, five of which are inhabited. The main island, St Mary's, is the first port of call for most visitors and the hub of inter-island travel. The islands offer something for everyone from ancient history and staggering bird life to subtropical gardens and dramatic lighthouses. For the active, there are challenging swimming events, sea kayaking expeditions and snorkelling with seals. For families, the pristine beaches and clear waters are perfect for exploring, rockpooling or simply relaxing. Great food is a Scilly speciality too, with excellent restaurants, cafes and characterful inns along with home-made ice cream from one of England's smallest dairy herds and the freshest of local food plucked from the surrounding ocean and island gardens.

ISLES OF SCILLY

Opposite St Agnes, views across Porth Conger to Gugh
Overleaf Samson, view of North Hill from South Hill

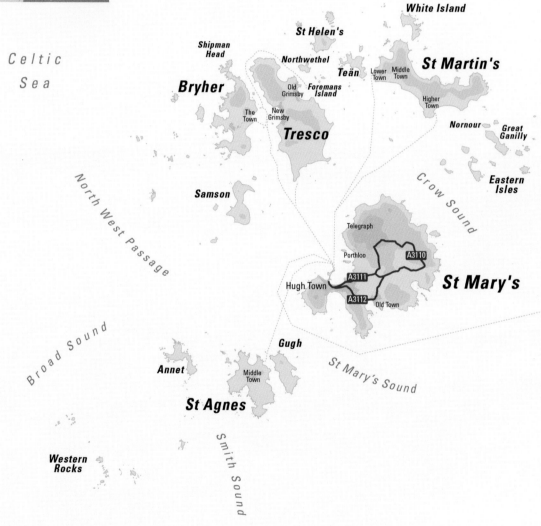

Celtic
Sea

Shipman
Head

St Helen's

White Island

Northwethel

Bryher

Old
Grimsby

Foremans
Island

Teän

Lower
Town

Middle
Town

St Martin's

The
Town

New
Grimsby

Tresco

Higher
Town

Nornour

Great
Ganilly

North West Passage

Samson

*Eastern
Isles*

Crow Sound

Telegraph

Porthloo

A3110

Hugh Town

A3111

St Mary's

A3112

Old Town

Broad Sound

Gugh

Annet

Middle
Town

St Mary's Sound

St Agnes

Smith Sound

*Western
Rocks*

N

0   3km

St Mary's

ACCESS FERRY; PLANE; HELICOPTER

The largest island of the Scilly archipelago and home to around 1,800 Scillonians, this is the beating heart of Scilly and the gateway to the other islands. Its wonderful beaches, local food, charming lanes, music and culture are a celebration of what these enchanted isles are all about. Hugh Town is the main centre with its cluster of shops, banks, post office, pubs, restaurants and cafes as well as the main supermarket on the archipelago. It has three lovely beaches and The Quay, where the daily *Scillonian III* arrives from Penzance and the inter-island ferries depart. Alternatively, small Skybus planes arrive year-round at the tiny airport on St Mary's from the mainland. The impressive fortification of The Garrison dominates the south-west peninsula, while the island's north coast is a string of deserted sandy beaches, incredible ancient sites and stunning seascapes. There are also four small islands off St Mary's that can be accessed at low tide. The island has every type of accommodation to suit a range of budgets; from coastal self-catering cottages, luxury hotels and inns to glamping and camping. Sampling St Mary's delicious food is an island highlight. Getting around the island is a laid-back affair with plenty of paths, including the beautiful coastal path, and quiet lanes to cycle or traverse by electric golf cart. There are taxis on the island and a community bus service that circles the island several times a day. Ferries run by the St Mary's Boatmen's Association to the off-islands generally depart from The Quay at 10.15 a.m. and 2.00 p.m. as a minimum (Easter to the end of October), with additional departures at busier times and wildlife and circular island tours on offer. Check the blackboard at The Quay or the association's Facebook page for the changing daily ferry times.
www.stmarysbikehire.co.uk
www.scillycart.co
www.scillyboating.co.uk

Circumnavigate the island

Hiking the sixteen-kilometre coast path around the perimeter of St Mary's is a great way to explore the island and sample the great island hospitality. From Hugh Town the route follows the defensive walls of The Garrison around the western peninsula, with a pit stop at the cafe-lined promenade and sandy beach of Porthcressa, before reaching the other-worldly rock formations of Peninnis Head and quaint Old Town with St Mary's Old Church where Harold Wilson, who served as Prime Minister of the United Kingdom in the 1960s and 1970s, is buried. Reaching the island's south-east corner, Porth Hellick is a special place for nature and history with the largest body of freshwater on the island just inland from the shingle sandbar and the Bronze Age cemetery of Porth Hellick Down. The beautiful sand beach of Pelistry Bay on the east coast is the starting point for a low-tide walk to Toll's Island, while the north coast has the highest concentration of incredible prehistoric remains, along with superb views of Tresco and the other islands. The high point of the island in the small settlement of Telegraph is located a few hundred metres off the coast path at the intersection of Pungies Lane and Telegraph Road and can be bagged on the return to Hugh Town.
www.islandeering.com

Prehistoric lives and death

St Mary's has the best range of surviving pre-historic sites in the Scilly archipelago with ancient homes and burial sites. A visit to them is a thought-provoking experience as you gaze across fantastic seascapes and wonder what life must have been like when the islands you see before you were vast plains, and the sea levels much lower. On the north-west coast the remains of a number of interconnecting stone houses from the Iron Age and Roman period can be seen at Halangy Down Ancient Village. Close by, the Bronze Age entrance grave of Bant's Carn has an impressive burial chamber covered with massive capstones. Further examples of Bronze Age burial chambers can be seen on the north-east coast

near Innisidgen and the south-east coast near Porth Hellick Down. All can be reached via the coast path.

Explore small islands linked to St Mary's

There are four small islands off the coast of St Mary's that can be accessed at low tide. **Toll's Island** is the largest at 300 metres long and 175 metres wide. It sits in the north-east of St Mary's, 100 metres off Pelistry Bay, to which it is linked by a sand tombolo. A number of overgrown paths weave through the island's interior of grass, heather, gorse and brambles. In the west, wind-stunted trees sit within a walled area. For the eagle-eyed there are four small stone-lined kelp pits, marked on the Ordnance Survey map, just back from the shoreline on the south side of the island. They were used to burn seaweed to make soda ash for glass, soap and alum production. The remains of an English Civil War gun battery, Pellew's Redoubt, can also be seen on the sixteen-metre high point of the island.

Innisidgen is a small tidal island that sits 100 metres off the north-east coast of St Mary's. This grass-topped island can be reached by an easy scramble from the mainland, just below the Bronze Age remains. Of no particular note, it is still a must for island baggers. Just north of Hugh Town, **Taylor's Island** is a small, rocky tidal island joined to the north end of Porthloo Beach at low tide, with a high point of fourteen metres. At the south end of the same beach, **Newford Island**, only cut off for an hour or so around high tide, has a dilapidated market garden in its centre. The island is a Scheduled Monument by virtue of its defensive wall and gun battery, dating to the English Civil War, on the western half of the island. In addition, **Rat Island** was joined to St Mary's by the harbour wall in Hugh Town, a building project undertaken as part of the quay extension in the nineteenth century. It is now home to the Isles of Scilly Steamship Group's ticket office and facilities; there is also a good restaurant and inter-island boats depart from here.

On the scent of narcissi

A much-coveted Scilly speciality, these cut flowers and bulbs are a gift that keeps on giving. Definitely not daffodils, narcissi have up to fifteen flowers on each stem, and are uniquely scented. With Royal Connection, Scilly Valentine, Scilly White, Soleil d'Or, Cheerfulness and many others to choose from there is a scent for every occasion. Nine family-owned flower farms make the most of St Mary's ideal climate to grow these delights in small hedge-lined fields for the global export of hand-picked flowers. Visit the narcissi exhibition at Scented Narcissi near the airport or buy bulbs around the island. Seaways Farm Shop is a favourite, particularly when combined with a visit to adjoining Juliet's Garden Restaurant with its good food and drink and stunning views over St Mary's Harbour.

Swimming, coasteering and kayaking

There's plenty to do on St Mary's for the more adventurous. Enjoy the freedom of jumping from rocks into the Atlantic and exploring the surreal granite cliffs and oddly-shaped tors of Peninnis Head on a coasteering trip. St Mary's also has a number of unique wild swim events. The toughest, Scilly 360, is a complete circumnavigation of St Mary's, about fifteen kilometres, with a well-earned party afterwards. The island's water sports centre at Porth Mellon has instruction and paddleboards, dinghies and windsurfing boards are available to hire. A sea kayak expedition is also a great way to explore all the islands in the archipelago.

www.kernow-coasteering.co.uk
www.scillyswimchallenge.co.uk
www.sailingscilly.com
www.expeditionpaddler.com

Carreg Dhu Garden

Tranquil Carreg Dhu is a subtropical community garden in an old quarry near Longstone Terrace in the centre of St Mary's. Started in 1986, this volunteer-tended oasis brims with colourful plants. An area of the garden has been set aside for the Historic Narcissus Collection contained in six hexagonal borders to preserve the traditional varieties grown on the islands. Easily reached from Hugh Town, entry is free and there are plenty of quiet corners to explore.

Spot dolphins

If you travel to the islands on the *Scillonian III*, you'll very likely see dolphins and porpoises riding the bow wave and, if you are lucky, basking sharks. There are several wildlife trips that operate from St Mary's and pods of hundreds of dolphins can be spotted, often west of the archipelago.

Island gin and wine ⭐

The Scilly Spirit Gin School is the perfect rainy-day activity. At the distillery in Old Town you can go on a short guided tour to see the beautiful stills, Bishop and Daisy, and learn about distillation and the history of gin. You can make your own gin in a personal mini still. With

tutoring on flavour profile and a choice of over sixty botanicals, you can create your perfect gin. St Mary's also has its own vineyard in the tranquil and beautiful Holy Vale. The Cellar Door is well worth visiting and wine tastings (of world wine) are informative and entertaining.
www.scillyspirit.com
www.holyvalewines.co.uk

Walk around The Garrison

Dominating the whole western peninsula of St Mary's, it is hard to miss one of the most impressive coastal defence systems in England. Here you can wander around the defensive walls and explore the tunnels, as well as sample the excellent food and accommodation at Star Castle, once the nucleus of the defensive system initially developed by Elizabethans to defend against the Spanish Armada. Using the strategic promontory, known originally as The Hugh, The Garrison became a Royalist stronghold during the English Civil War and

1

was further developed in the seventeenth and early eighteenth centuries with continued threat of invasion by the French and Spanish. Many of the surviving batteries, barracks and buildings date from this time. The Garrison was re-armed in World War I and used again as a signal station and barracks in World War II. The Garrison walk starts in Hugh Town and passes through The Garrison gateway, the original arched gateway with a bellcote and parapet above, and a sunken powder magazine called the Rocket House. It then follows the coast and ends along a wooded path to Porthcressa Beach which is accessed via hidden stairs and a tunnel.

Watch a gig race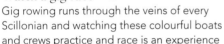

Gig rowing runs through the veins of every Scillonian and watching these colourful boats and crews practice and race is an experience to behold. Heralding from the late eighteenth century, when local pilot boats guided sailing ships to the Cornish shores, these boats have always been built for competition – as the pilot gig that got to the ship first got the job and the wage. Gig racing can be watched on Wednesday and Saturday evenings any time of the year, with the racing calendar culminating in the World Pilot Gig Championships in the waters off St Mary's. The event attracts thousands of rowers and supporters from across the globe for a weekend of passionate rowing and revelry alike. The Mermaid Inn and the pubs on the smaller islands are full of merriment, sea shanties and beer fumes. For events check notice boards around Hugh Town. *www.gigrower.co.uk/events*

Choose a festival

Whatever your interest you'll find a fabulous festival to attend on St Mary's: Walk Scilly; Taste of Scilly; Scilly Folk Festival; Creative Scilly; Scilly Dark Skies and Wild Scilly, to name just a few.

Western Rocks

ACCESS NOT PERMITTED; NON-LANDING BOAT TRIP
Once of shipwrecking notoriety, the jagged jaws
of this tiny archipelago, on the outer south-
west edge of Scilly, are now a birdwatcher's
paradise. The only other land between these
skerries and North America is nearby Bishop
Rock and its lighthouse. An Isles of Scilly
Wildlife Trust reserve for breeding European
shag and European storm petrel, it is also home
to breeding seals and other seabirds including
puffin and kittiwake. It can be visited as part of
a non-landing boat trip and wildlife tour.
www.scillyboating.co.uk

Annet

ACCESS NOT PERMITTED; NON-LANDING BOAT TRIP
Known as 'bird island', this is the main seabird
breeding site in Scilly. In early summer the skies
and seas around it are full of puffins, razorbills
and gulls, but its real fame arises from its large
colonies of Manx shearwater and European
storm petrel. It is also an important breeding
site for the Atlantic grey seal. Just one kilometre
west of St Agnes, it is managed by the Isles of
Scilly Wildlife Trust. Landing is prohibited, but

St Agnes Boating run weekly trips with an Isles
of Scilly Wildlife Trust ranger on board.
www.stagnesboating.co.uk

St Agnes

ACCESS SMALL FERRY
The astonishing rock formations, idyllic sandbars, secluded coves and uninterrupted swells
pounding the west coast leaves you in no doubt
that this is an island for adventure. Home to
the most southerly settlement in the United
Kingdom, this is as far away from the mainland
as it gets, yet its remoteness makes its hospitality
warmer with its much-loved inn, self-catering
cottages and cafes along the quaint jumble of
small lanes and a superb ice-cream-making dairy
with adjacent beach-side camping. St Agnes
Boating and St Mary's Boatmen's Association
run regular boats to and from St Mary's.
www.stagnesboating.co.uk
www.scillyboating.co.uk

Walk the coast path
This generally easy-graded, seven-kilometre
coast path takes in most of the island's highlights. It starts at the Quay, where the inter-
island boat arrives, passes The Bar across to
Gugh then takes in the wind-pruned heath

of Wingletang Down at the southern tip of St Agnes and the fantastical granite outcrops, including Nags Head. The wild west coast feels within touching distance of the fearsomely jagged Western Rocks and the swirling bird colonies of Annet. Troytown Farm and Campsite provides a great opportunity for refreshments before a walk out to tidal **Burnt Island** and then on around the north part of St Agnes to return. *www.islandeering.com*

Ice cream from one of the smallest dairy herds in the country

One of the joys of life is swinging gently from the fishing net hammock strung between two rocks above the shoreline on Troytown Farm and deciding which ice cream from among the thirty flavours to try next – rose geranium, Baileys or chocolate and cherry? Troytown Farm is the only dairy farm in Scilly and, with only nine milking Jersey and Ayrshire cows, it may also be the smallest in the country. Grazing on the island's lush grasslands full of birdlife, butterflies and flowers, the milk they produce must be good for you. Butter, clotted cream and deliciously creamy yoghurt are also available.
www.troytown.co.uk

Camp and watch the sun go down

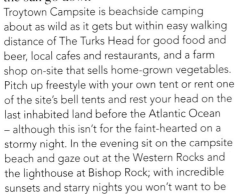

Troytown Campsite is beachside camping about as wild as it gets but within easy walking distance of The Turks Head for good food and beer, local cafes and restaurants, and a farm shop on-site that sells home-grown vegetables. Pitch up freestyle with your own tent or rent one of the site's bell tents and rest your head on the last inhabited land before the Atlantic Ocean – although this isn't for the faint-hearted on a stormy night. In the evening sit on the campsite beach and gaze out at the Western Rocks and the lighthouse at Bishop Rock; with incredible sunsets and starry nights you won't want to be anywhere else in the world.

Snorkel The Cove

This magical hidden cove, just south of The Bar across to Gugh, is fringed by fragrant trees and shrubs. The talc-white sand beach gives way to rocks of the seabed and makes a perfect spot for snorkelling and rockpooling at low tide. For refreshments, The Turks Head is just a short walk away.

Wingletang Down

This wild southern headland is a fascinating boulder-strewn landscape held together by wind-pruned heather dotted with plant life that can be found nowhere else in the UK. The weathered granite outcrops form weird and wonderful shapes that animate the landscape, with Nags Head (grid reference: SV 877078) probably the most remarkable. Standing at 4.5 metres tall, this ancient stone has an extremity that looks like an old horse's head.

St Warna's Well

To the north-west of Wingletang Down, above Porth Warna, a stone-lined well (grid reference: SV 880078) dedicated to St Warna is the only holy well on the Isles of Scilly. St Warna was a saint from Ireland whose role was thought to be to direct ships away from the rocks. Occasionally, during hard times, islanders were thought to have made offerings to the well in the hope that her protection would fail and the goods from the wrecked ships could be plundered.

Troy Town Maze

South of the campsite, on Long Point, the seven-ring turf and stone maze is thought to have been originally made on the shore to protect sailors by sending them fair winds; its structure is a common occurrence throughout Europe. The current maze is thought to be the work of Amor Clarke, a lighthouse keeper on the island in the 1790s, but excavations in the 1980s uncovered a much older maze on the site. It is a magical place for a full moon foray and impossible to get lost, as there are no dead ends.

An island murder mystery

St Agnes' squat lighthouse is visible from most points on the island. The light, originally a coal fire in an open casket, is one of Britain's earliest lights but the building holds a dark secret. Two squabbling keepers tended the light but one disappeared without explanation one night. He was found forty years later buried beneath the foundations of the lighthouse buildings, identified only by his teeth. It is also said that this light was deliberately involved in wrecking, so there may be more than one ghost.

The Turks Head Inn

A characterful pub inside with a terraced garden offering beautiful views across the small harbour of Porth Conger to the island of Gugh. The inn is a destination in itself – evening boat trips are often run to the inn from St Mary's – as well as being a great pit stop for a refreshing pint while you wait for the ferry or simply sit and watch the island's comings and goings.

Gugh

ACCESS TIDAL CROSSING

Accessed via an exotic white sandbar at low tide, this tiny island offers fabulous views across the crystal-clear waters of Porth Conger to St Agnes. There is a faint path around the island's perimeter which includes an impressive standing stone, the Old Man of Gugh at three metres tall, and Obadiah's Barrow; there's also a path to the high point of the island at Kittern Hill (thirty-four metres) for incredible views of the Western Rocks, Annet and the foreboding stone walls of The Garrison and rock formations at Peninnis Head on St Mary's. The nearest food and accommodation are on St Agnes.

Samson

ACCESS SMALL FERRY
(RESTRICTIONS APRIL–SEPTEMBER)

A true castaway experience, this idyllic tiny island has deserted white sands, sparkling sea, stunning wild flowers, birds, seals and around eight thousand years of living history. The largest uninhabited island in the archipelago is formed by two hills connected by a sandy isthmus and is managed by the Isles of Scilly Wildlife Trust as a nature reserve. Access to Bar Point from a St Mary's Boatmen's Association boat is either via transfer to a small RIB or to 'walk a plank' across to the sand. There are no facilities on the island. Access is by small ferry but is restricted from April until September on the south and west coasts. Access restrictions due to wildlife on the Isles of Scilly are determined by the Isles of Scilly Wildlife Trust. *www.ios-wildlifetrust.org.uk/making-space-for-nature*

Climb the island high points

The tops of North Hill and South Hill (the high point at forty-two metres) can be reached by paths that climb from the sandy isthmus that joins them. A Bronze Age stone burial chamber can be explored on North Hill which also offers a great vantage point to see the Samson Flats, a Bronze Age field system exposed at low tide. An ascent of South Hill reveals more prehistoric graves along with the ruined cottages of the forty or so people that once lived here. The last two surviving families suffered malnutrition from a diet of limpets and potatoes.

Idyllic beaches to relax or swim

Between the two hills, the path along the sandy isthmus weaves through beautiful wild-flower 'gardens' as well as the beaches of East and West Porth and the ruins of the boatsheds of the fishermen that once lived here. Further north, Bar Point, with its white sand beach and gently lapping waters, makes an ideal place to relax or take a swim.

1 Gugh, the Old Man of Gugh   **2 Samson,** ruins on South Hill

Low-tide walk to Puffin Island and Tresco

At extreme low spring tides it is possible to walk from Bar Point, initially heading west then out towards **Puffin Island**. For the adventurous and strong swimmer, it is also possible to walk back to Tresco via the Channel Ledge – although be prepared to wade through the numerous channels on your way. Check the tide times to ensure it is during one of the lowest spring tides.

Bryher

ACCESS SMALL FERRY; TIDAL CROSSING

An island of dramatic contrasts with thundering Atlantic waves pounding Hell Bay in the west, while tranquil bays and peaceful sand beaches line the south and east coasts. One of the smaller inhabited islands, it is known as 'land of the hills' due to its succession of prominent hills linked together by low-lying necks where farms and homes are clustered. The high point of the island is Watch Hill, at forty-three metres. Its main village, The Town, lies on the east coast opposite Tresco. The island has a luxurious hotel, a campsite, a B&B and a number of self-catering cottages. For many, the local food and drink are the main reason they visit, with local fish and shellfish, cafes, a pub, fine dining and a well-stocked island shop, along with a variety of home-grown produce. Bryher has two quays, Church Quay used at high water and Bar Quay used at low water, served by regular inter-island boats from St Mary's and Tresco.

Sample the island produce

The entire island is dotted with honesty stalls selling fresh produce including farm eggs, garden-grown salad and vegetables, strawberries, home-made chutneys and delicious island fudge. Together with freshly baked bread from the Bryher Shop you can fix yourself up with a tasty picnic and finish with the excellent tatty cake, which is only made on this island to a recipe handed down through generations. Island Fish sell freshly caught fish and shellfish daily, crab, lobster, mackerel, ready-made lobster and crab rolls and delicious home-made crab quiche to take away.

Hire a boat and explore the smaller islands

Bennett's Boatyard and Bryher Boatyard offer boats and kayaks for hire. You can have your own desert island adventure and paddle to Samson or simply explore the tiny islands in the tranquil waters of the Tresco Channel.
www.bennettboatyard.com
www.islesofscillyboathire.com

A pint in one of Britain's smallest bars

Fraggle Rock Bar is a destination in itself for many, especially on Fish and Chip Friday, and has been nominated by Jamie Oliver as a 'best British boozer'. With beautiful views across the Tresco Channel it is a pleasure to sit on one of the outside benches with a local ale and enjoy the views to Hangman Island and to Cromwell's Castle and King Charles's Castle on Tresco.

The Crab Shack

A must for seafood lovers, this rustic shed, part of the Hell Bay Hotel, is laid out with wooden benches serving simply prepared Bryher crab, mussels and scallops. You choose a crab and a flavoured butter, put on your apron and set to with a pair of crab crackers. Prepare to get very messy in this highly social affair.
www.hellbay.co.uk

Low-tide walk to Tresco

When sea levels were much lower, Bryher was once joined to Tresco, and on very low tides it is still possible to walk across the ocean floor between the two (see page 17 for full details).

Walk around the whole island

Bryher's eight-kilometre coast path is the best way to explore the whole island in a day. The undulating route is easy to follow and 'climbs' the three small hills of the island and descends into all of its coves and beaches; there are plenty of great pit stops on the way. Starting at Church Quay, the old bulb fields and quaint cottages of Old Town lead to the popular Fraggle Rock Bar before heading into the wilds of the moorland of Shipman Head Down and one of the largest Bronze Age burial sites in north-west Europe. From here ancient settlers believed their dead ancestors could keep watch over the living. Rounding the northern tip, the west coast is dramatic with cliffs and sentinel rocks exposed to the full power of the Atlantic. The aptly named Hell Bay is often a seething mass of white spume and thunderous waves. Heading south the landscape becomes much gentler at Stinking Porth, around the Hell Bay Hotel, with the brackish and calm waters of Great Pool a magnet for migrating birds. The path climbs again to reach the westerly points of Gweal Hill, Heathy Hill and Droppy Nose Point, a charismatic rock formation and a favourite haul-out site for seals. The dramatic, jagged Norrard Rocks can be seen from both hills. The south coast then becomes flatter with the sands of Rushy Bay before skirting around the base of Samson Hill, the location for the film based on *Why the Whales Came* by Michael Morpurgo, after which the route gently returns to Church Quay.
www.islandeering.com

Stained-glass windows of All Saints' Church

Designed by Scilly islander Oriel Hicks, the beautiful, colourful stained-glass windows of this church are best seen from the inside. The scenes of a gig rowing out to save a wreck and the flowers and birdlife of the island are a riot of colour even on a cloudy day.

Swim in Rushy Bay

The best beach and swimming spot on Bryher, Rushy Bay is a sheltered cove on the south side of the island, opposite Samson. Pristine white sands, private nooks amongst the tall marram grass and very calm, shallow water make for a great family beach. For the inquisitive there are plenty of shells to find, as well as the rare dwarf pansy. Building chortens with the pebbles on the beach is also a favourite activity with visitors here.

1 Bryher, tatty cake   **2** Bryher, walking towards the crossing to Shipman Head
3 Bryher, scrambling on the west coast   **4** Bryher, views across to Tresco

Find the longest cave in Scilly

Just north of Great High Rock, on Bryher's west coast, is the longest cave in Scilly. Thought to be used by smugglers in times gone by, it is hard to find. Its entrance is just one metre wide and nine metres high. This is not a trip for the faint-hearted. Scramble down to the base of the cliffs, then over the large boulder protecting the cave entrance. Only to be attempted during low tide, with minimum westerly swell.

Shipman Head

ACCESS TIDAL CROSSING
(RESTRICTIONS APRIL–SEPTEMBER)
Shipman Head is separated from Bryher's northern tip by a narrow channel of water

at the bottom of a steep-walled gully. In gentle seas, the gully is a thrilling place to jump into or swim for the more experienced. At low tide a large boulder protects the gully's western end from the breaking waves, creating a bubbling 'seawater spa'. The large kelp bed at the eastern end of the gully is also great to explore with a snorkel. Shipman Head itself can be accessed on foot at low tide via the jumble of rocks at the western end of the gully and its high point (at thirty-six metres) is readily climbed. As an important seabird colony, access is prohibited from April until September. If it is not possible to pass the gully, it is still well worth dropping down to the rock platform on Bryher above it to watch the water surging through.

1 Tresco, Tresco Abbey Garden **2 Tresco,** Cromwell's Castle

Tresco

ACCESS SMALL FERRY; TIDAL CROSSING; HELICOPTER
Renowned for its sophisticated vibe, beautiful beaches and world famous subtropical gardens, the second largest island of Scilly, and the only one privately owned, has plenty of wild places to discover amongst the great cafes, pubs and luxury accommodation on offer. An island of many contrasts, its exposed north coast is rugged with granite outcrops and heathland, while the east and south are mostly sand and shell beaches. Inland, the freshwater pools are a birdwatcher's paradise; the high point of the island reaches forty-four metres. The main settlements are New Grimsby and Old Grimsby on the west and east coasts respectively. The whole island offers accommodation of every type except camping, along with some lovely cafes, inns and restaurants and the well-stocked and upmarket Tresco Stores. Day trip boats from St Mary's dock at the Quay at New Grimsby, usually twice a day; they also arrive from St Martin's and St Agnes on a less frequent basis. From Tresco the inter-island boat is run by Tresco Boat Services.

There is no public transport on Tresco and the best way to get around is on foot. Bike hire is available in New Grimsby, while kayaks, boats and paddleboards can be hired from the sailing school at Old Grimsby.

Tresco Abbey Garden

This seven-hectare subtropical garden is home to over twenty thousand exotic plants from across the world that can be grown here, and nowhere else in Britain, because of Tresco's very mild climate. Built in the nineteenth century amongst the ruins of a Benedictine abbey, there are fishponds, a stone Gaia sculpture, glades of tree ferns and protea and succulent-lined terraces all nestled in a botanical paradise with beautiful ocean views beyond. The Mediterranean Garden, with its Agave Fountain and the Shell House decorated with seashell mosaics, is home to the Valhalla Museum and its collection of around thirty ships' figureheads and carvings. Most of the figureheads date from the late nineteenth century, and come from shipwrecks of merchant sailing vessels or early steamships that were wrecked on the archipelago.

Find the skeleton in Piper's Hole

Piper's Hole is a sea cave situated on the north-east tip of Tresco. Once a famous smugglers' haunt, the name may have derived from the clay pipes smokers once used. Legend states that Piper's Hole connects to a passage under the sea leading to a sea cave on St Mary's, and that men who entered it were never seen again; dogs emerged from the tunnel minus most of their fur. Access, only during low tide and low sea swell conditions, is via a small entrance packed with large boulders which have to be scrambled over before dropping down to the sea-level cave. It then opens up to reveal a small freshwater pool, often filled with the floating aids that previous cavers have used to stay dry during the crossing. In the pre-war years tourists visited the pool using a punt. Keep to the right of the pool where an underwater ledge makes it possible to wade rather than swim the pool. There's a gravel beach at the far end, on which the skeleton sits, beyond which is a narrow corridor of granite that peters out after about thirty metres. The roof of the cave glitters like small pieces of silver, thought to be a result of condensation supporting microbial communities, or salt and calcite deposits.

Walk the ocean floor to Bryher

Several times a year, on very low spring tides, the water level is so low in the Tresco Channel that it is possible to walk across the dryish seabed to Bryher and if you leave early enough you can also walk to Samson. The walk generally starts at the slipway on Tresco heading towards **Plumb Island** and crosses to Church Quay, Bryher. The committed island bagger can visit **Merrick Island** on the way. During the summer months the Tresco Estate organises a pop-up festival midway across, on a sandbar that is usually several metres underwater. There's a Hell Bay gin bar, mini pasties and cakes, as well as fish, shellfish and paella from Bryher's Island Fish to choose from.
www.tresco.co.uk
www.islandeering.com

Pizza at The Ruin

Nestled in Old Grimsby, this wonderfully laid-back eatery has idyllic views across the beach of Raven's Porth. Whether sitting on the wooden decking with a coffee or an evening meal, it's an experience that shouldn't be rushed. At the heart of this mosaic-decorated restaurant a wood-fired oven produces delicious pizzas, roast meats, fish and home-made bread. It takes its name from the ruined smuggler's cottage that forms part of its terrace.

Discover Tresco's castles

Cromwell's Castle is fabulously located on a rocky promontory to the north-west of the island, where it once guarded New Grimsby Sound and protected the heart of the archipelago. Built to deter Dutch invaders, it is a rare survivor from Cromwell's time. A staircase spirals within the walls of its tall round tower, taking the visitor to the roof for great views through any of its six gun ports. Cromwell's Castle superseded King Charles's Castle, which is located on the hill above it. The latter was so poorly sited that to hit enemy ships its cannons had to be aimed downwards and the cannonballs were said to roll out before they could be fired. Today it makes a romantic ruin to explore and enjoy the surrounding seascapes. Another fortification, overlooking Old Grimsby Harbour, is the sixteenth-century Old Blockhouse, built to protect against a French attack. It would have housed a battery of artillery pieces positioned on a gun platform on top of a rocky outcrop, with defensive banks and walls and tiny living quarters.

Walk around the island

This ten-kilometre walk starts at Carn Near Quay then gently wanders through New Grimsby and north to Cromwell's Castle on the boulder-strewn shore before ascending to the ruins of King Charles's Castle. It climbs Gun Hill and crosses the heather-clad moor of the island's north then dips into Piper's Hole and the ruins of the Old Blockhouse to reach the delightful, castaway cafe, The Ruin. The easy path south then follows the bone-white beaches to reach the dune-backed Pentle Bay, named one of the top 'under-the-radar' beaches by *The Wall Street Journal*. The route back to Carn Near Quay affords plentiful views of Tresco Abbey and, if time permits, many options for a detour to visit the world-renowned sub-tropical garden and wildlife-rich Abbey Pool. *www.islandeering.com*

St Martin's

ACCESS SMALL FERRY

Radiating an authentic simplicity and vibrant community spirit, the coastline of St Martin's is fringed with spectacular white beaches with steep granite cliffs to the east and vast tidal rockpools to the west. The northernmost inhabited island in Scilly, this island has three quaint settlements of Higher Town, Middle Town and Lower Town and two quays connected by the island's only lane. In the south, the narrow strip fields full of colourful flowers, vines and vegetables contrast sharply with the wild heathland areas of Chapel Down and the tidal White Island. Chapel Down, the island's high point at forty-eight metres, is topped by an iconic red-and-white-striped daymark; it is the most distinctive structure within the archipelago and is one of the first features visitors spot from the *Scillonian III*. There are several accommodation options ranging from a great campsite, farm cottages and chalets to B&Bs and a hotel. There are several options for food and drink including fine dining, an island bakery, charming pub, tea rooms, roadside honesty stalls and an island store. Boats arrive (usually twice daily) from St Mary's and about twice a week from Tresco, Bryher and St Agnes. The best way to get around St Martin's is on foot. Kayaks can be hired at Higher Town.

Tempt yourself in the bakery

Every morning a selection of organic loaves and rolls are baked, along with a weekly guest bread. With traditional Cornish pasties, tarts, pies, pizzas and home-made cakes to choose from, you can forage an excellent picnic here.

Pick a beach

The only difficult thing about St Martin's is deciding which beach to visit, as its whole coastline is fringed with spectacular white sands and crystal-clear water. Great Bay on the north coast is a long, wild stretch of sand that has often been voted the best beach in Britain. A family favourite is dune-backed Lawrence's Bay which stretches between Lower Town and Higher Town; its sands gently enter the shallows of St Martin's Flats making it perfect for a swim. For rockpooling, Pernagie Point at the northern tip of the island has large pools, as does Lawrence's Bay in the south, where you'll find anything from sea slugs, squat lobsters and pipefish to strawberry anemones, starfish, clingfish and crabs.

Meet 'Billy Idol'

Amongst the wild heathland of Chapel Down, home to the red-and-white-striped daymark, there are a number of ancient cairns and entrance graves. Amongst these sits 'Billy Idol', a locally-named, one-metre-tall standing stone that has a carved head similar to those found in Brittany and the Channel Islands. It was discovered in the early 1900s, lost and then found again in 1989 after a bracken fire. Grid reference: SV 942159.

Snorkel with seals

Scilly Seal Snorkelling run swimming-with-seals trips from St Martin's to the friendly seal colony of the Eastern Isles. The large males and the smaller, more sociable females often seek you out and like to play, usually by nipping your flipper or playing hide and seek in the kelp. October is the best time to swim with the seals as the water is still 'warm' and there are young pups to spot. Wetsuits, masks and fins are provided as well as advice on how to approach the seals responsibly. *www.scillysealsnorkelling.com*

1 St Martin's, tidal crossing to White Island   **2 St Martin's**, Lower Town Quay

Walk around the island

St Martin's fourteen-kilometre spectacular coast path weaves through the island's vastly contrasting landscapes. Starting at Lower Town Quay it follows the low-level wild west coast to Pernagie Point with its other-worldly rocky foreshore that extends around the headland to White Island. The extensive sands of Great Bay stretch along the north coast to the secluded Bread and Cheese Cove where the route then climbs to the heathland of Chapel Down and the high point of the island. The tranquil walk along the south coast passes once-thriving bulb fields, vineyards and flower farms to reach the shallow waters and sublime beach near Lower Town Quay.
www.islandeering.com

Sea shanties at the Seven Stones Inn

This rustic and quirky inn is a highlight for any visit to the island. With wood panels, old settles and a wood-burner in the big stone fireplace inside, and stunning seascapes from the stone terrace outside, it's the sort of place you can get very settled and soak up St Martin's island life. With live music, quiz nights, barbecues and film festivals, it is very popular with islanders and visitors and, during gig rowing championships, it's a great place to catch the buzz from the Cornish singers and their shanties.

White Island

ACCESS TIDAL CROSSING

An extraordinary, boulder-strewn causeway leads across from St Martin's to this tidal island. Once there, you can follow a faint path around the coast to see the rarely visited ancient, chambered cairns, prehistoric field systems and a dramatic chasm called Chad Girt. The high point (at thirty-one metres) at the north end of the island offers great views of the northern rocks of this archipelago. There's a very sheltered sandy beach at Porth Morran which makes for an excellent, secluded swim. If time permits, once back on St Martin's, head north and scramble 500 metres across the tidal rocks to nearby **Pernagie Isle**.

St Helen's

ACCESS BOAT TRIP
(RESTRICTIONS APRIL–SEPTEMBER)
This uninhabited island, formed as a single forty-four-metre hill, sits in the north of the archipelago between Tresco and St Martin's. The landing site is on a sandy beach on the south of the island where there are the remains

1 St Helen's, Pest House   2 Nornour, ruins of ancient village with Great Ganilly in the background

of a granite quay and low sand dunes at the top of the beach. St Helen's is home to one of the earliest Christian sites in Scilly, an eighth-century chapel, that sits on the island's south slope. A service is held there every August. The other building of note is the ruined Pest House, situated on a flat area behind the dunes. Also known as St Helen's Isolation Hospital, it was a quarantine station built to house plague cases from visiting ships calling at Old Grimsby. It was constructed after an Act of Parliament in 1754 decreed that any plague-ridden ship north of Cape Finisterre heading for England should anchor off this island. Visit as part of an organised tour from St Mary's or by private boat; access is restricted off the northern tip from April to September due to wildlife.

Teän

ACCESS BOAT TRIP
(RESTRICTIONS APRIL–SEPTEMBER)
Nestled between St Helen's to the north-west and St Martin's to the east, this tiny uninhabited island is composed of a series of granite tors, dune grassland, and sandy beaches. There are ruins of an early Christian chapel and graveyard and a nineteenth-century cottage to explore. Faint paths ascend Great Hill (the high point of the island at thirty-three metres) to visit a

Bronze Age entrance grave and to enjoy the expansive panorama. The rare dwarf pansy, a plant which only occurs on Scilly, can be spotted in the short coastal turf, in the sand dunes or at the entrances to rabbit burrows. Access as part of an organised tour from St Mary's or by private boat; access is restricted on the wildlife reserve in the centre of the island from April until September.

Other islands in the St Helen's Group

Accessible islands in the St Helen's Group include **Foremans Island** to the east of Tresco and **Northwethel** off Gimble Porth, Tresco. The latter consists of two hills connected by a low stretch of land with a sandy landing beach to the east and Bronze Age cairns, prehistoric field systems and hut circles at the island's highest point. Other islands where access is not permitted include the most northerly island of this group, **Round Island**, with an unmanned lighthouse on its summit, and **Men-a-vaur** to the north-west of St Helen's which consists of three granite slabs and is an important breeding site for the razorbill, fulmar and guillemot.

Nornour and Great Ganilly

ACCESS BOAT TRIP; RESTRICTIONS (GREAT GANILLY)
APRIL–SEPTEMBER

Nornour is an amazing island to explore for its incredible ancient ruins and outer edge feel. The whole island is a bracken-covered hill joined to Great Ganilly by a low-tide boulder tombolo. The views from its high point of twenty-three metres reach across most of the Scilly archipelago and back to mainland England and seals can be spotted in the sea below swimming in the kelp forest of the sheltered west coast. The island tells an incredible story of Romans re-using an Iron Age settlement for religious activity; which is a very rare occurrence. Uncovered in 1962 by a violent storm, an extensive settlement of ancient hut circles and a shrine to the goddess Sillina, who is linked to Sulis of Bath, were found along with Roman brooches, coins, glass beads, jewellery, spoons and clay figurines. It is thought that the Romans built this shrine to a local sea goddess so that Roman traders could assure their safe travel between mainland Europe and the British Isles by leaving an offering en route. Today, individual dwellings can be easily distinguished with room divisions, floors, hearth, entrance and courtyards clearly visible in these very atmospheric ruins. Great Ganilly consists of two hills joined together by a low sandy neck. The northern of the two hills is the high point at thirty-four metres. It has a ruined Bronze Age entrance grave on the summit, the stones of which have been used to make a navigational marker. Both islands can be visited as part of a boat tour from St Mary's; landing trips are available as part of organised tours and by private boat. There are landing restrictions on the wildlife-sensitive parts of Great Ganilly from April until September.

Other Eastern Isles

ACCESS BOAT TRIP; VARIED RESTRICTIONS

The Eastern Isles, including Nornour and Great Ganilly, are a group of twelve uninhabited islands located to the south-east of St Martin's that form a granite barrier to the east of the archipelago. Many of the islands are linked by sandbars or tombolos and the Eastern Isles has the largest assemblage of so-called tied islands outside of Shetland and Orkney. Most are covered by bramble and bracken with grass and pebbles or sand along their coastline. They have living histories that date back to the Bronze Age, Iron Age and Romans with field systems, cairns and entrance graves and a Roman shrine to explore. Wildlife is a big draw with grey seal pups in abundance and breeding colonies of gull, shag, cormorant, fulmar, razorbill and puffins. **Great, Middle and Little Arthur** are three rocky islands joined by two beaches forming a crescent around Arthur Porth with three entrance graves on the summit ridge connected by a prehistoric boulder wall. The high point of the group is at twenty-seven metres on Great Arthur. The Eastern Isles can be visited without landing as part of a boat tour from St Mary's; landing trips are available as part of organised archaeology tours and some islands may be landed on by private boat. There are complete restrictions on landing on **Menawethan**, **Innisvouls** and **Hanjague** and restrictions to landing during breeding season (April to September) on sensitive parts of **Little Ganinick**, Great Arthur and Great Ganilly, otherwise the other islands of this group are open all year. Check with the Isles of Scilly Wildlife Trust for details.
www.ios-wildlifetrust.org.uk/making-space-for-nature

For millennia, the exposed Cornish coast has been pounded by Atlantic swells splintering hundreds of tiny islands away from the mainland's rugged cliffs. Today, these islands are special places for seabirds, seals and rare plants. Some can be visited, others approached from the water and the wildest ones only viewed from the beautiful South West Coast Path. On the gentler south coast of Cornwall, St Michael's Mount, Looe Island and Drake's Island are popular destinations for day trippers. Many of these Cornish islands are close to the hotspot towns and villages, yet they are a world apart. Devon's islands are different again. Lundy and Burgh Island are packed with colourful human history, wildlife and family fun with the journey to them on a historic boat and a sea tractor an integral part of their appeal.

CORNWALL & DEVON

Opposite Lundy, coast path   **Overleaf** Asparagus Island

Bristol Channel

Porthcaw

Lundy
Rat Island

Barnstaple or
Bideford
Bay

Lynton

Ilfracombe

Barnstaple

Hartland Point

Bideford

Atlantic
Ocean

Bude

Launceston

Tavistock

Newland and The Mouls

Trevose Head

Padstow

Bodmin

Bedruthan Steps
Zacry's Islands
Flory Island
Porth Island
The Island

Newquay

Samphire Island
Crane Islands
Godrevy Island
The
Carracks

St Ives

Truro

St Austell

Camborne

Fowey

Looe

Plymouth

Ivybridge

Gribbin
Head

Looe Island

Rame
Head

Kingsbridge

Dodman
Point

Great
Mew Stone

Drake's
Island

Burgh Island

Salcombe

Penzance

Helston

Falmouth

Gull Rock
Inner Stone
Middle Stone
Outer Stone

Land's
End

St Michael's
Mount

St Clement's
Isle

Mullion Island

Lizard Point

English Channel

Asparagus Island

N

0   40km

The Carracks

ACCESS NON-LANDING BOAT TRIP; VIEW FROM MAINLAND PATH

This group of small rocky islands lie 200 metres off the northern coast of West Cornwall, between Zennor and St Ives. The largest island in the group is known as **Seal Island** as it is a major haul-out site for grey seals; the high point measures five metres. Popular wildlife-watching boat trips leave from St Ives, or the islands can be readily seen from the South West Coast Path on a great circular walk from Zennor – which has the added advantage of finishing at the atmospheric Tinners Arms.

Godrevy Island, Crane Islands and Samphire Island

ACCESS NON-LANDING BOAT TRIP; VIEW FROM MAINLAND PATH

These three tiny islands sit like gems along a spectacular eight-kilometre stretch of North Cornwall coastline between Godrevy Point and Porth-cadjack Cove. They can either be viewed from the South West Coast Path or directly explored with a little more effort. At the western end of this small chain, Godrevy Island lies just under 300 metres off Godrevy Point at the eastern side of St Ives Bay. The uninhabited island is dominated by Godrevy Lighthouse, thought to be the inspiration for Virginia Woolf's *To the Lighthouse*. This grass-topped island is home to seagulls, oystercatchers, pipits, primroses and sea thrift and the rocks at its base are a favourite haul-out spot for grey seals. Landing is only possible with permission from Trinity House, although the island can be circumnavigated on a boat trip from St Ives; one

option is aboard the historic St Ives Lifeboat, *James Stevens No.10*, that served in the early twentieth century, saving 255 lives. If viewing the island from the mainland, this popular National Trust-owned section of coastline has a cafe, toilets and swimming and surfing beaches close by. *www.stivesboats.co.uk*

To the east of Godrevy Island, the Crane Islands can be reached by a stunning six-kilometre walk from Godrevy Point, which includes the spectacular Hell's Mouth. The islands are at the bottom of a loose cliff which, despite faint paths, is not recommended for descent. Instead, the island can be reached by walking along the foreshore at low tide from Basset's Cove, slightly further to the east. The Crane Islands can also be accessed from the National Trust car park at Basset's Cove. This car park is also a convenient start point for a short walk north-east along the South West Coast Path to Samphire Island. Access to Porth-cadjack Cove is via a narrow grass path that turns left off the main coast path, following the line of a spring, then descending a steeper rocky scree slope, where a fixed rope is available, to reach the southern end of the beach. From here, at low tide, it is possible to scramble up steep-sided Samphire Island which was once farmed for the wild plant rock samphire. The high point of the group, at thirty-three metres, is located on Samphire Island.

The Island, Porth Island, Flory Island and Zacry's Islands

ACCESS FOOTBRIDGE; VIEW FROM MAINLAND PATH

Newquay, best known for its nightlife, famous surfing championships, beautiful beaches and

spectacular coastal scenery, also has a small clutch of islands that can all be reached from the South West Coast Path. The Island, closest to the town on Towan Beach, has an instantly recognisable holiday cottage perched high on its own rock and only accessible by a private suspension footbridge. Once a tea room, then a private home with astonishing Atlantic and beach views, it is now described as 'possibly the ultimate beach house' and can be booked for weekend or week-long breaks.
www.boutique-retreats.co.uk

Porth Island, north of family favourite Porth Beach on the eastern side of Newquay, is a peninsula connected to the mainland via a narrow footbridge. Low cliffs on the south side are contrasted by rugged high cliffs on the north side and the island boasts 'one of Cornwall's finest ancient monuments' – an Iron Age promontory fort with defensive ramparts and two round barrows dating from the early Bronze Age. There is also evidence of Iron Age smelting activity on the island with furnaces, ore roasting pits and slag excavated across the site, especially along the gully at the island entrance. The high point of this group (thirty-two metres) is on Porth Island. At the western tip there is an excellent blowhole and the views from here are spectacular looking back towards Newquay Bay and to Park Head in the north.

Flory Island (Black Humphrey Rock) near the steep steps on Whipsiderry Beach is a tiny island named after the smuggler known as Black Humphrey who lived in the mine workings at the base of this large, inaccessible sea stack before the sea eroded them to what they are today. Zacry's Islands are a pair of rock stacks between the hidden gem Whipsiderry Beach and Fruitful Cove that can be accessed by a low-tide walk from either beach. Both islands can be combined in a spectacular walk from Watergate Bay along the beaches to Whipsiderry Beach, crossing the rocks between Zacry's Islands and the cliffs, returning along the top of the cliffs on the South West Coast Path. There are some impressive caves, accessible from the beach, along this stretch of coast; the finest is The Cathedral Cavern, which

was once quarried for white marble and has a large pillar, a pool of water and several tunnels leading off. Another is Banqueting Hall, also known as Concert Cavern, where candlelit concerts have occasionally been held.

All three islands, Porth, Flory and Zacry's, can be visited in one walk (two hours either side of low tide) starting from Porth Beach, navigating through the cleft in the rocks from Porth Beach to Norwegian Rock, then on to Whipsiderry Beach and the rockpools and boulders between Zacry's Islands to reach Watergate Bay.
www.islandeering.com

Bedruthan Steps

ACCESS TIDAL CROSSING

A series of dramatic sea stacks between Newquay and Padstow. At low tide, a huge expanse of flat golden sand is revealed, allowing a visit to the base of each of the islands and their surrounding crystal-clear rockpools, as well as exploring the cliff caves along this spectacular stretch of coastline. The name Bedruthan Steps is taken from the legend of a Cornish giant, Bedruthan, who used the rocks on the beach as stepping stones. This tale was a Victorian ploy to encourage more visitors at the time. Each of the stacks is named. From north to south they are **Diggory's Island**, **Queen Bess Rock**, **Samaritan Island**, Bedruthan Steps, **Redcove Island**, **Pendarves Island** and **Carnewas Island**. Queen Bess Rock was so named as it was thought to resemble the outline of Queen Elizabeth I, although the head was lost after a storm in 1981; Samaritan Island was named after a ship, the *Good Samaritan*, which was wrecked here in October 1846; and Carnewas Island was named after the local iron mine. Bedruthan Steps is an accredited Dark Sky Discovery Site; the Milky Way can be readily discerned either from the beach or cliff tops. The islands are accessed by a steep cliff staircase, once used by silver, copper and iron miners in the late 1800s, off the South West Coast Path close to the

1 Godrevy Island   **2** Samphire Island, rope aid to descend cliff path   **3** Zacry's Islands   **4** Bedruthan Steps

National Trust car park, cafe and shop. At the time of writing, after rock falls in 2019, the staircase is currently closed. A steep track with a small scramble also leads down to Pentire Steps at the northern end of the beach.
www.islandeering.com

Newland and The Mouls

ACCESS NON-LANDING BOAT TRIP; VIEW FROM MAINLAND PATH
These two rocky islands that lie off Pentire Head, north of Padstow, are popular destinations for boat trips to see puffins, other seabirds and grey seals that haul themselves out of the sea on to the rocks. Bottlenose dolphins and basking sharks may also be seen on these trips. Newland, known locally as Puffin Island, is a prominent feature in the much-loved seascapes of Padstow and Polzeath. The Mouls (which has the high point of this group, at fifty metres) was visited during World War I by the poet Laurence Binyon; the island inspired some of his well-known work. Viewpoints of both islands from the mainland are best experienced from the trig point (grid reference: SW 929806) along the coast path walk around the dramatic coastline of Pentire Point. A six-kilometre circular walk around the headland starts at Lead Mines car park and offers great seascapes of Padstow Bay and beyond to Trevose Head. The Rumps can be reached across a narrow isthmus to see several outcrops of pillow lava and a prehistoric fort.

29

1 St Michael's Mount, the castle **2** St Michael's Mount, stained-glass windows in the chapel

St Clement's Isle

ACCESS SWIM; PADDLEBOARD; KAYAK

This tiny island lies 350 metres offshore from Mousehole, a sleepy fishing village on the outskirts of Penzance. The island's large square block of granite, with the inscription 'Lord of the Manor', is known as the Pepperpot and was erected in 1830 by J.A. Halse who possibly owned the island at that time. It is a popular destination for paddleboarders from Mousehole and swimmers. The island, which has a high point of five metres, is surrounded by sea life and offers an incredible underwater landscape to view as you swim. Mousehole is a magnet for visitors during the summer, and in the winter it is renowned for its winter traditions. Every December the harbour is illuminated with hundreds of Christmas lights, including the illumination of a Celtic cross on the island. Tom Bawcock's Eve is celebrated in the village every year on 23 December; it commemorates a local man who went out fishing in a ferocious storm to save the village from starvation. During the festival stargazy pie, with fish heads sticking up through the pastry, is eaten.

St Michael's Mount

ACCESS TIDAL CROSSING; NO DOGS

A tiny tidal island in Mount's Bay topped with a medieval chapel and turreted castle that form the heart of many local myths and legends. The island, named after the patron saint of high places, is a civil parish with around thirty islanders and is joined to Marazion by a granite causeway that is walkable at mid- to low-water. The Cornish counterpart of Mont Saint-Michel in Normandy, it is owned by the National Trust and is the family home of its previous owners, the St Aubyns. The island, which has a high point of sixty-two metres, marks the end of St Michael's Way, a twenty-kilometre walking route from Lelant, near St Ives. It is the only footpath in Britain that is part of a designated European Cultural Route and is part of a network of pilgrim routes that lead to Santiago de Compostela in Northern Spain.
www.nationaltrust.org.uk/st-michaels-mount

Extreme coastal gardening

The southern end of the island is a unique cliff-side garden where the effects of the Gulf Stream and the radiator effect of the granite rock in the sun allows plants such as agave, aloe, agapanthus, gazania and strelitzia to grow between the bedrock and the steep stone terraces. This spectacular garden has been designed to be viewed from above but there is a garden trail that can be followed. The sides of this garden are so steep that, to keep the granite free of invasive weeds, the gardeners need to abseil fifty metres down the castle walls.

Step on a giant's heart

As you climb the pathway to the castle, look out for the heart-shaped stone amongst the cobbles. Legend has it that it belonged to the giant Cormoran who, as the story goes, built the impressive castle atop St Michael's Mount, but he made a nuisance of himself by wading ashore every night to take children and cattle for his supper. Jack, a local boy, crept over to the island and dug a large 'giant-catching pit' which Cormoran fell into and disappeared with only his stone heart left. According to legend, if you are quiet, you can still hear the beat of the giant's unhappy heart.

Swim around the island

An organised annual three-kilometre high-tide swim from the beach at Marazion, around St Michael's Mount, offers great views of the causeway and rocks below the clear waters. *www.chestnutappeal.org.uk/events*

Visit the abbey

A spectacular sight perched on a rocky hill surrounded by blue water, it is well worth the climb to see the incredible views of the whole of Mount's Bay and explore the buildings here. The battlemented Chapel remains a peaceful place of pilgrimage with beautiful panels and a fifteenth-century rose window. The 1,300-book Library is replete with red velvet chairs, an Italian gaming table and a large fireplace and the Chevy Chase Room, perhaps the most impressive, contains a plaster frieze of hunting scenes that runs around the entire room with stained-glass windows made from fragments of Dutch and Flemish painted glass. The Blue Drawing Room displays portraits and landscape paintings by Cornish painter John Opie, while the Map Room is home to a model of St Michael's Mount made from champagne corks by Henry Lee, one of the castle's butlers. There is an eclectic display of weaponry including muskets, musket balls, Cromwellian armour and a Samurai suit of armour in the Garrison Room.

Mullion Island

ACCESS NOT PERMITTED; VIEW FROM MAINLAND PATH

This uninhabited island sits a short distance off picturesque Mullion Cove, on the eastern side of Mount's Bay. Composed of basalt and exposed pillow lava, this grass-topped island, which has a high point of twenty-two metres, was once used by local seine fishermen as a lookout post for passing shoals of pilchards. Currently owned by the National Trust, it is an important site for breeding great black-backed gulls, guillemots, shags and cormorants. Outside of nesting season it has been used in location shots for the 2015 TV series *And Then There Were None*, based on Agatha Christie's novel, that follows a group of strangers who were invited to a secluded island where they are murdered one by one for their past crimes. The harbour itself has a small, sheltered sand beach popular in summer with bathers. Although landing on the island is prohibited, it does make a good kayak circumnavigation from the harbour and there is some great diving around its base with deep gullies to explore and the remains of an iron cannon to find. The island can also be readily viewed from the tall cliffs of the South West Coast Path. There is a small cafe near the harbour and a car park nearby.

Asparagus Island

ACCESS TIDAL CROSSING
A small grass-topped tidal island named after the rare wild asparagus that grows here, lying within stunning Kynance Cove on the western side of The Lizard Peninsula. Made of translucent green serpentine blocks, invaded with granite and basalt, the island is flanked by two large rocks – **Gull Rock** and **The Bishop** – and sits below the impressive cliffs of the mainland to which it is linked by a tidal rock strand. The high point of the island is at twenty-nine metres. Asparagus has two blowholes, the Devil's Bellows and the Post Office, the latter named because the sea tunnelling along a fault creates enough suction to post a letter through the gap. Access is from the South West Coast Path, two hours either side of low tide, with a short scramble up the north-east tip of Asparagus Island; it is also possible to swim around all three islands. There is a National Trust car park nearby with a great cafe above Kynance Cove.

Gull Rock, Inner Stone, Middle Stone and Outer Stone

ACCESS SWIM; KAYAK
Located 600 metres off the gnarly headland of Nare Head, at the northern entrance to Gerrans Bay, the row of small, jagged islands are part of the infamous Whelps Reef and the scene of many shipwrecks. The largest is Gull Rock (which has the hight point of the group at thirty-seven metres), then Inner, Middle and Outer Stone. These rocky islands, especially Gull Rock, provide refuge, roosting and breeding places for many seabirds. From May to August they are home to a breeding colony of guillemots and razorbills, which bolster its roaming population of great black-backed gulls, herring gulls, cormorants and shags; landing is not recommended during this time. The islands can be approached by kayak or paddleboard leaving from the slipway at National Trust-owned Carne Beach. They can also be reached by a three-kilometre return swim from Kiberick Cove, either independently or via an organised swim. The islands are readily seen from the mainland along the South West Coast Path. A seven-kilometre route from Carne Beach, around Nare Head to Kiberick Cove, gives plenty of great views and interest on the way, including the deep rocky valley called Paradoe Cove where there is a cliff cave known as Tregagle's Hole and a Cold War bunker on the east side of Nare Head.

Looe Island

ACCESS SMALL FERRY; TIDAL CROSSING; NO DOGS
The island dream of two sisters, now a nature reserve and oasis of tranquillity away from the bustle of seaside Looe. Lying less than one kilometre off Cornwall's south coast, this island (which has a high point of forty-seven metres) is an unusual mix of woodland, grassland and beach all lovingly managed by the Cornwall Wildlife Trust. The fabulous views back to the mainland's coastline stretch from The Lizard to Prawle Point in Devon. The best way of experiencing the whole island is the gentle two-kilometre walk around the island's coast, which is packed with wildlife, smuggling legends and the fruits of self-sufficient living. A family yurt can be booked for a three-night stay on the island. To reach the island, a small passenger boat leaves Buller Quay, East Looe, tide and weather permitting (T: 07814 264 514). On the lowest spring tides, it is also possible to wade out to the island at low tide from near Hannafore Point.

1 Asparagus Island, sand tombolo at low tide   **2** Looe Island, in the hide   **3** Looe Island

Follow the island dream of two sisters

The spirits of the happy, self-sufficient sisters, Babs and Evelyn Atkins, who in the 1960s achieved their dream of owning an island, is all-pervasive – especially amongst the ramshackle vegetable plots, tales of elderflower champagne-making and their old home. All strongly conjure the sense of their bucolic yet harsh island life, more of which can be read about in Evelyn's book, *We Bought an Island*.

Seals and gulls

The Ranneys, small rocky outcrops on the eastern tip of Looe Island, are a popular haul-out site for grey seals and home to the largest great black-backed gull colony in Cornwall. The waters around here are a designated conservation zone, providing rich habitat for many fish species, pink sea fan, stalked jellyfish and cuttlefish. Along the island's south coast a small, green-turf-roofed bird hide is a good

1 Burgh Island, tombolo and sea tractor **2** Drake's Island

place to sit and watch the great black-backs, fulmars, herring gulls, cormorants and shags. The seals you'll spot here are individually named – Lucille, Duchess, Snowdrop and Sunrise. Inside the hide there is a helpful identification guide as well as shelves stacked with curious bottles of medicines used by previous inhabitants.

Drake's Island

ACCESS SMALL FERRY

This fortress island sits 500 metres away from the city of Plymouth in the Plymouth Sound and has only recently opened to the public. Named after Sir Francis Drake, who sailed from Plymouth in 1577 to circumnavigate the world and became the island's governor on his return, the island has a high point of twenty-five metres. Fortification began in 1549 as a defence against the French and Spanish and continued through to World War II. In the 1980s it was run as an adventure centre but today it is privately owned with tours of the derelict Napoleonic-era military buildings and tunnels available along with seasonal events. The admission charge includes the boat trip.
www.drakes-island.com

Great Mew Stone

ACCESS NOT PERMITTED; VIEW FROM MAINLAND PATH

A tiny, pyramidal island (which has a high point of fifty metres) with a surprisingly rich history just a short distance offshore of Wembury Point. Named after the old English name for the herring gull, it is often called 'Plymouth's mini Alcatraz' after a local man was sentenced to spend seven years living here in 1744 after committing a minor crime. His daughter, known as Black Joan, later moved to Looe Island and became one of its most notorious smugglers. In 1833, Samuel Wakeham negotiated to live his years of exile on Great Mew Stone instead of being transported to Australia as a criminal. He settled on the island with his family and enlarged an existing house to create the unusual turret-shaped building that can still be spotted today from Wembury Point. Wakeham created a garden and kept poultry and pigs and remained on the island until he was caught smuggling by excise men. The island then changed hands a few times until it was bought by the War Office after World War II; it was in the line of fire from gunnery school, HMS Cambridge, then based at Wembury Point. The restriction

3 Burgh Island, The Pilchard Inn   **4** Great Mew Stone

on public access greatly benefited the wildlife on the island; the National Trust purchased the island in 2006, to continue the protection of the nesting cormorants, great black-backed gulls, herring gulls, fulmars and Canada geese. Great Mew Stone is an important first landing and feeding site for migrant birds before they move further north. Landing on the island is prohibited, but it can be readily viewed from the stunning stretch of the South West Coast Path around Wembury Point.

Burgh Island

ACCESS TIDAL CROSSING

An iconic island located on the largest sandy beach in South Devon, directly opposite the popular village of Bigbury-on-Sea. There are several buildings here, the most prominent being the Art Deco Burgh Island Hotel, closely linked to Agatha Christie, and a bolt-hole in the 1930s for London's rich and famous, including Noel Coward. There's also an old smugglers' pub, The Pilchard Inn, three private houses and the remains of a building known as the huers hut along the high cliffs to the south of the island which was once used to watch out for shoals for the island's pilchard seine fishermen. The high point of the island is at forty-eight metres. Access is via a sea tractor ride during high tide or a walk across the causeway at low tide. There is a car park at Bigbury-on-Sea.

Paddleboard or swim around the whole island

It is possible to paddleboard around the whole island at high tide in good weather to explore the wilder side of the island with its hidden coves and caves and get glimpses of the hotel's grounds with its private tidal Mermaid Pool. Paddleboards are available for hire on Bigbury Beach. Alternatively, a full swimming circumnavigation is rewarded with a chance to swim through 'Death Valley', a rocky chasm between Little Island and Burgh Point that at specific tides amplifies the surf and becomes a maelstrom of water to challenge the stronger swimmer.

Walk around the island

There is an extensive network of footpaths that circumnavigate the island. Starting along the sand beach of the north, the tombolo is full of beachgoers during the summer months, especially when the tide starts to cover it and space becomes more restricted. The path ascends the island and passes between the inn and hotel to the rugged rocks and coves on the west coast and continues to ascend to the remains of the huers hut at the high point of the island, from which there is a precipitous cliff path across a narrow neck to Little Island. Returning, there are vantage points that overlook the hotel but the secretive Mermaid Pool remains hidden to all except for the hotel's guests.

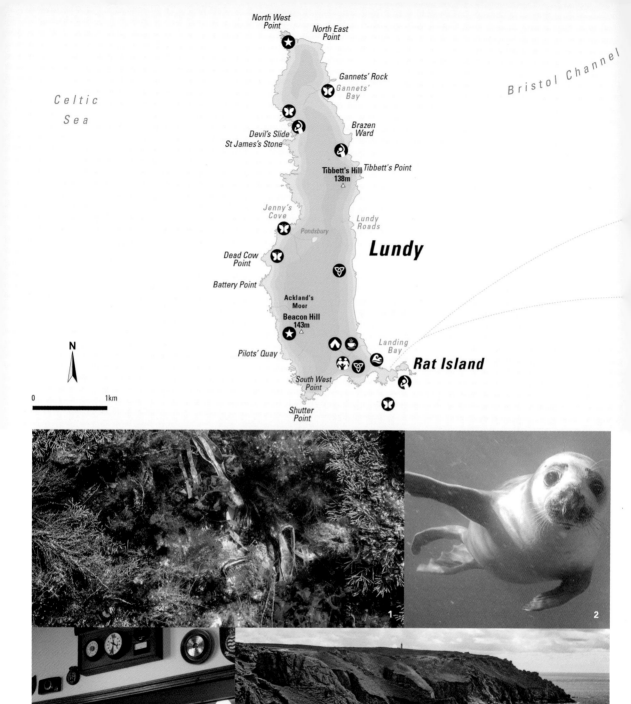

Celtic
Sea

Bristol Channel

North West
Point

North East
Point

Gannets' Rock

Gannets'
Bay

Brazen
Ward

Devil's Slide
St James's Stone

Tibbett's Hill
138m

Tibbett's Point

Jenny's
Cove

Pondsbury

Lundy
Roads

Lundy

Dead Cow
Point

Battery Point

Ackland's
Moor

Beacon Hill
143m

Landing
Bay

Rat Island

Pilots' Quay

South West
Point

Shutter
Point

N

0   1km

Lundy

ACCESS FERRY; HELICOPTER; NO DOGS

Once the haunt of pirates and chancers and now a haven for wildlife, this weather-battered lump of granite in the Bristol Channel packs well above its weight with things to see and do. The largest island in Devon, with a high point of 143 metres at Beacon Hill, it lies eighteen kilometres off the coast of North Devon at the point where the Atlantic Ocean meets the Bristol Channel. For hundreds of years this strategic position has attracted a number of unlawful profiteers. One of the most devious was the eighteenth-century North Devon MP, Thomas Benson, who was paid to deport convicts to the United States but instead dropped them on Lundy – several thousand kilometres short. A hundred years or so later the businessman Martin Coles Harman bought the island and declared himself the King of Lundy – he was later fined for setting up his own currency. The island's fortunes took a change for the better when Jack Hayward, the former owner of Wolverhampton Wanderers Football Club, bought Lundy in 1969 and donated it to the National Trust. Lundy is managed by the Landmark Trust. Today Lundy is a magnet for day trippers and holiday makers, who visit to get away from it all, relax and enjoy the wildlife, particularly the puffins and seals. The Marisco Tavern serves local beer and food and there is a full range of supplies in the general stores. Self-catering accommodation in restored buildings includes the old castle and lighthouse (none with TV, radio or internet) and there is also a rustic campsite. The historic *MS Oldenburg* is Lundy's own ferry and supply ship that sails at least three times a week (April to October) from either Bideford or Ilfracombe on a two-hour crossing, leaving four to six hours to explore the island depending on the day you choose to travel. In the winter a helicopter service runs from Hartland Point on Mondays and Fridays. *www.landmarktrust.org.uk*

Rockpooling

Between Lundy and Rat Island, Devil's Kitchen is one of the richest places in Britain for exploration of the seashore. Here, the slate bedrock has been worn away to form a series of rockpools and gullies bursting with marine life. You'll find brown, red and green seaweeds; barnacles and limpets; and beadlet, strawberry, and snakelocks anemone. Turning over small rocks also often reveals shore crabs, cushion starfish, pipefish, gobies and blennies as well as jewel anemone, sea squirts and clingfish. The lucky may spot a Lundy special – the nationally scarce scarlet and gold star corals. The island's wardens lead Rockpool Rambles to Devil's Kitchen and Snorkel Safaris in the shallow waters of Landing Bay.

Puffins and seabirds

The island's plateau of grass and heath is a haven for resident and migrant birds, while the rugged coastline supports some of the largest seabird colonies in Southern England. Spring (March to June) and autumn (August to November) are the periods of greatest interest for birdwatchers when thousands of migrant birds land on the island. Up to thirty-five bird species nest here during the spring season. Lundy is one of the best places in England to see puffins, the largest concentrations being around Jenny's Cove and St Peter's Stone on the western coast (April to July). Breeding guillemots, kittiwakes, Manx shearwaters and razorbills are equally abundant. Inland, skylarks are regularly spotted along with water rail in the wetter areas. With around 140 species recorded on Lundy each year, there's always something to be seen whether you're on a day trip or staying longer.

Swim with seals

The island has its own resident population of around 200 grey seals that can be seen all around Lundy hauled out on the rocks at low tide. Gannets' Bay is a popular spot for divers

1 Lundy, rockpool   2 Lundy, seal   3 Lundy, Marisco Tavern   4 Lundy, Jenny's Cove

and snorkelers; curious seals can often be spotted nipping the fins of divers and playing in the water. Bookings can be made through mainland boat trip operators.

While away an evening in the Marisco Tavern

The Marisco Tavern is a proper pub with excellent locally-brewed ales, food served all day, piles of board games and a dartboard. Originally the pub was in the old village stores built during the 1860s when the quarrying operation employed around 300 men and needed a 'refreshment room'. In the early 1980s the pub was redeveloped by the Landmark Trust and the bar moved into the former residence of islander Felix Gade. Today the pub provides a restaurant and social hub for island staff and guests and is a magnet for day-trippers wanting a pint of Dutch courage before they return to mainland on the *MS Oldenburg*. It's the only building on the island to have lighting after the generators shut down for the night with any walk back to lodgings illuminated by the starry canopy that shines so brightly away from light pollution.

Find the Lundy Letterboxes

A kind of treasure trail across the whole island with twenty-seven hidden letterboxes which can be found by following a set of clues. Each box contains a rubber stamp that is unique to its box and the objective is to discover all of the boxes and collect the stamps, including the elusive 'Lundy Bunny' which is a movable stamp. Letterbox packs are available to purchase from the shop, and compasses available for hire should you not have one. It is fun for adults and children alike.

Climb some tough routes

Some of the best climbing in the British Isles can be found on Lundy, the majority of which is located on the west coast between Old Light and Threequarter Wall. The immaculate granite cliffs of Lundy, some up to 120 metres high, provide over 1,000 documented routes. When high winds or big seas make climbing on the west coast impossible, there are good climbs on Halfway Buttress on the east coast, around the obvious Logan Stone. Iconic Lundy climbs include *Satan's Slip*, *Albion* and the *Devil's Slide* – a huge span of pristine granite which sweeps

1

down into the ocean and one of the UK's most famous slab climbs. To avoid disturbing nesting seabirds, access restrictions on some routes generally apply between the end of March and August.

Lundy coast path ⚡ ★ 🦋

The fourteen-kilometre circular coast path can be completed in a day trip from the mainland and is mostly well off the beaten track. With its starkly contrasting coastlines and views to the Gower Peninsula and Exmoor, this is the best way to get a real feel for Lundy. The route starts at the pier at The Landing Beach and heads north along the gentle slope of the east coast. The only buildings along this stretch are the restored buildings of the Lundy Granite Company. Further north, spectacular rock formations lead to Gannets' Bay from where there is a steep ascent to the plateau at the north end of the island. The North Lighthouse makes for an exhilarating detour down steep stone steps and across two iron bridges. Walking south down the western coast, the precipitous cliffs are home to some of the UK's most iconic sea cliff climbs and the island's hotspots for seabird watching. Slightly inland,

the geological feature known as the Earthquake is formed from two deep fissures in the rock with several deep chasms which are great to explore. Towards the island's south-west tip the Old Light, on the highest base for a lighthouse in Britain, is a good place to climb up the cantilevered staircase to enjoy the views of the whole island from the deckchairs in the glazed lantern gallery. Along the south coast you can find a smugglers' cave and the ruins of Marisco Castle before arriving at the village. *www.islandeering.com*

Rat Island

ACCESS TIDAL CROSSING; NO DOGS

Accessed at low tide from the coast path in the south-east corner of Lundy, this tiny island offers an atmospheric walk through its subterranean tunnel. The island's high point of thirty-four metres can be reached from the rocks on its south side and heading towards South Light. The short scramble is well worth it for views of Barnstaple Bay and the east coast of Lundy and the possibility of spotting dolphins in the water. Not to be attempted if seals are on the access beach.

Britain's South Coast between Swanage and Chichester contains a series of wonderful natural harbours within which are a fabulous array of islands. Poole Harbour is Europe's largest natural harbour and is fringed with unspoilt woodland and coastal walks. The jewel in its crown is Brownsea Island, famed as the birthplace of the Scouting movement and home to a thriving population of red squirrels. Across The Solent, the Isle of Wight fits like a jigsaw piece to the coastline near Southampton. The largest island in England, it has hundreds of kilometres of paths and cycle routes, extraordinary nature, great beaches and a burgeoning foodie scene. Further east, Portsea Island is the most populated island in Britain and holds over 800 years of British naval history. The south coast of neighbouring Hayling Island is the birthplace of windsurfing as well as a training ground for the epic missions of World War II heroes.

ISLE OF WIGHT & THE SOUTH COAST

Opposite Portsea Island, Spinnaker Tower **Overleaf** Isle of Wight, Watcombe Bay

Isle of Wight

ACCESS FERRY; HOVERCRAFT

A county in itself and the largest island in England, this sunshine-rich island gem is a treasure trove of attractions, natural wonders and outdoor activities. Lying just three kilometres across The Solent, it is also easy to reach from the mainland. There is huge diversity and character in its Victorian-era holiday resorts and quaint rural settlements, from the county town of Newport to the stylish port of Cowes. Its patchwork of landscapes rolls seamlessly from the dramatic, fossil-packed chalk cliffs, wild beaches and deep chines of the south coast to the wildlife-filled estuaries of the north. There is downland, old forests and bucolic farmland to explore in the island's interior; the high point of the island at St Boniface Down reaches 241 metres. With so many important habitats, the whole island is a UNESCO Biosphere Reserve. The island is also rich in history and culture. As the front line

of coastal defences through the ages it has a wealth of historic places to visit. It is also an entertainment destination with a multitude of high profile annual festivals and a local food offering that is undergoing a bit of a revolution with quality cafes and some great restaurants. There is plenty of outdoor action too. Criss-crossed by footpaths and cycle routes, it is a very popular destination for walkers and cyclists and, with its maritime heritage, it is per-ennially popular with sailors and water sports enthusiasts alike. There are several transport links from the mainland including the hovercraft from Southsea and ferries from Southampton, Lymington and Portsmouth.

Spot a white-tailed eagle 🦅

In the last few years eagles have been re-introduced to the Isle of Wight with plans for up to sixty in the coming years. With a wing-span of up to 2.5 metres, they have earned the nickname of 'flying barn doors'. They can be spotted all over the island but, with a favourite diet of fish and water birds, they are often seen hunting over The Solent and surrounding estuaries. The woods and cliffs of the island make quiet areas for them to rest. Under a joint conservation project between Forestry England and the Roy Dennis Wildlife Foundation, the chicks are collected under licence in Scotland and the birds are reared at a secret location on the island before release to the wild. They can fly significant distances in a day and the island's eagles have been found as far away as southern Scotland, Norfolk and Yorkshire before returning to their home.

Walk or cycle around the whole island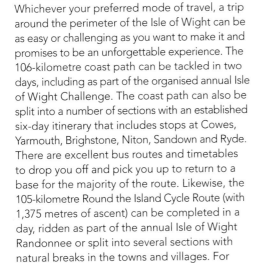

Whichever your preferred mode of travel, a trip around the perimeter of the Isle of Wight can be as easy or challenging as you want to make it and promises to be an unforgettable experience. The 106-kilometre coast path can be tackled in two days, including as part of the organised annual Isle of Wight Challenge. The coast path can also be split into a number of sections with an established six-day itinerary that includes stops at Cowes, Yarmouth, Brighstone, Niton, Sandown and Ryde. There are excellent bus routes and timetables to drop you off and pick you up to return to a base for the majority of the route. Likewise, the 105-kilometre Round the Island Cycle Route (with 1,375 metres of ascent) can be completed in a day, ridden as part of the annual Isle of Wight Randonnee or split into several sections with natural breaks in the towns and villages. For the leisurely rider, the Taste Round the Island Route follows the same route but gives cyclists the chance to discover the Isle of Wight's cafes, restaurants, inns and local foods, while burning off the extra calories in the process.
www.isleofwightchallenge.com
www.cycleisland.co.uk
www.visitisleofwight.co.uk/things-to-do/cycling/bicycle-island/taste-round-the-island-route

Go fossil hunting

The Isle of Wight, or 'Dinosaur Island', is one of the richest places in the UK for dinosaur remains. There are several top spots for finding fossils of all different sorts. Along the south coast large dinosaur foot casts can be seen at Compton Bay; they are also scattered along the coast slightly east of Hanover Point and Fossil Forest. Rocken End, west of Niton, is a quiet and stunning location and is a good place to find ammonites and other molluscs, either on the foreshore or in the small inland quarry; this makes for an excellent day out for all the family. On the north coast between Yarmouth and Hamstead, at the base of Bouldnor Cliff, the foreshore and cliffs are great for finding fossils of mammals, crocodiles, turtles, crustaceans, fish, molluscs, plants and seeds – look out for the giant fossilised oysters here too. The Isle of Wight also has some remarkable geology at locations such as Alum Bay with its multi-coloured sand cliffs.

Find the hidden beach at Watcombe

Just west of Freshwater Bay, remote Watcombe Bay is cut into the chalk cliffs below Fort Redoubt. Its sand and pebble beach is often deserted and there are caves to explore through the cliffs. Not for the faint-hearted, the only way to get there is to swim or kayak from Freshwater Bay on a calm sea; at the lowest of spring tides it is also possible to scramble around the headland. The bay can be spotted from the cliffs above, along the Isle of Wight Coastal Path.

Rockpooling at Bembridge

The raised beach between Bembridge and Foreland is a rockpooling mecca of vast, shallow pools full of life. Depending on the time of year you might find brittle star, snakelocks anemone, crabs, periwinkles, starfish or goby. You might even be lucky to find one of the famed edible Bembridge crabs, lobsters and spider crabs – or, if not, there are plenty of places to buy them in the town.

Gull Island

Portsea
Island

Gosport   Portsmouth

The *S o l e n t*

Cowes

Osborne Bay

Lymington

Thorness
Bay

Wootton   A3054   Ryde   Seaview

St Helen's P

Hamstead   Newtown   Parkhurst
Forest   A3020

Yarmouth   A3054   Newport   A3055   B3330   Bembridge

Colwell
Bay   B3401   *Foreland*

Totland   Brading   B3395

Freshwater   B3401   Arreton

Alum Bay   **Brighstone**
Forest   A3056   Sandown

The Needles   *Compton*
Bay   Brook   B3323   Rookley   A3020   *Sandown*
Bay

Brighstone   Godshill   Shanklin

Isle of Wight   A3055   B3399   *St Catherine's*
Down   B3327   Ventnor

N

Atherfield
Point   Niton

0   5km   *Chale*
Bay   St Lawrence

St Catherine's
Point   *English Channel*

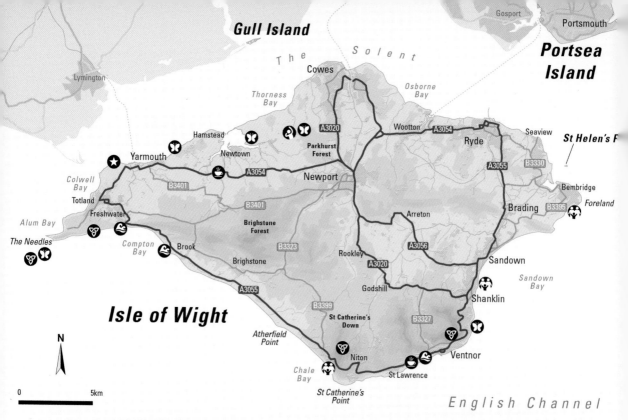

Giant crickets at St Boniface Down

St Boniface Down is the highest point on the Isle of Wight with great views over the coastline at Ventnor. It is also home to the seven-centimetre-long great green bush-cricket which, from May to October, can be seen in the trees and grassland or their very loud sewing machine-like 'song' may be heard. Cricket-spotting may be combined with a fabulous circular walk from the car park at Ventnor Downs, across Luccombe Down, Bonchurch Down and St Boniface Down. Some sections are steep, but it is worth it for the views to Sandown Bay, Culver Cliff and across the island towards Portsmouth. There is also the chance of bumping into the island's feral herd of Old English Goats on Bonchurch Down and Coombe Bottom. The walk passes various World War II buildings and the RAF Ventnor radar station, which played an important role in the Battle of Britain.

St Catherine's Oratory

This romantic ruin, also known as the 'Salt Pot', high on St Catherine's Down and overlooking Chale Bay, is reputed to be the only medieval lighthouse in England and the subject of a colourful local legend. It was built in the fourteenth century when the Pope ordered the Lord of the Manor, Walter de Godeton, to build an oratory and beacon on Chale Down as penance for his theft of wine from a French ship that ran aground on the rocks below. After this original structure fell into disrepair, building work was started on a lighthouse in 1785 but was never completed because the hill is so often shrouded in mist. A more functional lighthouse was built on the coast at St Catherine's Point in 1838.

Ventnor Botanic Garden

These gardens boast a large collection of rare and exotic plants; they lie at the heart of The Undercliff, which has a remarkable microclimate, as it is protected from cold northerly winds. 'Britain's Hottest Garden' talks of itself as an experiment to understand which plants are likely to thrive in the warmer UK of the future. Founded by Sir Harold Hillier, it is the site of various national collections and some of the biggest specimens of giant Amazonian water lilies in the world are grown in its large tropical house. The warmer climate has also attracted amazing wildlife such as wall lizards, slow worms and Iberian ants. Guided tours of a Victorian tunnel which leads down to the sea (dating from when the site was a hospital) are available.

www.botanic.co.uk

Crab sandwich in Steephill Cove

A pretty, hidden sandy cove along The Undercliff near Ventnor with a handful of traditional shacks, cottages and cafes that feels like a step back in time. With no road access, it is a tranquil spot to indulge in fresh lobster and crab, people-watch and laze in a deckchair with a coffee. The cove's Beach Shack cooks up the day's catch from local fishermen and the Crab Shed features the catch of the day, fresh mackerel and the popular, albeit small, crab pasties. Access by walking the coast path around the cove is highly recommended; otherwise there are car parks along the A3055.

Explore a chine

These steep-sided coastal ravines, where a river flows through eroding cliffs to the sea, are common features of the Isle of Wight's south coast. Each has its own character depending on geology and wildlife and over the ages they have been used to access the sea by smugglers, wreckers and pleasure seekers alike. There are about twenty chines to explore on

1 Isle of Wight, Watcombe Bay **2** Isle of Wight, white-tailed eagle
3 Isle of Wight, Dinosaur foot cast near Hanover Point **4** Isle of Wight, Whale Chine

the island, although access does vary if storms have altered their features. The main chine for visitors is Shanklin Chine, a lush tree- and fern-lined ravine that cuts its way from Shanklin Old Village to the sandy beach and Esplanade far below. This pay-for-entry family-friendly gorge first opened in 1817 and is the longest established attraction on the island. It can be enjoyed by day or at night, when hundreds of lights illuminate the narrow paths, streams and waterfalls. Nearby Luccombe Chine, between Shanklin and Ventnor, is a deep, wooded chine that leads to a remote beach. A footpath runs down to Luccombe Chine where it is possible to scramble down an old landslip on to the beach. Whale Chine, above Chale Beach, is another scramble down a few steps and a rope to a deserted beach, or can be viewed from the coast path.

Circular walk to Tennyson Down, The Needles and Alum Bay

Experience a number of the island's highlights in this ten-kilometre circular walk. Start at Freshwater Bay and follow the coast path west to climb the chalk downland above Fort Redoubt and on to Tennyson Down. From this vantage point there are great views of the island's south and north coastlines, and it's one of the only places in the world to find the rare early gentian. There are also Bronze Age burial mounds and a mortuary enclosure, where bodies of the dead would have been left exposed to the elements and their bones subsequently collected and buried. Continue past the large Celtic cross of Tennyson's Monument and on to The Needles, with its lighthouse and iconic chalk sea stacks which are best viewed from the National Trust's pay-for-entry Needles Old Battery – a Victorian-era coastal defence. Further up the headland, the free-to-enter underground rooms of the Needles New Battery tell the fascinating story of the secret British rocket testing programme here between the 1950s and 1970s. The route continues towards Alum Bay with its famous multi-coloured sands. From here, walk east to Headon Warren Barrow to re-join the coast path at Tennyson's Monument via the popular Highdown Inn.

Watch a sunset

There are plenty of special spots to finish off the day on the island with an incredible sunset view. On the west coast Colwell Bay, near Freshwater, offers spectacular sunsets and views back across The Solent to mainland England, and is also a generally calm bay for a sunset swim. Just south of this, Totland Bay is a pebble beach – enjoy a pint from The Waterfront pub as you watch the

sun sink over the horizon. The Needles area has three good vantage points. The first is from the raised decking at the north end of The Needles car park; the second is up the hill from the car park to the Needles New Battery; the third is from Headon Warren. Along the south coast, great sunsets can be caught from the top of the cliffs along the Military Road, especially around Whale Chine. Gurnard is a great spot on the north coast where you can also enjoy the good local food and the buzz of its sailing scene.

Look for the Milky Way

There are plenty of opportunities to stargaze on the island, especially along the Military Road in the south. The best spots with car parks are Freshwater Bay, Compton Bay, Brook Chine, Whale Chine, Yaverland and Culver Down. More remote locations with darker skies include Brighstone Cliff, The Needles Headland, St Catherine's Down, Brading Down and Mottistone. The Isle of Wight Observatory, near Newchurch, is frequently open to the public for regular stargazing sessions along with the Island Planetarium, near Yarmouth, which also has an astrodome theatre.

Wildlife walks around Newtown National Nature Reserve

This large natural harbour on the island's north-west coast offers tranquillity, unspoilt beauty and a huge variety of wildlife that thrives in the estuary, mudflats, salt marsh, wild-flower meadows and woodlands of the reserve. Managed by the National Trust, there are waymarked trails with plenty of opportunities for birdwatching in the various hides. The walks start from the hamlet of Newtown which in medieval times was a thriving borough with a busy harbour, saltworks and many oyster beds until it started to decline as a result of the combination of the Great Plague and a French raid. Today the Old Town Hall is the only evidence of Newtown's former importance and it stands alone on a grass area that was once a wide street. Nearby is Newtown's oldest house,

known as Noah's Ark, which refers to the boat and lion illustrated on the seal above the front door. It was formerly a pub called the Newtown Arms Inn, which closed in 1916. The large ponds around the Quay were formerly used for salt production. The walk can be extended along the coastal path, via Cassey Bridge, along the roads and tracks to Shalfleet and on to its Quay, from where you can enjoy more fine estuary views and a potential stop for refreshments at the excellent New Inn.

Red Squirrel Trail and Parkhurst Forest

The Red Squirrel Trail is a fifty-one-kilometre mostly traffic-free cycling route from Cowes to Sandown and Shanklin that passes through estuaries, woodland, farmland, downland and coastline. Many people start at Shanklin and cycle the family-friendly twenty-three-kilometre section of the route through Wroxall, Merstone and Sandown. Parkhurst Forest near Newport is a popular extension to the main trail. This mix of remnant ancient woodland, heathland and Forestry Commission plantation woodland offers kilometres of footpaths and gravel tracks to enjoy while you watch out for the island's famous red squirrels. The best place to spot them is from the Red Squirrel Hide, to the north-west of the forest car park.

St Helen's Fort

ACCESS TIDAL CROSSING

Lying one kilometre east of St Helens village just north of Bembridge, St Helen's Fort is the smallest in a chain of Palmerston Forts built in The Solent to protect Portsmouth from Napoleon III and the French. Although private and not open to the public, on the lowest spring tides there is an unofficial mass walk from St Helens Beach out to the fort and back along a causeway, usually followed by a beach barbecue. Walking access is also possible from the spit from Bembridge. The island has a high point of less than five metres.

Brownsea Island

ACCESS SMALL FERRY; KAYAK; NO DOGS

A flourishing wildlife haven with woods, lagoons and unspoilt beaches, a world apart from the bustle of Poole Harbour. Sitting serenely just 400 metres away from the glass-fronted mansions and urban foreshore of 'Millionaires Row' at the mouth of the harbour, Brownsea bursts with flowers and wildlife and was recently voted the best nature reserve in the UK. A string of eccentric owners has shaped this island's character and most famously it is the spiritual home to Scouts worldwide. Today it is in the joint ownership of the National Trust and the Dorset Wildlife Trust; part of the island is leased to the John Lewis Partnership. A National Trust cafe on the island serves all the usual fare and there are hot drinks and ice cream at the Scout camp. Overnight visitors can stay in one of the two National Trust self-catering cottages on the water's edge; or spend a night under the stars at the campsite which also has tree tents. The high point of the island, located at Lincoln Cliff Head, is twenty-seven metres. Regular ferries for foot passengers leave from Poole Quay and Sandbanks for the short crossing. It is possible to kayak or swim to the island but watch out for the ferries and other boating traffic.
www.brownseaislandferries.com

Circular walk 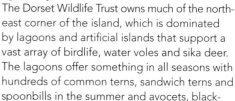 around the island

The nine-kilometre walk around the edge of the island passes through a wide range of habitats and offers ever-changing coastal vistas as well as a visit to most of the island's highlights. Starting at the landing pier and kiosk, it passes the statue of Robert Baden-Powell, the founder of the Scouting movement, before entering the Dorset Wildlife Trust reserve with its hides offering a close-up peek at the bountiful bird life on the lagoons and the island's famed red squirrels seen jumping from tree to tree. Pottery Pier, on the west coast, is full of the ceramic fragments of the ill-fated porcelain works. Then, along the south coast, the site of the original Scout camp still offers nights under the stars for Scouts, Guides and members of the public. From this stretch of coastline there are multiple access points to South Shore, a great place to bathe and swim. The route returns to the pier via a peacock-filled lawn in front of the church which is a great place for a picnic.
www.islandeering.com

Spot a spoonbill

The Dorset Wildlife Trust owns much of the north-east corner of the island, which is dominated by lagoons and artificial islands that support a vast array of birdlife, water voles and sika deer. The lagoons offer something in all seasons with hundreds of common terns, sandwich terns and spoonbills in the summer and avocets, black-tailed godwits and wildfowl in the winter.

Watch red squirrels

Brownsea Island is a safe haven for red squirrels with over 200 living in its woodlands. The Dorset Wildlife Trust's reserve is one of the best places to watch for red squirrels. An interpretation centre is located in The Villa, which is a great place to sit on the benches in the sun, watching birds and squirrels nibbling seeds from the nearby feeders. They can also be spotted hopping along the boardwalks that hover over the creeks of primordial-looking water and fern-covered logs before reaching the entrance to the reserve.

Camp where the Scouting movement started

Spend a night under the stars on the very spot the first Scouts camped over 100 years ago. This unique campsite on the south side of Brownsea Island overlooks the Purbeck Hills, with Old Harry Rocks in the distance, and is within easy reach of the sandy beach on the southern shore. The campsite is well placed for a variety of paths around the island which are a joy to walk once all of the day visitors have left and you have the island to yourself. There are showers, toilets and drinking water but no food shopping facilities so bring your own supplies.
www.nationaltrust.org.uk/holidays/campsite-brownsea-island-dorset

Brownsea Swim

The Royal Life Saving Society (RLSS) Poole Lifeguard club runs this annual charity event for around 300 swimmers to swim 6.5 kilometres of open water to circumnavigate the island. With appropriate support and knowledge of tidal flows, especially with Poole Harbour's unique tides, it is also possible to swim around the island as a private group.
www.brownseaswim.org.uk

Open air Shakespearian theatre ★

Brownsea Open Air Theatre performs a Shakespeare play on the island during July and August. Boats are laid on to ferry theatre goers to and from Poole Harbour.
www.brownsea-theatre.co.uk

Other islands in Poole Harbour

ACCESS ROUND ISLAND ONLY (PRIVATE BOAT/KAYAK)
Poole Harbour is a large natural shallow harbour and home to a wealth of wildlife and secluded places as well as being a busy commercial port and centre for a wide range of recreational activities. There are nine islands within the harbour, and its smaller channels and inlets. The largest, Brownsea Island, sits at its sea entrance. To the north of the harbour, Holes Bay is a shallow, inland tidal lake between Poole Bridge and Twin Sails Bridge that is home to the wild and uninhabited **Pergins Island**. Part of the Upton Estate and owned by Poole Borough Council, this island sits just offshore and yet is an increasingly important stopping off point for migrating ospreys, especially between April and August.

South of Holes Bay, in Poole Harbour itself, uninhabited **Long Island** lies just off the Arne Peninsula. Owned by a property developer, access is not permitted. Neighbouring privately-owned **Round Island** has a large house, pier and rentable holiday cottages. Harry Paye, a fifteenth-century pirate, is said to have lived here and an annual fun day in Poole is held in his name. As the story goes, Paye intercepted hundreds of French ships for gold, wine and exotic fruits which he distributed to the people of the town. Old Harry Rocks, off the Isle of Purbeck, are named after him; it's alleged that he used them for cover before attacking passing merchant ships. From 1940, Round Island was requisitioned by the Royal Navy and combined as a training ground with *HMS Turtle* at the Marines base in Hamworthy.

Green Island, the third largest in Poole Harbour, has the high point of this group of small islands (twenty metres). It lies to the east of the harbour and is again a private island with a huge family eco-house. It was previously run by a charity giving outdoor experiences to people with spinal injuries. Today it is an important nature reserve. In 2004, Channel 4's *Time Team* found the remains of an Iron Age furnace and evidence of the production of shale jewellery that was thought to have been exported to Europe. Pine-clad **Furzey Island**, between Green and Brownsea islands, is the second largest in the harbour and home to twenty-two oil wells on the Wytch Farm Oil Field. This is the largest inland oil field in Britain and its pipeline delivers oil directly to Hamble on Southampton Water.

In the west of the harbour, near the River Piddle outlet, **Gigger's Island** is owned by the Dorset Wildfowlers' Association whose members shoot teal, wigeon, mallard and pintail. **Stone Island** is a ridge of gravel and sand, possibly the remains of an old, recurved shingle spit, which is only visible between high tides. It sits to the west of the chain ferry at the harbour's mouth. Finally, **Drove Island**, a small marshy island, lies in the south of the harbour in Brand's Bay. All of these islands, along with the whole of Poole Harbour, can be explored by kayak all year round.

1 Old Harry Rocks

Old Harry Rocks

ACCESS KAYAK; PADDLEBOARD

These three iconic chalk formations, including a stack and a stump, are located at Handfast Point on the Isle of Purbeck at the easternmost point of the Jurassic Coast, a UNESCO World Heritage Site. The rocks, owned by the National Trust, can be viewed from the South West Coast Path at Ballard Down. Old Harry Rocks used to be part of a long stretch of chalk between Purbeck and the Isle of Wight before large parts of this seam were eroded away. They are an excellent destination for sea kayakers, where the small caves and huge stacks can be experienced up close.

Gull Island

ACCESS NOT PERMITTED; VIEW FROM MAINLAND PATH

A small, uninhabited island at the mouth of the Beaulieu River in The Solent that rises shallowly (to a high point of less than five metres) above the tidal sands to the east of Needs Ore Point. Consisting primarily of salt marsh, it is part of the North Solent National Nature Reserve and an important breeding site for birds. It is illegal to land on the island. Great views of the island can be seen along the coast path to the west of Lepe Country Park, best completed at low tide to permit walking along the shingle beach.
www.hants.gov.uk/thingstodo/countryparks/lepe

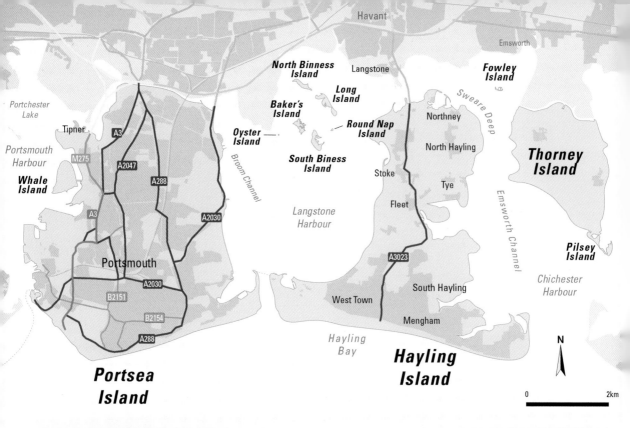

Portchester
Lake

Tipner

Portsmouth
Harbour

Whale
Island

Portsmouth

**Portsea
Island**

Havant

Emsworth

**North Binness
Island**

Langstone

**Long
Island**

**Baker's
Island**

Oyster
Island —

**Round Nap
Island**

**South Biness
Island**

Stoke

Broom Channel

Langstone
Harbour

**Fowley
Island**

Sweare Deep

Northney

North Hayling

Tye

Fleet

**Thorney
Island**

Emsworth Channel

**Pilsey
Island**

Chichester
Harbour

West Town

South Hayling

Mengham

Hayling
Bay

**Hayling
Island**

N

0   2km

Portsea Island

ACCESS ROAD BRIDGE; FOOTBRIDGE; FERRY

Home to the waterfront city of Portsmouth, this island vividly chronicles 800 years of British naval history through its historic dockyard, King Henry VIII's ship the *Mary Rose* and a wide variety of fascinating military museums and historic buildings. Portsea is the most populated island in Britain; it is separated from the mainland by the narrow tidal Ports Creek. Surrounded by Portsmouth and Langstone harbours, with the Spithead area of The Solent to the south, it is a very popular spot for sailing and water sports and was recently endorsed by Ben Ainslie who made it his British Racing headquarters. Portsea is an island for the good times too, with a string of summer festivals, sporting events, great food and drink and plenty of space on its beaches for everyone. Some of the best views on the South Coast can be seen from the top of the iconic Spinnaker Tower. The high point of the island (measuring eight metres) is at St Mary's Church. The island is connected to the mainland by three main road bridges and a foot and cycle bridge; it also has four railway stations. Ferry services leave Portsea bound for mainland Gosport, Hayling Island, the Isle of Wight, the Channel Islands, France and Spain.

Spinnaker Tower

Modelled on a sail, this iconic tower is the tallest publicly accessible structure in the United Kingdom outside of London. The views of Portsmouth, Southsea and the Isle of Wight from the viewing deck are fantastic at any time, but at sunset are truly special. Walk across the vertiginous glass Sky Walk and watch the boats below. The Sky Garden has an open roof and is a unique place to have coffee, 105 metres above the harbour. For the adventurous, it is also possible to abseil down the side of the building.

Go crabbing in Canoe Lake

With its swan-shaped boats to hire, a bronze statue of an angel and colourful flowerbeds, Canoe Lake is good to walk around and fun for the children. Grab a bucket and fishing line and catch crabs in the lake. It's also just across the road from Southsea Beach if you fancy a swim.

Viviers Fish Market

On the historic Camber Dock, adjacent to The Point, Viviers sells some of the freshest seafood on the South Coast. With tantalising displays of fresh fish, crab, lobster and shellfish you can also watch the comings and goings of the boats of the small fishing fleet based here if you get up early enough. Ben Ainslie's racing headquarters are also located on Camber Dock and The Dolphin, reputed to be Portsmouth's oldest pub, is almost next door.

Portsmouth Historic Dockyard

Any trip to the UK's most significant naval port must include a visit to at least one of its celebrated landmarks or museums. Portsmouth Historic Dockyard is a good starting point. It is home to the Mary Rose Museum which includes the ship itself, once Henry VIII's favourite before she capsized in The Solent, taking her crew of around 500 with her. She is possibly more famous for the huge salvage operation in 1982, when she was returned to the surface on live television, along with hundreds of objects that lay with her. Next door, onboard *HMS Victory*, it's hard to not be struck with awe as you experience the low-ceilinged lower decks and the gold plaque on the upper deck that marks where Horatio Nelson was struck by the fatal shot whilst commanding this ship. Close by, *HMS M.33* is the only remaining British veteran of the Battle of Gallipoli in World War I and the Russian Civil War which followed. The ship is one of just three British warships from World War I still in existence and was built on the orders of the First Lord of the Admiralty at the time, Winston Churchill. The dockyard

1 Poole Harbour   **2** Portsea Island, Royal Navy warship in dock   **3** Portsea Island, *HMS Victory*

is also home to the National Museum of the Royal Navy which tells the whole story of the British Navy's 800-year history. It displays an extraordinary diversity of exhibits, from the Enigma machine and Nelson's table and chair from the Great Cabin of *HMS Victory* to an Exocet missile. There are also interactive screens that show the position of the British fleet today.

Stories of wartime subterfuge and elite forces

There are numerous other museums dedicated to more recent military and wartime history. The excellent D-Day Story on Clarence Esplanade is the only museum in the UK dedicated to the Allied Invasion in 1944; it interprets the events from the perspective of the people involved – from the stories of subterfuge that kept the Germans from knowing the details of the operation to the factors that led to such a large attack being necessary. Some of it is hard to hear, especially the tales of lives lost and families quite literally blown apart. It is full of memorabilia from the pencil which Lt Cdr John Harmer used to sign the order to start the invasion to the tanks and landing craft used. It is also home to the Overlord Embroidery that was commissioned as a tribute to the sacrifice and heroism of those men and women who took part in Operation Overlord, the codename for the Battle of Normandy. It is the largest of its kind in the world.

Swim off Southsea and Eastney beaches

All three sections of lively Southsea Beach – Southsea East, West and Central – have lifeguards during the summer, meaning you can go for a safe dip. Choose Eastney Beach for a quieter swim.

Cycle the island's perimeter

This twenty-six-kilometre cycle ride around Portsea Island mostly uses routes 2 and 22 of the National Cycle Network. The ride starts at the Portsea–Hayling Island ferry and

uses a traffic-free path along the Esplanade, past the major historic military buildings to Southsea Castle. From here it heads north to Clarence Pier and the historic area of the city and Spinnaker Tower. It then weaves around the naval yards, past the Charles Dickens' Birthplace Museum and cross-Channel ferry terminals to reach the waters of Portsmouth Harbour and the fortifications, woodland and meadows of the Hilsea Lines. The final stretch heads south down the east coast with fine views over Langstone Harbour. This route can be combined with the Hayling Island route (see pages 59–60).
www.islandeering.com

Step back in time in Old Portsmouth

With cobbled streets, historic houses, traditional pubs and quaint cafes, the historic Portsmouth Harbour of today is a world away from the press gangs, vice and debauchery of its past that earned The Point the name 'Spice Island' for its reputation as the 'Spice of Life'. Located on the eastern side of the narrowest point of Portsmouth Harbour, you can almost touch the huge cross-Channel ferries (or warships!) as they glide past the many bars and restaurants that line its streets. The area between Clarence Pier, replete with its nostalgic Wimpy restaurant, and The Point is the most historic part of the city and contains the majority of its remaining early defences.

Walk a section of the Solent Way

This two-kilometre walk from the southern tip of the island to The Point, along a stretch of the Solent Way, is packed with interest and great pit stops. Start at Southsea Castle (free entry; open March–October), once part of Henry VIII's ambitious coastal defence system and where he watched the sinking of his favourite ship, the *Mary Rose*. Within the outer bailey there is a working lighthouse and steps up to the ramparts. The views from the roof of the keep stretch across The Solent to the Isle of Wight with **Spitbank Fort**, a private island

1 Portsea Island, Spinnaker Tower and Old Portsmouth

with a premium hotel, in the foreground. Recently a microbrewery has been set up within the walls of the castle and during the summer a champagne bar serves 'bubbles on the barracks'. Walk north-west along the promenade to the small, but interesting, Blue Reef Aquarium, which is a good stop for the kids, before continuing along this surprisingly undeveloped stretch of Portsmouth Harbour. Inland, Southsea Common's Portsmouth Naval Memorial, which is dedicated to around ten thousand sailors of World War I and almost fifteen thousand of World War II, is a prominent landmark. Next up is Southsea Hoverport, which houses the only commercial passenger hovercraft service still operating in the UK – it takes just ten minutes to cross The Solent to the Isle of Wight – then Clarence Pier, which has many rides and arcades.

Further north, Spur Redoubt marks the start of the outer fortifications of Portsmouth. A narrow passage through the ramparts, known as a sally port, is the route Nelson took to avoid the supportive crowds on his way to board *HMS Victory* for the Battle of Trafalgar in 1805. His statue stands where he took his last steps on dry land. This part of the seafront would also have been lined with bathing machines – small, walled, wooden carts which were rolled out into the sea so people could take a dip without being seen. The walk continues to a large, paved area with lots of benches where thousands of people gathered to welcome the Royal Navy back after the Falklands War, then on to the Tudor-era Square Tower, one of Portsea's oldest fortifications, and the rest of The Point. This walk is part of the Solent Way, a ninety-six-kilometre footpath along the Hampshire coast, that links Milford on Sea with Emsworth Harbour.

Whale Island

ACCESS NOT PERMITTED; OPEN DAYS

A small island in Portsmouth Harbour that is home to HMS Excellent, the oldest shore establishment, known as a 'stone frigate', in the Royal Navy. It is the headquarters of the Royal Navy and its most senior officer, the First Sea Lord, is stationed here. Originally constructed with the aid of prisoners from the Napoleonic Wars using material dredged from Portsmouth Harbour during the construction of the dockyards, it is largely a reclaimed island (with a high point of eleven metres) connected to Portsea Island via a road bridge. Before World War II, Whale Island was the site of the Royal Navy's zoo. It housed polar bears, lions and elephants amongst many other exotic creatures. The zoo was started as a place to house animals presented as official gifts to ships or those adopted as mascots. Today the site of the zoo is a garden with a small cemetery containing the remains of many animals. The island is also the home of the gun carriage that carries the coffin in British state funerals. As an active naval base, the island is generally closed to the public but has very occasional open days.

Hayling Island

ACCESS ROAD BRIDGE; FERRY

Hayling Island has all the attractions of a traditional seaside holiday yet has kilometres of unspoilt coastline and countryside. Linked to the Hampshire coast by a road bridge, this T-shaped island is completely surrounded by sea with the narrow channel of Sweare Deep separating it from the mainland in the north, Langstone Harbour to the west and Chichester Harbour to the east. Its western coast is tranquil with views across the nature-filled Langstone Harbour and is easily walked or cycled along the Hayling Billy Trail. The south coast is the most built-up area. Expect funfairs, kiss-me-quick and fish and chips shops. The south-west corner is quieter and

home to the island's vast shingle beach, a mecca for windsurfers. Nearby, the grasslands of Sinah Common (which is the high point of the island at thirteen metres) are stacked with military history. Most of the east coast is indented by silent creeks and is largely the preserve of sailing clubs, farmed land and nature. There is a full range of accommodation and food on the island. Access is via the road bridge from Langstone; the Hayling Ferry is a small pedestrian ferry connecting to Portsea Island.

Oldest yew and a Russian princess

A couple of island churchyards offer some quirky historic gems. Standing in St Mary's churchyard, along Church Road towards the south of the island, one of the oldest yew trees in England arches over its porch. It is thought to be 2,000 years old and boasts a nine-metre girth. The mortar of this ancient church is also decorated with shells and pebbles from the nearby beaches. For something completely different, the churchyard at Northney in the north of the island is the final resting place of Princess Catherine Yorievskaya, who was the daughter of Tsar Alexander II. She was born in 1878 and, after her father was assassinated, she fled the country, wandered around Europe and eventually settled on Hayling in 1932. She fell on hard times though and after her last servant died, a retired Southsea cafe owner volunteered out of pity to act as an unpaid handyman around the house. She had a weekly standing order for spirits at a Havant off-licence, and reportedly sold her last piece of jewellery for £40 and a bottle of gin.

Windsurf in the birthplace of this sport

Hayling Island is the recognised birthplace of windsurfing after Peter Chilvers assembled his first board with a sail here in 1958. Today the island boasts some of the best kitesurfing conditions in the world. It has a dedicated kitesurfing beach with a large sandbank that creates a natural bay offering a good mix of flat

1 Hayling Island, cycling the Hayling Billy Trail

water and waves to play in. At low tide, there are large, waist-deep, flat-water lagoons perfect for beginners, freestyle and wakestyle tricks. There is a private member's club here so you will have to either join the club or arrange a day pass. The beach is situated on the Sea Front, opposite Chichester Avenue. Lessons and equipment hire are available. Hayling is also a mecca for stand-up paddleboarders, with a variety of conditions to suit. There are plenty of sea kayaking adventures to be had around this coastline too. Hayling hosts the annual National Watersports Festival, a three-day event with its hub at the Inn on the Beach celebrating everything to do with windsurfing and stand-up paddleboarding. It is quite a spectacle with over 500 competitors, mingling with the surf-Gods, floodlit night-surfing events, live music and plenty of fun.

Seals, seabirds and the mysterious sea path

Langstone Harbour is a tranquil and beautiful place and a rich haven for nature, particularly wading birds, wildfowl and seabirds. The harbour also provides one of only two haul-out sites for The Solent's twenty-five-strong population of harbour seals and the two grey seals that occasionally visit. The tidal mudflats, salt marsh and seagrass meadows of the old oyster bed lagoons on the island's north-west shoreline are the best place to get close to the wildlife. Here, at low tide, you can also see the wooden markers of the Wadeway, a submerged Medieval crossing between Langstone and the promontory north of Stoke Common. A popular way to enjoy the sights of Langstone Harbour is along the island section of the Hayling Billy Trail. This trail is also part of the twenty-three-kilometre Langstone Harbour Waterside Walk which starts from Ferry Point at Eastney, circumnavigates the whole loop of Langstone Harbour, including the stretches along Portsea Island and the Hampshire coastline, then uses the Hayling Ferry to return.

Cycle around the island

This twenty-five-kilometre, flat, coastal cycle route around Hayling Island uses trails, roads and lanes. Starting at Langstone Bridge, head south along the Hayling Billy Trail, then explore the lanes of the western tip of the island, with options to cross on the ferry to Portsea or continue around Hayling's southern shore along beach tracks (suitable for mountain

bikes and hybrids), the Sea Front and promenade. The route goes through the houses
at the eastern tip then turns north on the busy
main road before branching off along the idyllic
Yew Tree Road through farmland to re-join the
coast at Langstone Bridge. There are great
views and seascapes throughout as well as several
great places to stop off for food and drink.
www.islandeering.com

Clandestine operations and secret canoes

The World War II Heritage Trail along the coast
of South Hayling is a walk through an important
part of British wartime history, when members
of the armed forces lived in the holiday camps,
hotels and large houses here. Starting at the
Hayling Ferry there are six information points to
see, including the COPP Memorial. The World
War II Combined Operations Pilotage Parties
unit, code-named COPP, is one of the greatest
clandestine operations in history and the key to

the success of the Normandy landings. The
Hayling Island Sailing Club was once the base
for this top-secret unit of less than 200 men who
won over ninety medals and commendations
for their secret reconnaissance missions to
enemy-held beaches. The secluded waters
around Hayling Island were perfect for testing
specialised military canoes to extract secret
agents, gather intelligence and mount guerrilla
attacks all around the world. The canoes' most
ingenious low-tech feature was the outrigger
support floats which were filled with ping-pong
balls to retain their buoyancy if hit by a bullet.
The most famous canoe mission was Operation
Frankton at Bordeaux Harbour, undertaken by ten
Royal Marine commandos who became known
as the Cockleshell Heroes – as their canoes were
codenamed 'cockles'. They entered the harbour
unnoticed and sunk one ship, severely damaged
four others and disrupted the use of the harbour
for months in a sortie that Winston Churchill said
helped to shorten World War II by six months.

1 Hayling Island, beach **2** Hayling Island, windsurfing

Grab some local food

Stoke Fruit Farm in the island's centre is bursting with local produce, including Hayling tomatoes and honey, and is a good place to assemble a picnic for the beach. For its artisan ice cream, Northney Farm uses milk and cream from their own island dairy herd to make traditional flavours as well as caramel toffee crunch, bubblegum and wild cherry. It also has a great tea room serving delicious home-made and often homegrown fare. A top spot for breakfast is the barbecued breakfast at the Salt Shack Cafe, overlooking Northney Marina and Chichester Harbour.

A day at the beach

Hayling Island has nearly five kilometres of beach running along the south coast of the island. It is split into three beaches – West, Beachlands Central and Eastoke. They are mostly shingle with long stretches of sand below the high-tide mark and safe places to swim or splash in shallow water at low tide. They shelve steeply so at high tide it does get deep quickly. All three have great open views across The Solent to the Isle of Wight with a huge variety of yachts, cruise ships and ferries to watch in between. East Winner is a sandbank that stretches for over a kilometre into Hayling Bay, which shelters West Beach from the larger waves and creates a 'warm' lagoon on certain tide states and is a popular place for swimmers. Beachlands Central Beach is the handiest beach for family-friendly facilities. Heading east, Eastoke Beach has pebbles, sand and a nice grass area for picnics and leads to Sandy Point Nature Reserve. All the beaches on Hayling Island combine great water quality with traditional British seaside traditions. There are car parks all along the seafront, with plenty of cafes.

Other islands in Langstone Harbour

ACCESS LONG ISLAND ONLY (BY PRIVATE BOAT/KAYAK)

Langstone Harbour, between Portsea and Hayling islands, contains six islands along with the extensive tidal mudflats, all of which are owned by the RSPB. Seabirds including the black-headed and Mediterranean gulls and common, sandwich and little terns breed on the islands during the summer; in fact the harbour is the largest nesting site for Mediterranean gulls in the UK. At other times the islands become high-water roosts for seabirds which are either stopping off during migration or are overwintering in the harbour. **North Binness Island** is the largest of this group of islands with oak woodland and gorse. The remaining islands – **Baker's Island**, **Long Island**, **Oyster Island** and **South Binness Island**, to which **Round Nap Island** is connected via a tidal causeway – are gradually eroding away (the current high point of the group is less than five metres). No landing or close approach is permitted on these islands except on the southern end of Long Island, and only during daylight, to avoid disturbing birds.

Thorney Island

ACCESS FOOTBRIDGE; ROAD BRIDGE

With access via a security intercom, a military heartland and true wilderness around its perimeter, this island is one of a kind. Separated from the West Sussex mainland by the narrow channel of the Great Deep, Thorney Island sits secretly in Chichester Harbour. The charming hamlet of West Thorney lies on the east coast and is part of the military base. The coastal mudflats and the creeks of Thorney and Emsworth channels are a haven for wildlife and the beach on the southern tip is a glorious place to swim. A coastal public footpath, part of the Sussex Border Path, circumnavigates the island and forms the only public access from Prinsted or Emsworth. The high point of the island measures six metres. Walkers need to request access to the island at the east or west security gates on the south side of the Great Deep.

www.islandeering.com

St Nicholas Church

Halfway down the east coast in the tiny hamlet of West Thorney, St Nicholas Church is a peaceful oasis and, open to the public, is the only place that offers shelter on the island. It dates mostly from the late twelfth century and its graveyard is the resting place for World War II servicemen, both Allied and German, who now lie side by side.

Pilsey Sand beach

Pilsey Sand at the southern tip of Thorney Island is one of the most remote beaches along this otherwise busy stretch of the South Coast. It can only be accessed via a five-kilometre walk from Prinsted or by private boat. At low tide it is a large area of mudbanks and cockle-beds fringed by a long white sand beach. As the tide comes in the water is warmed by the mudbanks, making it a great spot to swim.

Pilsey Island

ACCESS NOT PERMITTED

Off the southern tip of Thorney Island, Pilsey Island encloses an area of salt marsh with low sand dunes on its west coast. The island, which has a high point of less than one metre, is an RSPB Nature Reserve with no direct public access permitted either from Thorney or adjacent Pilsea Sand. The area is a great place to watch out for passing avocets and ospreys along with overwintering wildfowl and waders either from the bird hide at Longmere Point on Thorney Island or the beach adjacent to Pilsey Island.

1 **Thorney Island**, Pilsey Sand   2 **Langstone Harbour**, Mediterranean gull
3 **Thorney Island**, salt marsh plants   4 **Thorney Island**, path alongside Chichester Harbour

Fowley Island

ACCESS NOT PERMITTED

A small uninhabited island in Chichester Harbour, around 900 metres south of the coast at Emsworth between Hayling Island and Thorney Island. It rises to a high point of less than one metre above the tidal sands between Sweare Deep and Emsworth Channel and has a number of man-made lagoons within it. An ancient causeway, known as Fisherman's Walk, is thought to have been built for the oyster farms in the area. It runs along the sands from the Emsworth coast to Fowley Rithe, a narrow channel that runs 200 metres to the north-east of Fowley Island. Fishermen would have stored oysters in large man-made ponds before taking them back to the mainland to sell. The whole area was home to an important and large-scale oyster industry until the Dean of Winchester died of typhoid after dining on Emsworth oysters and further sales were banned for a period of time. The island can be approached by kayak from Emsworth.

Two large river estuaries – the Swale and the Medway – create an important wilderness haven amongst the surrounding urban life and modern industry. With the exception of the Isle of Sheppey, which is packed with historic and natural gems along with walks and great cycleways, these low-lying islands are largely uninhabited. The salt marsh and mudflats support an impressive and diverse ecosystem, providing the perfect habitat for thousands of protected birds and diverse marine wildlife. Throughout history these estuaries have been a main trading route and the strategic position of their islands have been exploited to protect nearby Chatham Naval Dockyard and defend against the Luftwaffe during World War II. Some also hold more macabre tales.

KENT

Opposite Isle of Sheppey   **Overleaf** Hoo Island

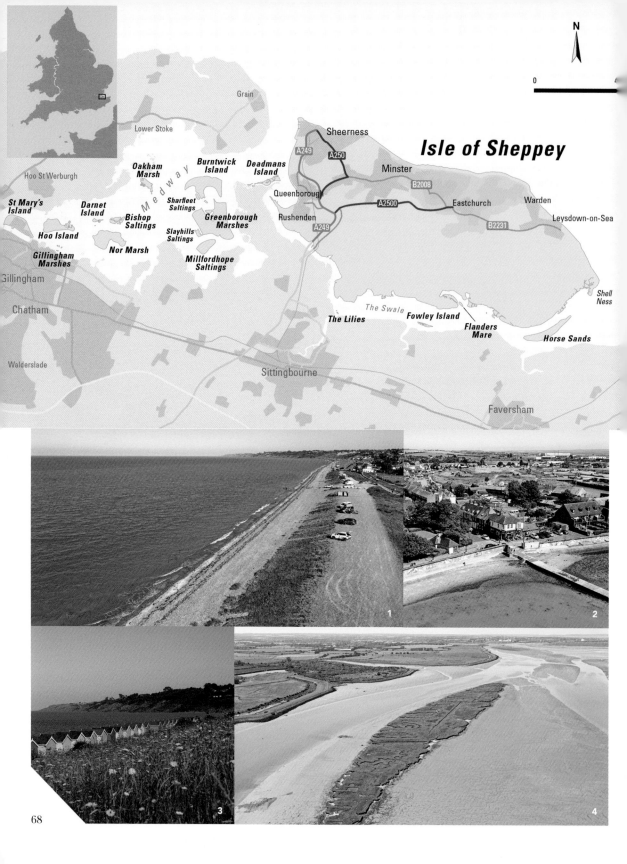

Isle of Sheppey

Grain

Lower Stoke

Hoo St Werburgh

St Mary's Island

Darnet Island

Hoo Island

Gillingham Marshes

Gillingham

Chatham

Walderslade

Oakham Marsh

Bishop Saltings

Nor Marsh

Medway

Burntwick Island

Sharfleet Saltings

Slayhills Saltings

Greenborough Marshes

Millfordhope Saltings

Deadmans Island

Sheerness

A249 A250

Queenborough

Rushenden

A249

Minster

B2008

A2500

Eastchurch

B2231

Warden

Leysdown-on-Sea

Sittingbourne

The Swale

The Lilies

Fowley Island

Flanders Mare

Shell Ness

Horse Sands

Faversham

0

N

Isle of Sheppey

ACCESS ROAD BRIDGE

Full of surprises, secret wild places and strong community spirit, there is plenty to do on this island for a weekend or more. The southern half is a medley of marshland comprised of two other islands, **Elmley Island** and the **Isle of Harty**, which make up a vast nature reserve. The north is a mix of industrial landscape, long beaches, a sprawling commercial port and holiday camps. It is loved by traditional holidaymakers and birdwatchers alike and offers plenty of adventure, escape and quirky things to do. The high point of the island, The Mount, measures seventy-six metres. The island is criss-crossed by a network of footpaths and quiet cycle routes that pass the places that made aviation history as well as nostalgic music halls and heritage centres and places linked to the life of Lord Nelson. Access is via Kingsferry Bridge from the north coast of Kent.

Aviation museum and cafe – in a prison

The Isle of Sheppey has three prisons in total and one of them, HMP Standford Hill, is an open prison. Known as the Old Mill Village, it hosts a large variety of community training opportunities for offenders. The village also includes the Eastchurch Aviation Museum which celebrates the aeronautical history of Sheppey with the plane-manufacturing activities of the Short Brothers. The museum and village are open to the public, with a prisoner-run cafe and a shop that sells honey, beeswax and recycled wood items made by the prison's residents.

Elmley Nature Reserve

Elmley Island in the south-west of the Isle of Sheppey is unique in being the only privately-owned National Nature Reserve in the UK. Its 1,335 hectares of salt marshes, freshwater, mudflats, hay meadows, woodland and the

glistening waters of The Swale host one of the most important sites for birds in the country. In winter tens of thousands of lapwings, redshanks, golden plovers, teals and wigeons fill the skies, while short-eared owls are also common. Birds such as oystercatchers and marsh harriers can be seen here year round while autumn sees migrants such as green sandpiper and whimbrel stop over on their way to Africa. On the reserve there is an accessible route to the main bird hide, with walking trails to three further hides. Elmley was once a village which consisted of the Turkey Cement Works, a school, church, a pub and thirty houses. Today, the last surviving building is the Kingshill Farmhouse and its barn. This nature reserve is unique because visitors can stay overnight. With several comfortable huts dotted around the reserve and over three kilometres to drive to the nearest public road, this is a full-on immersion in nature. There are walking routes and cycling is permitted on all permissive paths from June to September although a through route is not possible. Note that dogs are not allowed in the nature reserve.
www.elmleynaturereserve.co.uk

Sail on a Thames barge

The *Edith May* is a beautifully restored 1906 Thames barge that once used to transport grain and bricks along The Swale to the centre of London, returning with horse dung for the fields. Today, she sails from the Elmley Nature Reserve to explore the tranquil Swale around the reserve. For the more adventurous she also sails around the whole island. This highly varied trip reflects the diversity of island landscapes and history. It starts in the tranquillity of Elmley and Harty, sails into the Thames Estuary near to the famous Red Sands Fort and then heads around the outside of the Isle of Sheppey, past Minster Cliffs and into the port of Sheerness before Kingsferry Bridge lifts to allow it to sail underneath on its return.
www.tillerandwheel.com

1 Isle of Sheppey, Barton's Point   **2** Isle of Sheppey, Queenborough   **3** Isle of Sheppey, Minster Leas   **4** Fowley Island

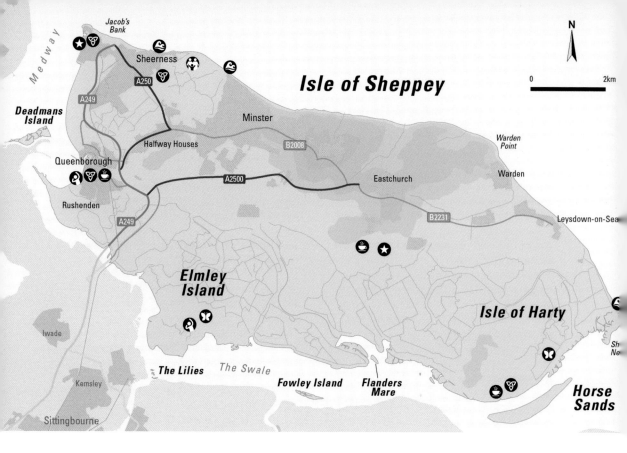

Explore the island by cycling on traffic-free routes

The Isle of Harty Trail and the Sheerness Way are flat, circular, family-friendly routes that are mainly traffic-free, off-road and a great way to see more of Sheppey's top spots. The Isle of Harty Trail starts at the small lively seaside resort of Leysdown-on-Sea and passes the wild beach of Shell Ness to the statue of the Short Brothers who designed and built the first British-powered aircraft that completed a circular mile flight in 1909. Nearby, Muswell Manor Inn was once the headquarters for the early aviators; it subsequently became the base for the Royal Aero Club of Great Britain from which the first pilot's licence was issued. Today the Grade II listed building is a popular holiday centre. The marked trail continues to the Isle of Harty with Harty Church and the Ferry House Inn.

The Sheerness Way is again family-friendly and mainly traffic-free but with some sections on road. Starting at Sheerness-on-Sea station and following the blue cycle signs the route includes the Queenborough Lines, a mid-

nineteenth-century ditch fortification built to protect Sheerness Naval Dockyard from invaders, and Barton's Point Coastal Park. It heads along the sea wall, where the dockyard is visible to the west and the masts of a sunken World War II vessel, the *SS Richard Montgomery*, can be seen offshore. Loaded with explosives when it sank it was too dangerous to blow up due to its proximity to the town. The route returns to Sheerness, with its clock tower built to commemorate King Edward VII's coronation and the Blue Town Heritage Centre where you can discover the history of the island.

Explore historic docks, Blue Town and its music hall

Historic and atmospheric Blue Town sits alongside the walled former Royal Navy Dockyard at Sheerness. It grew during the Napoleonic Wars and it earnt its name from the grey-blue naval paint used on the exteriors of the dock-builders' homes which became known as the Blue Houses, a name eventually

corrupted to Blue Town. When the dockyard closed in 1960 the entire site was passed to a commercial port operator and much of the dock's history was demolished. Today, the preserved area is a collection of late-Georgian buildings that was the residential quarter of the dockyard and includes the Chief Superintendent's House, the pretty Boatswain's House, a terrace of officers' houses and the derelict dockyard church. Blue Town is the home of the nostalgic Criterion, a restored Victorian music hall where you can watch classic cinema, listen to live music and order cream teas. It also has an excellent heritage centre to learn more about this fascinating and hidden slice of England's history.
www.thecriterionbluetown.co.uk

Find your perfect gnome ⊗
Established in Blue Town in 1974, Whelans is now the largest concrete ornament manufacturer in the UK. Whatever you are looking for from concrete frogs and lanterns to windmills, full-scale naked Romans and five-tier water fountains, you'll find it here. It's a fascinating place to walk around. There are also plenty of gnomes to buy, in every possible colour scheme you can think of.
www.whelansgardenornaments.com

The Isle of Harty's church and inn ⊕ ⊗
In the hamlet of Harty sits the 900-year-old St Thomas the Apostle Church. Inside, the church is lit by oil lamps as there is no electricity and the delightful stained-glass windows depict the four seasons. The farmland around is managed for wildlife with marsh harriers and barn owls readily seen. At the very end of this road through the Isle of Harty is the popular Ferry House Inn near to the old ferry landing where, until 1947, a regular ferry crossed to the mainland.

Discover the hidden history of Queenborough ⊕ ⊕ ⊗
This once thriving port, where the Swale and Medway rivers meet, still retains a strong sense of its eighteenth-century seafaring history and remains the only English town where a foreign flag has flown. On the island's west coast, Queenborough's significance started when Queenborough Castle was built during the Hundred Years' War with France to protect the thriving wool and chemical trade. The castle was then left to deteriorate and was unable to protect the town from Dutch occupation in the seventeenth century after they captured nearby Sheerness Fort and attacked Charles II's fleet in the worst defeat in the Royal Navy's history. Today nothing of the castle remains. Queenborough's maritime heritage is also cemented through its strong connections with Lord Nelson in both his life and death. Lady Hamilton, his mistress, resided here and it was to nearby Sheerness that *HMS Victory* bought his body to after his death at the Battle of Trafalgar. Placed in a brandy-filled barrel, it inspired the age-old sea shanty 'Oh, a drop of Nelson's blood wouldn't do us any harm'. From Sheerness, Nelson's body was then transported up the River Thames for his funeral in St Paul's Cathedral. Today, Queenborough Harbour makes for a lovely walk with its range of small pleasure craft, birdlife, seals, low-tide stone beach and stunning sunsets. There are some great pubs and restaurants, including the delightful microbrewery, the aptly named Admiral's Arm.

Other islands in the Swale Estuary

Other islands of salt marsh, salting and mudbanks in the Swale Estuary include **The Lilies, Fowley Island, Flanders Mare** and **Horse Sands**. Landing is not recommended as they are important nature reserves. It is possible to explore the surrounding estuary via kayak, paddleboard or private boat at high tide.

Deadmans Island

ACCESS NOT PERMITTED; VIEW FROM ISLE OF SHEPPEY COAST PATH

Opposite Queenborough on the Isle of Sheppey, this uninhabited mudbank in the River Medway, with a high point of less than five metres, has a mysterious past and horror stories that have been handed down the generations. Local legend suggests that 'hounds with glaring-red eyes that ate the heads of buried bodies' stalk the land. Then, in 2016, the horrors of this island finally emerged. Skulls, bones and open coffins started to slowly rise to the surface. They are believed to be from men and boys who died of contagious diseases on board floating prisons, known as prison hulks, which were moored off the Isle of Sheppey more than two hundred years ago. Now owned by Natural England it is an important bird breeding and nesting site leased to two people and public access is not permitted.

Burntwick Island

ACCESS KAYAK; RESTRICTIONS DURING NESTING SEASON

A raised area of marshland (with a high point of less than five metres) among the tidal sandbanks on the southern side of the Medway Estuary that at high tide becomes several smaller islands. Once used for smuggling tea and spirits, it was a hideout of the infamous group of smugglers known as the North Kent Gang who were eventually captured and either executed or deported to Tasmania. Now the property of the Ministry of Defence, a gun and searchlight battery was built here during the early years of the twentieth century. A torpedo school later became established with a barracks building and ammunition depots with target practice taking place during World War II. There is little to see on the island today except for the grave of Dr Sidney Bernard, which sits amongst the wild sea purslane. He tended the crew of a yellow fever-infected naval ship in 1845 then succumbed to the disease himself. The remains of the seawall, built to protect the shepherd's house from the tides, is also evident and Victorian pottery and glass can be spotted from when the island was used as a refuse dump. Now a haven for seabirds, access is restricted during nesting season.

Hoo Island and Darnet Island

ACCESS KAYAK

On two lone embankments in the River Medway (both with a high point of less than five metres)

the circular forts of Hoo and Darnet share a fascinating history. Built in 1872 to counter the threat of invasion from France, and to defend nearby Chatham Naval Dockyard, they were fitted with guns and an underwater boom was strung between them to catch invading ships. They never saw military action, although they were used as observation posts during World War II and played a vital role in keeping the German Luftwaffe at bay, particularly during the Battle of Britain which was fought over Kent's skies. Long since abandoned, the lower levels of both have been deliberately flooded to keep out vandals, though anyone is able to visit them by boat or kayak at high tide from Whitton Marina, south of Hoo village or The Strand at Gillingham. Hoo Island can also be viewed from the Saxon Shore Way, accessible from Vicarage Lane in Hoo.

St Mary's Island

ACCESS ROAD

Scratch the surface of this island and discover a rich naval history amongst today's attractive waterside development. Originally a marshy area (with a high point of less than five metres) to the north of Chatham Naval Dockyard, it went on to have many uses over the years, from brickfields and a prison to a burial ground for French prisoners housed in the hulks of boats in the River Medway, a place to change the

reactor cores of the Royal Navy's submarines, a nuclear waste dump and now, a modern housing estate. The three ship-building basins, which divide it from the mainland, were used to build Nelson's flagship *HMS Victory*. There are riverside walks and cycle paths on the island, including a circular walk around the perimeter which offers great views of Upnor Castle and the River Medway. With a ten-metre-high sail, The Mariners makes for a stunning sculpture that marks the millennium and reflects local maritime heritage. Its 'Jack Tar' bronze figure, the nickname for a seaman of the Royal or Merchant Navy, represents the past life of the river while a woman in a wetsuit represents the river's future.

Other islands in the Medway Estuary

Other salt marsh islands and salting in the estuary are inaccessible except by boat and kayak and include **Hoo Salt Marsh**; **Bishop Saltings**; **Nor Marsh**; **Gillingham Marshes**; **Oakham Marsh**; **Sharfleet Saltings**; **Slayhills Saltings**; **Millfordhope Saltings**; and **Green-borough Marshes**.

3

4

The River Thames is the longest river entirely in England. It rises in Gloucestershire and flows into the North Sea via the Thames Estuary, draining the whole of Greater London on the way. The tidal, salt water section reaches as far inland as Teddington Lock. The small islands closer to London were historically associated with the cultivation of osier willows and the trapping of eels; others were used to service the working boats that once plied these waters; those further upstream were the playground of day-tripping Londoners. Many of these are now vibrant houseboat communities where people live off-grid within a few kilometres of the capital. By contrast, the Isle of Dogs offers some of the best riverscapes in the capital and the story of its evolution from marshland to the greatest docks in the world to one of the global financial capitals is a staggering insight into how the River Thames and its islands helped build London's fame and fortune.

THAMES ESTUARY, LONDON & THE RIVER THAMES

Opposite Lot's Ait **Overleaf** Angler's Ait

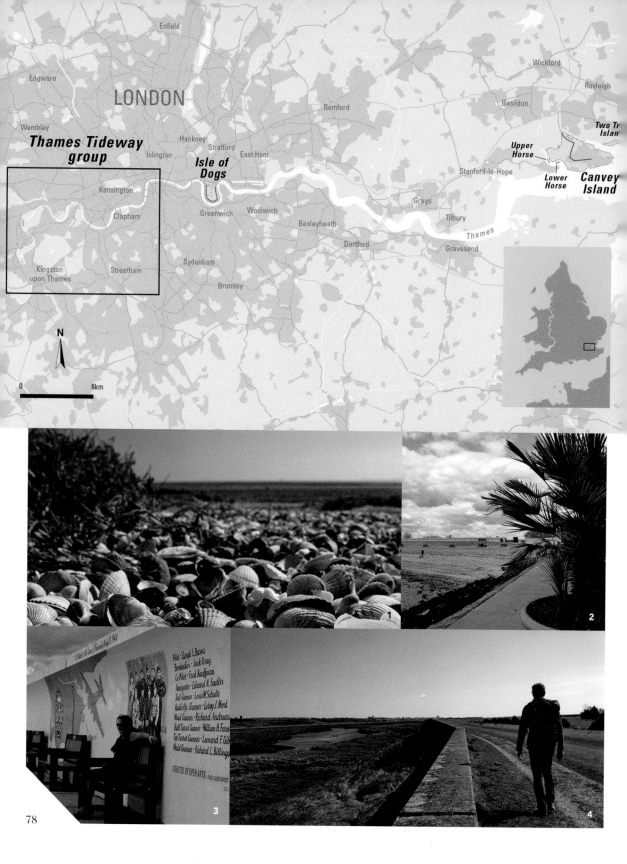

Canvey Island

ACCESS ROAD BRIDGE

Quirky, independent and defined by the Thames Estuary, Canvey offers wild marshes, ancient inns and arty promenades all with a nostalgic dash of rhythm and blues. Separated from the mainland of south Essex by a network of creeks and lying just above sea level (the high point of the island reaches sixteen metres), it is built on land reclaimed by Dutch engineers. Discovered by Victorian beach lovers from the East End of London, Canvey became the fastest-growing seaside resort in Britain until competition from the burgeoning holiday package industry halted its further development. Today, the south coast strongly reflects this golden era with beaches, promenades and cafes. Its interior is built up, while its coastal areas contrast between the petrochemical industry and vast nature reserves of the west, to the wild marshes of the north and marinas and country parks in the east. Access is via two road bridges; the closest train station is at South Benfleet.

Canvey Point

At the eastern tip of the island a low-tide footpath leads out past the Island Yacht Club into the wild expanse of Chapman Sands. These sands were the last natural hazard for ancient mariners to navigate before entering the safe waters of 'Old Father Thames'. Today they offer a surprising area of wilderness, with gentle shell bays and low-lying mud sculptures etched by the gentle tides. Locals often wade way beyond the path's head to collect the cockles, clams, mussels and samphire that sit abundantly on the banks.

Murals along the sea wall

After the 1953 storms and floods that led to fifty-nine deaths and the whole population of Canvey being moved to safety, a huge 22.5-kilometre sea wall was built around the whole island. The floods have been depicted on panels along a mural on Concord Beach, painted by professional artists and Canvey residents. The mural also depicts the impact the flooding had on the Netherlands, where more than 1,800 people died. There are many other colourful murals here too, including a memorial to three American airmen killed in a crash over Canvey Island during World War II and a homage to the island's most famous natives, the legendary 1970s R&B band, Dr Feelgood.

Concord Beach,
Art Deco and the tidal pool

Concord Beach and the Western Esplanade are the main destinations for families looking for a bit of seaside fun. The children's tidal pool is always popular, as is its nearby beach cafe. For a slice of history there's also the Grade II listed Art Deco Labworth Cafe, which resembles the bridge of the *Queen Mary*. Its architecture and views are as much a pull as its great menu.

Cycle around the island

A flat, off-road, twenty-six-kilometre cycle ride around the sea wall of the island's perimeter that starts across the bridge from Benfleet station. The route hugs the creeks and winds through the peaceful green marshes in the north alongside Benfleet Creek. It passes the colourful murals of the Thames seawall and beaches in the south and skirts Oil City and the nature reserves of Canvey Wick and West Canvey Marsh.
www.islandeering.com

1 Canvey Island, banks of shells on Canvey Point **2** Canvey Island, Thorney Bay
3 Canvey Island, sea wall mural **4** Canvey Island, walking along the sea wall

Oil refinery ruins and RSPB Canvey Wick

Inland from Hole Haven, this reserve forms one of Europe's most important areas for bug life. Previously the site was the prototype for storing imported liquid natural gas from America and was later dismantled after the discovery of gas in the North Sea. Today, the 1.5-kilometre pier is all that remains of the original site and nature has taken over. There are more than 1,000 invertebrate species – estimated to be as many species per square metre as is found in a tropical rainforest. You might be lucky enough to hear the high-pitched buzz of the aptly-named shrill carder bee, one of Britain's rarest bumblebees. There are some fearsome predators to watch out for too, like the bee wolf and exploding bombardier beetles. When disturbed, these iridescent blue, green or orange beetles detonate an explosion inside their abdomen, spraying hot liquid at attackers, whether insect or human. There are also plenty of plants to discover including clumps of sea aster – the food of the rare sea aster mining bee that builds a waterproof lining around its underground cell so it can survive an unexpectedly high tide.

Secret Cold War station

On the east side of Thorney Bay, the strange-looking building which houses The Bay Museum was once a Cold War defence building, built between 1962 and 1963, due to the Cuban Missile Crisis. At that time there was concern that the Soviet Navy may deposit magnetic mines along the Thames if the crisis escalated. Steel warships, as used by the British Royal Navy, create an invisible magnetic signature as they sail and, if detected, the mines detonate even when they are tens of metres underwater. The function of the building was to degauss (remove the magnetic signature) British ships before they entered unprotected waters. Wire loops placed in the middle of the Thames were connected to surveillance equipment in the building. Fortunately, the Cold War never escalated and magnetic mines were never

placed by the Soviets so the station was never used. Not many degaussing stations exist in the UK so The Bay Museum is fairly unique. The site was classified up to 1993 and, although the building itself is now declassified, the equipment it contained and the technology that lay mid-channel remains classified. The museum is packed with memorabilia and well worth a visit. *www.the-bay-museum.co.uk*

Two Tree Island

ACCESS ROAD BRIDGE

A peaceful salt marsh wilderness almost on London's doorstep, Two Tree Island is a popular destination for birdwatchers, walkers, water sports lovers and model airplane pilots. The land (which has a high point of seven metres) was reclaimed from the sea in the eighteenth century when a seawall was built around the salt marsh and the land used for farming. Now managed as a nature reserve and just a short walk from Leigh-on-Sea, it is a firm favourite as a walking destination. The east of the island is dominated by the reed beds of Leigh Marsh with paths that can be followed to explore this nature reserve. There is a large car park but no other facilities on the island itself. Leigh-on-Sea has the closest facilities (some may be available at the golf club at the entrance to the island).

Enjoy the island's nature

During the winter months the mudflats are the perfect habitat for thousands of wildfowl and waders, including large flocks of dark-bellied brent geese that feed on areas of eelgrass. From Lagoon Hide, on the west of the island, you'll spot curlew, dunlin, avocet, redshank, black-tailed godwit and possibly a short-eared owl. The eastern section is part of Leigh National Nature Reserve, where the salt marsh is one of the best in the Thames Estuary. There is an array of salt marsh plant species such as golden samphire, sea purslane, common sea-lavender and sea aster. In the summer, the island is full of rare insects and butterflies,

1 Two Tree Island, view from Leigh-on-Sea

including the incredibly rare shrill and brown-banded carder bee and butterflies such as the marbled white and Essex skipper. You may also see sun-bathing adders or slow worms.

Stand-up paddleboarding trip 🐾

Two Tree Island is one of the best paddleboarding spots along this stretch of coastline. It is one of a very few places in the area that can be paddled at low tide and, protected from the prevailing southwesterly winds, offers generally flatter water. A popular low-tide trip departs from the island's slipway on the south coast and heads east along Hadleigh Ray to Seal Point and Southend Pier beyond. Alternatives on a flooding high tide are to paddle west towards South Benfleet or cross Hadleigh Ray to investigate 'The Maze', then return as the tide turns. The slipway is also a good starting point for a wild swim in Hadleigh Ray, going parallel to the island's southern shore in either direction. It will be a less energetic swim around thirty minutes before high tide; it is always best to wear a bright-coloured cap and take a tow-float to be seen by the numerous boaters.

Upper Horse and Lower Horse

ACCESS VIEW FROM MAINLAND PATH; KAYAK OR STAND-UP PADDLEBOARD

'Horse' is a local name given to a raised area of land surrounded by water. There are two 'horse' islands at the Thames end of Holehaven Creek between the west of Canvey Island and Shell Haven; both are marshland islands with high points of less than five metres. Upper Horse contains possible Roman earthworks, which was likely part of a fortified camp for around 200 men. The central area of Upper Horse has lagoons that were probably Roman saltings. Lower Horse is another small uninhabited island segmented by numerous creeks. Both are only accessible by kayak, packraft or paddleboard.

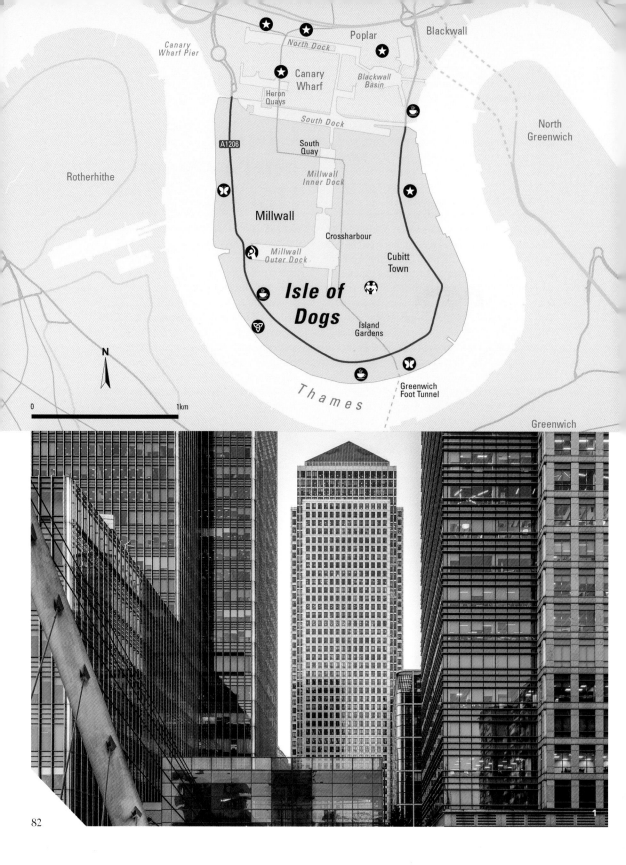

Canary Wharf Pier

Canary Wharf

Heron Quays

North Dock

Poplar

Blackwall

Blackwall Basin

South Dock

South Quay

A1206

Millwall Inner Dock

Millwall

Crossharbour

Cubitt Town

Isle of Dogs

Millwall Outer Dock

Island Gardens

Rotherhithe

North Greenwich

T h a m e s

Greenwich Foot Tunnel

Greenwich

N

0   1km

Isle of Dogs

ACCESS ROAD/FOOTBRIDGE; GREENWICH FOOT TUNNEL; RAIL (LONDON UNDERGROUND AND DOCKLANDS LIGHT RAILWAY); RIVER BUS

On a large meander and bounded on three sides by the River Thames, the Isle of Dogs is delineated from the mainland in the north by the South Dock with its eastern lock gate and western drainage culvert. Once the bogs of Stepney Marsh, then drained by the Dutch, it grew to become one of the busiest docks in the world. These thrived until the 1970s when a shift towards the use of shipping containers moved the UK's docks to the coast and the subsequent closure of the wharves on the island led to a massive downturn and subsequent dereliction of the area. Following a massive regeneration project in the 1980s it is now home to one of the most important financial districts in the world as well as the largest city farm in Europe and some of the best views in London. Wandering the Thames Path, stopping for a pint in historic pubs with stories still told of dockside life or craning your neck to see the gleaming heights of the financial behemoths all give a strong sense of the role this island played in putting London on the world map.

Walk the island circuit

This fascinating seven-kilometre waterside route follows the Thames Path for most of the southern loop and then takes the easy city paths through the colourful high-rise buildings of Canary Wharf at South Dock. There is plenty of green space for picnics including the Sir John McDougal Gardens, Island Gardens and Mudchute Park and Farm, a short deviation from the Thames Path. There's lots of fascinating history to uncover here too – all shaped by the presence of the mighty River Thames. There's the historic Docklands Sailing and Watersports Centre; old wharf buildings once the centre for chemicals, paints, drugs and oils; the Ferry

House inn (one of the oldest buildings on the island); historic pumping stations and more to explore. The view from the Isle of Dogs across the Thames to Greenwich is one of the best in London with many famous landmarks to spot, including the glass dome at the south entrance of the foot tunnel, the wooden masts of the *Cutty Sark*, the majestic buildings of Greenwich Hospital and the parkland topped by the Royal Observatory. This walk will entertain the whole family with plenty of great pit stops along the way. ***www.islandeering.com***

Enjoy the island's green spaces

There are plenty of parks on the Isle of Dogs enjoyed by local communities, city workers and visitors alike. Favourites include the Sir John McDougal Gardens which were built to allow public access to the river, when huge flour mills dominated the foreshore, and were designed to make the most of the expansive views of the Thames. The Island Gardens also provide a lovely green space and a strong sense of community. They are the northern access point to the Greenwich Foot Tunnel, a mighty engineering feat for its time and a Victorian architectural delight if you decide to walk through it. These gardens were built so that the views from Greenwich across to the Isle of Dogs were easier on the eye and a bit of a nod to the world of the 'haves' and 'have nots' of history. Inland, Mudchute Park and Farm is the largest city farm in Europe with thirteen hectares of open space, a medley of farm animals and a cafe. Clues to the origins of the site can be interpreted from its name – the overspill from excavating Millwall Dock was dumped here through a chute system.

Historic Millwall

Millwall, on the southern and western side of the Isle of Dogs, is an area probably better known for its football club than its surviving nineteenth-century industrial heritage when flour mills and windmills lined the walls of the

1 Isle of Dogs, One Canada Square seen from South Dock footbridge © Shutterstock/I Wei Huang

Thames and the area was full of thriving factories and ship-building ironworks. Here the *SS Great Eastern*, the largest ship of its time, was launched sideways into the River Thames on account of it being too long to launch forwards. A section of the launch site is preserved at Napier Avenue. Slightly further east is Burrells Wharf, once an important trading centre for chemicals, paints, drugs and oils; it is now a smart residential complex. The brick chimney used by the colour-makers here often belched out pink smoke that left the local pigeons with pink-tinted feathers. The pigeon-racing locals saw a pink pigeon as lucky, though maybe the opposite was true if it had inhaled the toxic fumes from this industry. The Docklands Sailing and Watersports Centre with its historical twin cranes borders the west end of Millwall Outer Dock. Further south, on Westferry Road, the curious façade of St Paul's Presbyterian Church was designed to look like the west front of Pisa Cathedral. Today, St Paul's is the performing arts centre known as The Space, whose highly-rated bar serves great food and coffee.

Canary Wharf

The name 'Canary Wharf' was requested by Fruit Lines Ltd, the shipping company that unloaded fruit from the Canary Islands on this dock. Today it is the headquarters of some of the world's largest corporations – Barclays, Citigroup, J.P.Morgan and HSBC – all housed in the towering, angular, reflective buildings that make up this city within a city. Frenetic during the week with suits, heels and busy bars, yet quiet at the weekend, there is a whole underground world that operates below the skyscrapers with over 300 shops, restaurants and bars. The glass canopy and futuristic design of Canary Wharf's underground station has been used as a filming location for *28 Days Later* and *Rogue One: A Star Wars Story*. You can't miss spotting One Canada Square, once the tallest building in England before The Shard stole its thunder. In complete contrast, you'll still find fishermen on the dockside as you walk the length of the South Dock.

Billingsgate Market

Just north of the Isle of Dogs proper, the UK's largest inland fish market sits across five hectares of buildings in the shadow of the Canary Wharf skyscrapers. An early morning foray here is a must-do for fish lovers who are visiting the island. The action starts at 4.00 a.m., when the traders buy fish by the boxful, and continues until 8.30 a.m. Around 150 different species of fish and crustacean – live, fresh, frozen and salted – from all over the world are sold here. There are live lobsters and crabs, salmon, plaice, scallops, clams, mussels, squid, octopus, oysters, prawns, mackerel, sardines, halibut, swordfish, turbot and herring to name but a few. Exotic fish like mahi-mahi, barramundi and blue shark are often sold alongside local cockles and jellied eels. There are around 100 stalls and thirty shops for visitors to see the very freshest of fish and shellfish. Experience the lifestyle of the East End trader and hear their banter and salty language across the market floor. A visit wouldn't be complete without breakfast in one of the cafes for a mug of tea and a scallop and bacon bap.

Postmodernist pumping station

John Outram's 'Temple of Storms' pumping station, listed as one of the UK's finest postmodern buildings, is a hidden gem found along the Thames Path in the north-east of the island. Completed in 1988, it was designed to deal with the water run-off from the new streets created when the surrounding area was redeveloped. The building, full of complex iconography, is fronted by a pair of grandiose columns and features decorative eaves and a gable covered in corrugated cladding. It looks like a classical temple rising from a river.

Visit an East End boozer

There's nothing quite like the atmosphere of an East End boozer and the Isle of Dogs has some real hidden gems. The Ferry House, the oldest on the island, is a cosy wood-panelled pub with a welcoming fire. Located on the River Thames since Tudor times, its present incarnation was built in 1822 as a home for the ferryman whose wife served pints to people waiting for the ferry to Greenwich. Nearby, the Lord Nelson was originally built as a grand pub in contrast to the Victorian beer houses that were there to serve the dockers. It still has paintings of its namesake sailor adorning the walls. In one corner it has a London speciality – a rare East End fives board. Originating in medieval times, it is believed to have started as an indoor version of archery; it is the predecessor of the modern 'clock' dartboard. With just twelve segments, the wider sections give more opportunity to hit a maximum score of 180, which would make life easy if it wasn't for its extremely narrow trebles and the longer throwing distance. Another historic watering-hole sits just across the lock from the north-east tip of the island along the narrow cobbled Coldharbour. The Gun, an eighteenth-century tavern, is an atmospheric building that harks back to a time when London was the greatest port in the world. Named after the cannon fired to celebrate the opening of the nearby West India Import Docks in 1802, it is now a great place to sit in the snug next to the fire in winter or on the terrace looking across the Thames to the O2 in the summer. Lord Nelson was a regular drinker here, frequenting it whenever he visited the area to inspect the nearby docks. It was also the haunt of smugglers and pirates who would offload and distribute their contraband via a secret tunnel here. A spyhole, once used as a lookout for the authorities, remains in one of the pub's staircases.

Museum of London Docklands

Covering 2,000 years of history, through the story of the River Thames, this brilliant museum will delight, horrify and inform. Housed in a Georgian warehouse amongst the modern buildings and workplaces of Canary Wharf, it is hard to imagine how this was once a destination for slave ships which, along with the sugar trade, shaped London. An immersive display recreates the atmosphere of the dark alleyways and shops of Sailortown.

This ramshackle London district, close to the docks, once centred around Wapping, Shadwell and Ratcliffe. The City and River gallery then takes you on a tour of the huge docks complex built on the Isle of Dogs and how it enabled Britain to become the centre of world trade. Learn how Docklands survived as the first target attacked by the Luftwaffe in 1940 and then went on to aid the war effort through the role it played in events from Dunkirk to D-Day. Since World War II, London's Docklands has had its ups and downs, culminating in its closure from the 1960s through to the early 1980s before it became the site of Europe's largest regeneration projects and the headquarters of the financial industry that it is today. The Museum of London Docklands is excellent, free and needs at least half a day.
www.museumoflondon.org.uk/museum-london-docklands

Mudchute Park and Farm

A working farm in the middle of the city, Mudchute Park and Farm on the Isle of Dogs is just a stone's throw from Canary Wharf and forms a local nature reserve and a Site of Metropolitan Importance for Nature Conservation. Farm animals range from grazing cows and sheep to alpacas. The cafe serves locally-sourced food.

Crossrail Place Roof Garden

One of London's largest roof gardens, this has exotic plants, hidden pathways and an amphitheatre that hosts a variety of shows. It sits almost exactly on the meridian line and planting is arranged according to which hemisphere they originate from. Asian plants such as bamboos are planted to the east, and plants such as ferns from the Americas to the west. This is a beautiful, peaceful and leafy oasis within one of London's busiest districts. Open daily to the public until 9.00 p.m. or sunset in summer.

LONDON

Brentford
Ait
Chiswick
Chiswick
Eyot
Kensington
Oliver's Eyot
Hammersmith
Westminster
Brentford
Lot's Ait
Fulham
Thames
Isleworth Ait
Hounslow
Isleworth
Richmond
Clapham
Corporation Island
Wandsworth
Eel Pie Island
Glover's Island
Twickenham
Swan Island
Teddington Lock Ait
Angler's Ait
Teddington
N
Kingston
upon Thames
0   5km

Thames Tideway group

86

Chiswick Eyot

ACCESS TIDAL CROSSING

Hidden in a backwater in Old Chiswick village, this narrow, uninhabited, tree- and reed-covered island appears on television in every Boat Race – the green pole at its south-west end marks the halfway point of the race. Once the haunt of eel fishermen and osier cutters, it now sits silently opposite the ancient terrace of elegant Georgian and Regency houses with their beautifully manicured riverside gardens. Owned by the local council, at low tide it can be reached across the mud on foot, while high tides cover most of the island (the high point of the island is less than five metres). Tours are available at the neighbouring Fuller's Brewery.

Oliver's Eyot

ACCESS NOT PERMITTED; VIEW FROM MAINLAND PATH

Close to Kew Railway Bridge, this thickly-wooded islet derives its name from an unlikely story that Oliver Cromwell took refuge here and set up temporary headquarters at the Bull's Head, in Strand on the Green, which he reached via a secret tunnel. Later the islet was used as a tollbooth for passing river traffic, then as a smithy and storage facilities. It is now owned by the Port of London Authority and is a haven for herons, cormorants and Canada geese. Landing is not permitted, other than during Thames Tide Fest. It can be approached by stand-up paddleboard, hired or launched from the north end of Kew Bridge. The island, which has a high point of less than five metres, is also easily seen from the lovely walk along the Thames Path on both the north and south banks.

www.thamestidefest.net

Brentford Ait

ACCESS VIEW FROM MAINLAND PATH; PADDLEBOARD

Inconspicuous on a bend in the Thames opposite the Royal Botanic Gardens at Kew, this tree-covered island was once home to a notorious pub called the Three Swans – the pub closed in 1796 and no trace remains of the building today. An island of two halves at low tide, separated by Hog Hole, it is a significant heronry and home to kingfishers, wading birds, cormorants and grebes. The fact that it still exists, rather than having slowly eroded away, is due to the obligation of Richmond Council to buy and maintain it to block the views of the Brentford Gas Works from the gardens. The island, which has a high point of less than five metres, can be approached by stand-up paddleboard or kayak launched from the slipway at Kew Bridge or viewed from the Thames Path.

Lot's Ait

ACCESS NOT PERMITTED; VIEW FROM MAINLAND PATH

Next door to Brentford Ait and hidden behind Brentford High Street, the smaller, privately owned Lot's Ait is dominated by Lot's Ait Boatyard with its workshops and tidal dock that has been restored to its former glory by John's Boat Works. Its thriving boat-dwelling community live across the footbridge from the north bank, while the area of the island fronting the Thames remains untouched to provide a natural habitat for the local wildlife; including the rare two-lipped door snail. Once well known for its osier beds and willows, the island has featured in Humphrey Bogart and Katharine Hepburn's 1951 film *The African Queen*, as well as the 2017 British action thriller *Stratton* and the Channel 4 TV series *George Clarke's Amazing Spaces*. Public access to the island, which has a high point of less than five metres, is only permitted as part of Thames Tide Fest; or the island can be viewed from the Thames Path.

www.thamestidefest.net

1 Oliver's Eyot **2** Chiswick Eyot, neighbouring Fuller's Brewery **3** Chiswick Eyot **4** Glover's Island, view from Richmond Hill

Isleworth Ait

ACCESS NOT PERMITTED; VIEW FROM MAINLAND PATH
This island is one of London Wildlife Trust's most remarkable sanctuaries, sitting in the middle of the River Thames, opposite the Royal Botanic Gardens at Kew. This undisturbed wooded island (which has a high point of less than five metres), once a centre for osier production, is now home to more than fifty-seven species of birds, including the treecreeper, kingfisher and heron; two rare species of air-breathing land molluscs, the two-lipped door snail and the German hairy snail; and several rare species of beetles. Owned by Thames Water, it is the discharge point into the Thames of the purified effluent from Mogden Sewage Treatment Works which treats waste water from around 1.9 million people. Access to the island is only possible on a London Wildlife Trust workday. From the riverbank the best views are from the beer gardens of either the London Apprentice or Town Wharf on the Thames path.
www.wildlondon.org.uk

Corporation Island

ACCESS NOT PERMITTED; VIEW FROM MAINLAND PATH
Opposite Richmond's impressive river frontage, almost in the shadow of Richmond Bridge, this undisturbed island (with a high point of less than five metres) is home to herons, coots, moorhens, ducks and geese and its peace is in sharp contrast to the bars and promenades of the northern bank of the Thames here. One of the last photographs of The Beatles together was taken in 1969, with the band sitting on Corporation Island. Two further eyots, collectively known as the **Flowerpot Islands**, sit between Corporation Island and Richmond Railway Bridge. These tiny, circular, tree-topped mounds have had no other purpose than to be ornamental and the current owners, Richmond Council, are bound by deed from Queen Victoria to keep them in good repair. Public access is not permitted but the islands can be readily viewed from the Thames Path.

Glover's Island

ACCESS NOT PERMITTED; VIEW FROM MAINLAND PATH
Between Richmond Lock and Teddington Lock, Glover's Island rises in the Thames to a high point of less than five metres. The view of this heavily-wooded islet from the top of Richmond Hill is the only view in Britain protected by an Act of Parliament and it is one of the most famous views in Greater London. The story behind it is less tranquil than the view of the gentle meander of the River Thames, flanked on one side by the Petersham Meadows and the Middlesex plains on the other, with the island a beautiful, natural centrepiece. In the 1890s Richmond Hill was a very desirable place to live and some local landowners wanted to profit from it. Glover's Island was put up for sale twice, its owner suggesting that Pears Soap should buy it to erect a giant advertising billboard there. The ongoing threat of development led in 1902 to the Richmond, Petersham and Ham Open Spaces Act to protect the view from Richmond Hill. Today the viewpoint is best enjoyed from the pedestrianised, tree-lined balcony on Richmond Hill called the Terrace, where you can find a plaque that records those who helped to preserve 'the rural tranquillity of this celebrated view'.

Eel Pie Island

ACCESS FOOTBRIDGE
Named after the eel pies once served by the island's inn in the nineteenth century and home to the UK's largest hippie community in the 1970s, some say this is the true home of British R&B. Located in the River Thames at Twickenham it has always been a destination for the good times. Its musical heyday was during the 1960s when the Eel Pie Island

1 Teddington Lock Ait

Hotel hosted a stream of the great and good from Rod Stewart, Acker Bilk and The Rolling Stones to The Who, Pink Floyd, Black Sabbath, Genesis and Hawkwind. The hotel is now long gone and replaced by a vibrant and eclectic community, two or three boatyards and artists' studios. There are nature reserves at either end of the island, which has a high point of less than five metres. The public can access the island's main pathway from the footbridge along The Embankment, Twickenham. The other walkways are private, except on certain days when the Eel Pie Art Studios are open to the public. The excellent Eel Pie Island Museum on nearby Richmond Road is well worth a visit as it really brings the island's history to life.
www.eelpiemuseum.co.uk

Swan Island

ACCESS FOOTBRIDGE
At the southern end of Radnor Gardens, Twickenham, the centre of this island is occupied by Newman's Boatyard while its perimeter is home to the long-established community living on houseboats, yachts, barges and floating homes. The island, which has a high point of less than five metres, was built on top of mudflats by a local builder using clay excavated during the construction of the London Underground in the 1890s. There is a cafe in Radnor Gardens and a microbrewery for takeaways at the mainland entrance to the island.

Teddington Lock Ait and Angler's Ait

ACCESS FOOTBRIDGE
Located 109 kilometres along the River Thames from the sea, Teddington Lock is the largest lock system on the river and forms the boundary between the tidal and non-tidal Thames. It is here that fresh water from the west meets the salt water from the east and the Environment Agency takes over control of the river from the Port of London Authority. Wooded Angler's Ait is accessed across the decorative footbridge that spans the Thames. There is a small sandy beach immediately adjacent to the bridge and a kayak and stand-up paddleboard launch point at the north end of the footbridge. Teddington Lock Ait is accessed via a further small footbridge from the north bank of the Thames, off the Thames Path, and is a great spot to sit and watch the boating activity along the river. The high point of the group is less than five metres. There are wooded and riverside trails in adjacent Ham Lands Nature Reserve. Two inns are located along the southern approach to the footbridge, including The Anglers, which dates back to 1795, as well as the excellent riverside Flying Cloud Cafe.

Essex has around thirty islands (more than any other English county); they differ in character, wildlife and geology. The larger islands of Foulness and Mersea are known for their long human histories, buildings and attractions. Many of the other islands are smaller, uninhabited and completely wild and offer a safe haven for birds, rare insects and flora that thrive in the maze of salt marsh and other special habitats. Beaches, salt marsh, sea walls and saltings characterise the islands here as do the daily activities of oystermen, farmers and sailors. Every year the coastlines change as these delicate places erode a little more; some all but disappear under the waves at high tide. Suffolk has just one island which is an incredible bird reserve, while Norfolk's Chedgrave Island is a great way to immerse yourself into the wilds of the Norfolk Broads and Scolt Head Island is a family wilderness adventure.

THE ESSEX ESTUARIES, NORFOLK & SUFFOLK

Opposite Cobmarsh Island **Overleaf** Tollesbury Wick Marshes

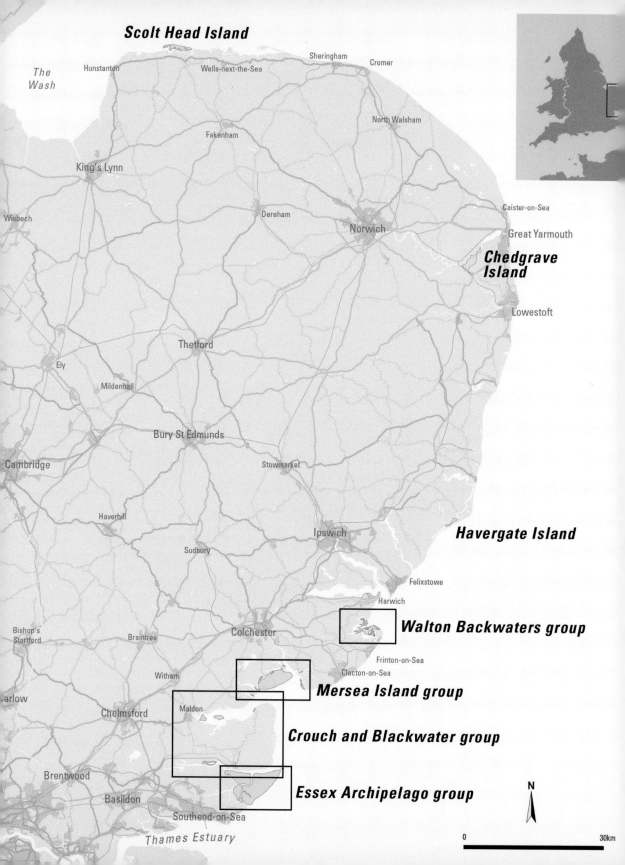

Foulness Island

ACCESS ROAD BRIDGE; TIDAL WALK
(ACCESS RESTRICTIONS)

Foulness, Essex's best kept secret and just up the coast from Southend-on-Sea, can be accessed via The Broomway, a treacherous path through the tidal sands that has also been named The Doomway. Foulness, the largest island in Essex and the fourth largest in England, is owned by the Ministry of Defence and inhabited by civilians who live in its quaint weatherboard and brick houses. The island has a high point of less than five metres. The landscape is dotted with the watchtowers, launch towers, domes and fenced compounds of the military munitions-testing facilities, which adds a surrealness to the otherwise bucolic farmland and traditional buildings. The island can also be accessed through the security gate at Great Wakering and open to the public on the first Sunday of the month (April to September); home-baked cakes in the Heritage Centre await those that venture on to the island. A flat, four-kilometre road, perfect for cycling, leads through the firing range to a car park in the village.

Visit the Heritage Centre

Housed in the former school in Churchend, its eclectic displays range from wedding gowns to gas masks and tell the island's story with poignant images of the North Sea flood of 1953. This is a great place to meet the friendly islanders whose local dialect, an Australian-like twang, is peppered with native Foulness terms such as *stringies*, *cadgers* and *doggies*. The islanders make great home-made cakes to be enjoyed in the garden and, from here, it is possible to explore the paths around the village. During the summer this centre is open once a month.

Walk The Doomway

Stepping out on to Maplin Sands to follow the legendary ten-kilometre-long Broomway, where the incoming tide moves faster than most people can run, requires some planning and nerve. Those that attempt it will be rewarded with a fabulous wilderness experience. Start from Wakering Stairs and track along the sands to Fisherman's Head on Foulness Island. This isn't for the faint-hearted and the largely featureless landscape requires good map and compass skills, with GPS back-up, and good knowledge of walking speed and tides.
www.islandeering.com

New England Island and Havengore Island

ACCESS NOT PERMITTED

The government-built road from the mainland to Foulness Island crossed and joined the islands of New England and Havengore so that now they are generally treated as one larger island under the ownership of the Ministry of Defence. Havengore Island was the original military site, used towards the end of World War II. It was involved in the testing of rockets, tackling oil storage fires and understanding the effects of close-range bomb explosions on Anderson Shelters – the air raid shelters that were erected in people's gardens. Today the island is farmed and the creeks that surround it are a popular spot for boating. A lifting bridge spans Havengore Creek between Havengore and the mainland which allows boats to sail through the creek from the River Thames to the River Roach. Public access to the island itself is limited to the road that passes through it on the way to Foulness Island. New England Island was once a prosperous centre for sheep farming with the export of wool, skins for parchment, meat, butter and cheese. Today it is uninhabited and Ministry of Defence restrictions essentially prevent free access, except for passing through it on the road to Foulness Island. The high point of the group is less than five metres.

Essex Archipelago group

Rushley Island

ACCESS NOT PERMITTED; VIEW FROM MAINLAND PATH
Fitting like a puzzle piece between the
mainland and the Ministry of Defence islands
of Havengore and Potton, this uninhabited and
isolated island is little-visited. It has a surprising
history – local entrepreneur John Harriot
bought it and in 1781 set about a plan to
enclose the whole island with a sea wall to use
the highly fertile land to grow crops. He built
a farm and dug several wells. For his efforts he
was presented the gold medal by the Society
for the Encouragement of Arts, Manufacturers
and Commerce, and was invited to meet King
George III. He did successfully grow crops here
but after a run of bad luck and flooding he ran
out of money. Since then the island, which has
a high point of less than five metres, has been
continually used for agriculture. There is a low-
tide ford across to the island which is not open
to the public. It can be easily seen from the
mainland via a lovely 3.5-kilometre creek-side
walk heading north-east from Great Wakering
to Oxenham, then north along the seawall,
returning south from Mill Head. This can be
combined with the walk to see Potton Island.

Potton Island

ACCESS NOT PERMITTED; VIEW FROM MAINLAND PATH
In the west of the Essex Archipelago, Potton
Island has been inhabited since Neolithic times.
It was home to several arable farms which
through history went through a cycle of flooding
and rebuilding but generally prospered.
During World War II the island had its own
Home Guard who were properly exercised by
the dropping of over 250 bombs from planes
heading back to Europe following bombing
sorties on London. The island was acquired by
the Ministry of Defence in 1955 and formed
part of its blast and fragmentation range,
used to test controlled explosions in cars.
The knowledge gained was to become useful
in Northern Ireland. Today, the island, which
has a high point of less than five metres, is
managed by tenant farmers with crops, grazing
and horse stabling. There is a road from Great
Wakering Common to the island's bridge with
a small security building manned by a Ministry
of Defence employee whose job is to raise the
bridge when boats wish to pass. Public access
is not permitted. Good views of the Ministry
of Defence buildings and the southern shore
of the island can be seen from a 4.5-kilometre
walk from Great Wakering along the sea wall
footpath. This can be combined with a walk to
see Rushley Island or can be extended with a
loop around Fleet Head.

Wallasea Island

ACCESS ROAD; SMALL FERRY
One of the most tranquil places in Essex, this
island is in the process of being returned to
nature with magical landscapes of marshland,
lagoons and ditches packed with wildlife in
a nature reserve twice the size of the City of
London. It feels like it has truly earned its peace
after being originally drained by fifteenth-
century Dutch settlers, with sea walls built and
the land converted to farmland which went on
to produce for the nation during both world
wars. Today, the RSPB's Wallasea Island Wild
Coast Project has seen the sea walls breached
and the land re-wetted with the ambition
of bringing back species like the spoonbill
to colonise and breed. Today the island's
enchanting interior is evolving into wetland,
mudflats, saline lagoons and artificial islands
to create new habitat for wading birds. This
landscape creation was aided by shipping more
than three million tonnes of earth, excavated
during the development of the Crossrail scheme
in London, to raise the island above sea level.
A tiny hub of a marina, bar, cafe, campsite

1 **Foulness Island**, start of The Broomway   2 **Foulness Island**, walking The Broomway
3 **Rushley Island**, flat landsape across Havengore Creek   4 **Wallasea Island**, Half Moon Viewpoint

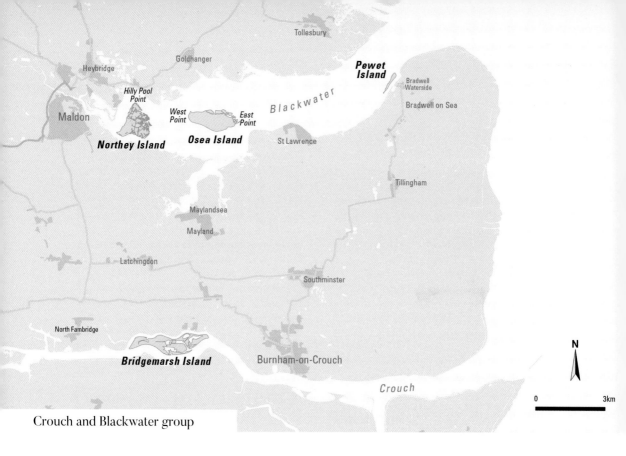

Crouch and Blackwater group

and timber yard is nestled in the north-west corner where the wharf operates regular timber shipments from Riga. Access to the island, which has a high point of less than five metres, is via a road bridge or seasonal ferry from Burnham-on-Crouch.

Walk one of the island's many trails

The island has a network of waymarked trails along public footpaths and permissive paths – it is a great way to experience the wilds of the island. A ten-kilometre circuit starts at the reserve's car park (grid reference: TQ 955945) and follows the sea wall along the island's northern shore. From here there are great views across the River Crouch to quaint Burnham-on-Crouch. The route heads south to the wilds of Jubilee Marsh with views across the River Roach to the military buildings of Foulness Island before reaching the shelter of the Half Moon Viewpoint at the island's south-east tip. It then continues along the sea wall along the island's southern boundary with the River Roach to Beagle Viewpoint with views across to the

boats moored along tranquil Paglesham Reach. Heading north-west, the route passes the Water Vole area and returns to the car park through more marshland. Three shorter routes are also on offer – Jubilee Marsh, Allfleets Marsh and Marsh Flats. At the ends of the Allfleets Marsh and Jubilee Marsh trails, shelters provide a comfortable place to sit overlooking the river. Details of all these walks are available online. *www.rspb.org.uk/reserves-and-events/ reserves-a-z/wallasea-island*

Wildlife watching

There is plenty to see year-round in the island's incredibly rich wildlife habitats. Spring brings migrants including whimbrels, green sandpiper, avocets and common terns with hundreds of skylarks singing, gull-packed islands and hares playing in the grassland. In the summer terns dive for fish, marsh harriers hunt, butterflies and bees collect nectar and water voles scurry around the ditches. Common seals are often seen hauled out on the banks of the River Roach. Autumn brings new migrants including

1 Wallasea Island

ringed plovers, dunlins, greenshanks, black-tailed godwits and redshanks along with teal, wigeon and brent geese that overwinter on the Essex coast. The greatest spectacle though is in the winter when the size of the flocks of waders and wildfowl on the lagoons and mudflats is astounding. There are a number of hides around the island to watch the birds without disturbing them.

Bridgemarsh Island

ACCESS KAYAK; PADDLEBOARD; VIEW FROM MAINLAND PATH
The only proper island on the River Crouch outside of the Essex Archipelago is close to the river's mouth. Like many other Essex islands it has gone through the cycle of flooding and reclamation and today almost disappears at high tide (the island has a high point of less than five metres). It was once an island used for grazing animals with an intact sea wall and its source of clay led to the construction

of a brickworks. All that remains today are remnants of the sea wall, seen at low tide, and the brickwork's chimney. Its marshland is an important site for wildfowl and is currently managed by the Bridgemarsh Island Trust. The island can be approached by stand-up paddleboard or kayak along the River Crouch, which is also a popular spot with sailors. Smaller craft can explore the creeks that cut through the island at high tide. Most of the island can be seen along the peaceful coast path walk from Althorne station and marina or, for a longer walk, from Burnham-on-Crouch.

Pewet Island

ACCESS KAYAK; PADDLEBOARD; VIEW FROM MAINLAND PATH
Pewet Island lies on the southern side of the Blackwater Estuary, just 100 metres across the boat-filled Bradwell Creek from the hamlet and marina of Bradwell Waterside. There is a great walk around the wild Dengie Peninsula to see it. Privately owned, it is a strip of low-lying salt marsh (the high point of the island is less than

1 Northey Island, salt marsh   **2** Northey Island   **3** Northey Island, tidal causeway

five metres) notable for the remains of Saxon-era timber fish traps. Author Michael Morpurgo lived in nearby Bradwell-on-Sea as a child, and lovingly described this as an area of 'infinite beauty'. One of the best ways to appreciate it is an incredible ten-kilometre walk along mudflats, salt marshes and beaches as well as the Dengie National Nature Reserve. Starting at Eastlands (grid reference: TM 023078), the route passes the seventh-century Chapel of St Peter on the Wall, one of the oldest surviving churches in England and built of materials from the pre-existing Roman fort of Othona. The chapel marks the end point of the pilgrim path, St Peter's Way. The walk continues north around the coast, through the nature reserve and past the bird observatory, salt marshes and the decommissioned Bradwell Nuclear Power Station from where there are fine views of Pewet Island across the creek. Continue to the marina then head to the historic village of Bradwell-on-Sea, past the Bradwell War Memorial, in remembrance to the World War II pilots from the airfield here that never returned. There are three pubs and a village shop en route.

Northey Island

ACCESS TIDAL CAUSEWAY

A wild National Trust-owned island in the Blackwater Estuary a stone's throw from the historic town of Maldon. It is accessed via a tidal causeway, which is the oldest recorded battlefield in Britain after the Vikings fought local forces here in the Battle of Maldon. Northey Island has a high point of eight metres and is surrounded by creeping tides and salt marsh, which is the origin of the famous Maldon sea salt used in cookery worldwide. The fringes of the island are home to thousands of shelduck, godwit, avocet, greenshank and plover along with brent geese which overwinter here and graze Northey's pastureland. Northey House is the former home of Sir Norman Angell, an English Nobel Peace Prize winner. Access is via the tidal causeway (not passable for two hours either side of high tide). No food is available on the island but there are plenty of options in Maldon, including the riverside Queen's Head inn.

Wilderness walk

The views of the mudbanks either side of the causeway are fantastic. Once on the island there is an easy lane to follow to the Warden's Cottage (free for National Trust members). There is a gap in the hedge on the left just before the cottage (signed *Private*) to reach the path that then follows the perimeter of the island back to the causeway.
www.islandeering.com

Be a castaway

The annual Castaway event is a weekend where you'll be cut off from the world to experience Northey Island at high tide and camping in its purest form. Run by the National Trust there are stalls and activities, a beer tent and hot food, live music and themed activities for the family.

Osea Island

ACCESS PRIVATE TIDAL CAUSEWAY

A privately owned island that hosts celebrities and families who can enjoy the peaceful paradise of this coastal gem. Lying in the Blackwater Estuary with a high point of seven metres, and joined to the mainland by a tidal causeway, Osea first opened in 1903 as a retreat for city alcoholics. It repeated history as a detox clinic in its turreted manor house with guests including Amy Winehouse. It closed again and re-emerged as a recording studio, a hideaway for the renegade spy David Shayler and a party island for hipsters. Today, families and mainland escapees can enjoy staying in the cottages in the 'village', a cluster of Victorian weatherboard cottages, outdoor swimming pools and peaceful beaches. Access is restricted to guests staying at the island's accommodation.

Mersea Island group

Mersea Island

ACCESS TIDAL ROAD BRIDGE; SEASONAL FOOT FERRY
Mersea Island lies in the Blackwater and Colne estuaries to the south of Colchester. The island is split into two main areas: the populated and seafaring West Mersea and the rural East Mersea which also includes Cudmore Grove Country Park. The north of the island is wild salt marsh and mudflats packed with wading and migratory birds while the south is the key holiday destination with several holiday parks and the photogenic rows of pastel-coloured beach huts along the shore. The high point of the island reaches twenty-one metres. Mersea is famed worldwide for its native oysters and is a foodie destination that boasts its own vineyard and brewery. It is also a very popular sailing and water sports centre. Access is across the Strood and Pyefleet channels via a road bridge that closes when tides are higher than five metres; allow up to one and a half hours either side of a tide of this height to travel safely.

Mersea Week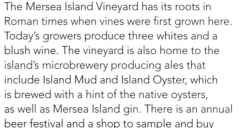
Mersea Week is an annual sailing festival which attracts hundreds of boats and thousands of spectators every August. The festival includes the Round the Island Race where competitors navigate the island's coastline, with a short stretch where they have to take their boats out of the water, with the help of family and friends, and run down the road to cross Strood Channel. This fun race ends with the Town Regatta, an event which dates back to 1838.
www.merseaweek.org

Vineyard and brewery
The Mersea Island Vineyard has its roots in Roman times when vines were first grown here. Today's growers produce three whites and a blush wine. The vineyard is also home to the island's microbrewery producing ales that include Island Mud and Island Oyster, which is brewed with a hint of the native oysters, as well as Mersea Island gin. There is an annual beer festival and a shop to sample and buy the products.

1 Mersea Island, fresh seafood at West Mersea

Walk round the island's coast

This twenty-two-kilometre, flat walk along the coast path starts amongst the salty hubbub and traditional clapperboard-clad houses of West Mersea. It quickly follows the sea wall along the island's north coast, parallel to the gentle tidal creeks of the Strood and Pyefleet channels. The wild salt marsh and mudflats here are packed with wading and migratory birds. Heading around the eastern tip of the island the low fossil-rich cliffs and woodland of Cudmore Grove Country Park are popular destinations for families. The route continues along the south coast past the ribbon of holiday parks and pastel-coloured beach huts that mark the return to civilisation.
www.islandeering.com

Enjoy a seafood feast

There are a number of lively eateries in West Mersea, full of foodies tucking into piles of shells, but a firm favourite is the legendary Company Shed, a wooden shack where tables are laid with just salt, pepper and Tabasco sauce. Bring your own wine and bread and tuck into the best seafood around. The 'common' rock oysters are available all year but connoisseurs are drawn here to taste the native oyster. Sourced from local waters and brought to the laying beds around the island to grow naturally, they have been cultivated here by the Haward family since the 1700s. The current generation of the Haward family export their prize-winning oysters all over the world as well as selling at London's Borough Market.

Beach huts

The much-photographed string of pastel-coloured beach huts along West Mersea Beach are a hark back to the modesty of Victorian bathing and the ultimate seaside home from home. Each has its own small, nautically-themed stained-glass window and ornate railings and offer the perfect daytime refuge from inclement weather and a place to make your own cup of tea. A few of the huts can be rented for the day.

Explore by paddleboard

The waters around Mersea Island are ideal for most water sports. This sailing Mecca is popular with paddleboarders and kayakers who enjoy the endless opportunities offered by the varied waters of the Blackwater Estuary and its numerous channels and creeks. Favourite trips from West Mersea Marina include heading north along the Strood Channel to the road bridge and south to Packing Shed Island. Both trips weave through moored boats and houseboats and pass numerous small creeks. Equipment hire and instruction are available in West Mersea.

Visit the Radio Caroline ship

Radio Caroline, founded in 1964, was the first pirate radio station that challenged BBC Radio's dominance in the 1960s. The station played pop music all day, while the BBC only played pop records for a few hours a week. It stayed legal by broadcasting from a ship, the *Ross Revenge*, moored in international waters until it ran aground in 1991 off the Kent coast. The ship has now been refurbished and, in 2017, the station re-started broadcasting from her on medium wave – ironically using a previously redundant BBC World Service mast at Orford Ness. Radio Caroline now offers regular trips from West Mersea Marina to visit and tour the *Ross Revenge*, often during live broadcasts and led by Radio Caroline DJs.

Great Cob Island and Little Cob Island

ACCESS KAYAK; PADDLEBOARD

South-west of Mersea Island, at the entrance to Tollesbury Fleet, these two long, narrow islands lie adjacent to each other in the middle of the river. They are two of the largest raised areas of marshland (the group has a high point of less than five metres) in this popular waterway for leisure craft, and provide sheltered boat anchorages. They can be approached by kayak or paddleboard or can be viewed from the coast path to the north side of Tollesbury Wick Marshes, by walking from the picturesque village and marina of Tollesbury.

Packing Shed Island

ACCESS KAYAK; PADDLEBOARD

One of West Mersea's best known landmarks, this Blackwater Estuary island (which has a high point of less than five metres) is a reminder of the sheer scale of the nineteenth-century oyster industry when Mersea Natives were sent to London by the barrel-load on board Thames barges and exported throughout Europe. Cleaning, sizing and packing the oysters was a key process and the Packing Shed was built here in 1890 when sixty or so fishermen worked on the island. It was restored in the 1990s by the Packing Shed Trust and today is a popular destination on open days. It is also used by various local groups for camping, birdwatching and art classes. An annual highlight is the Oyster Dredging Match which celebrates the opening of the native oyster season at West

Mersea. A fleet of restored smacks, bawleys and bumkins compete under sail to see which boat can dredge the largest number of oysters. Boat trips are available to the island from West Mersea or it can be reached by paddleboard or kayak.

Cobmarsh Island

ACCESS KAYAK; PADDLEBOARD

Low-lying (with a high point of less than five metres) and mostly salt marsh, this island was once used for oyster cultivation. East of Packing Shed Island, and larger, it can be easily seen and reached from West Mersea by kayak or paddleboard. Plant life thrives on the shingle banks and marsh and includes the nationally scarce shrubby sea-blite and golden samphire as well as sea purslane and common sea-lavender. Landing is not advisable during the summer bird breeding season.

Sunken Island

ACCESS KAYAK; PADDLEBOARD

In Salcott Channel, just west of Packing Shed Island and Cobmarsh Island, this island has a dark past. It was the location for the murder of a boat full of excisemen that caught smugglers red-handed one night during the smuggling days of Mersea Island. Their ghosts are said to still haunt the island today. The island, which has a high point of less than five metres, can be visited by kayak or paddleboard from West Mersea.

Ray Island

ACCESS TIDAL WALK; KAYAK; PADDLEBOARD

Hidden in the Strood Channel, between Mersea and the mainland, this uninhabited and rarely visited island offers a bit of an adventure. Its atmospheric marshes have inspired a number of Gothic novels including the classic *Mehalah,*

1 Ray Island, crossing from Bonner's Saltings to the island

and *The Essex Serpent*. The island is said to be haunted, so watch out for the ghosts of escaped bears and Roman centurions – the hooves of their horses can apparently still be heard. Owned by the National Trust, the island is an important bird reserve, especially for the large flocks of overwintering wildfowl, waders and brent geese. Most of the island is rough grassland and the perfect hunting ground for the long-eared and short-eared owl, barn owl and hen harrier. The high point of the island is five metres; the only contour line on the Ordnance Survey map is a small thicket of blackthorn and hawthorn next to a freshwater pond near the western shore. The small paths that weave through here are great to explore and the shingle beach nearby offers the perfect landing spot for kayaks and paddleboards. The island's eastern fringe is mostly salt marsh with a wide range of plants including sea lavender, golden samphire and sea rush. As a National Trust-owned property, public access is permitted. Ray Island is reached via a footpath

from The Strood which starts almost opposite Pyefleet House. The route is accessible across Bonner's Saltings from 1 March to 31 August only but is not possible two hours either side of high tide. Alternatively, it is possible to kayak or paddleboard over from Mersea Island.

Pewit Island

ACCESS KAYAK; PADDLEBOARD; VIEW FROM MAINLAND PATH

Taking its name from the 'peewit', the local name for a lapwing, this uninhabited and low-lying island (the high point is less than five metres) once played an important role in Colchester's calendar as it was home to the oyster packing shed used by the town's mayor to conduct the annual opening ceremony for the oyster fishery on the first Friday of September. Today an old Nissen hut sits on the site, but the ceremony still takes place with the mayor and other officials in full civic dress,

floating on a Thames barge in the Pyefleet Channel. A flotilla of small boats carrying invited guests follows the mayor as he dredges and consumes the first oyster of the season. The mayor goes on to host an oyster lunch, with a toast to the Queen, to mark the season's opening of the fishery. The island is accessible by kayak or paddleboard or can be readily viewed from the coast path along the north-east of Mersea Island.

Rat Island

ACCESS KAYAK; PADDLEBOARD; NON-LANDING BOAT TRIP

This raised area of marshland and saltings (with a high point of less than five metres) in the mouth of the Geedon Creek is an important nature reserve with a large nesting colony of black-headed gulls and a small colony of common terns. Spoonbills and skuas have also been spotted passing through here. The island can be approached by kayak or wildlife-spotting boat trips from West Mersea; it is best seen from the mainland across the Colne from along the coast path that runs north-west from Brightlingsea.

Cindery Island

ACCESS KAYAK; PADDLEBOARD; VIEW FROM MAINLAND PATH

To the east of Mersea Island, across the River Colne in Brightlingsea Creek, Cindery Island was originally one long island. It was split into two to allow the owner of St Osyth Priory to take a shortcut in his yacht through the creek. It is full of disused oyster pits and today the south of the island makes a popular anchorage for boats, thus continuing Brightlingsea's maritime traditions; its waters were once home to a wartime military minesweeper base. The island, which has a high point of less than five metres, can be approached by kayak or paddleboard from Brightlingsea or can be seen from the coast path along the sea wall south of Brightlingsea.

Colne Bar

ACCESS FOOTBRIDGE

Made of an impressive expanse of salt marsh, creek and shingle, this island runs along the coastline at the mouth of the Colne Estuary and is separated from the mainland by Ray Creek. Managed by the Essex Wildlife Trust, it has a high point of less than five metres and is rich in plant and animal life including golden samphire, sea holly, sea bindweed, yellow horned poppy and sea kale. Its mudflats are a feeding ground for large flocks of geese and ducks, with grebes and divers offshore during the autumn and winter. Access on foot from the village of St Osyth or there is a small car park (grid reference: TM 108124) just inside the reserve, but it is liable to flood at very high tides. Alternatively, there is a public park at Seawick Holiday Park, next to the Sailor Boy pub, with a pleasant walk along the sea wall to Lee-over-Sands and the footbridge into the reserve. For non-members of the Essex Wildlife Trust, access is via day permit.
www.essexwt.org.uk/nature-reserves/colne-point

Stone Marsh

ACCESS WALK; RESTRICTIONS MAY–SEPTEMBER

At the northern tip of The Naze, Stone Marsh only becomes an island a few times a year when the highest tides flow over the sand spit at the eastern end of Stone Creek. In Arthur Ransome's book Secret Water, the children re-named Stone Marsh as Flint Island, most likely after the fact that Stone Age flint axes have been found on the beach here. Stone Marsh, which has a high point of less than five metres, is surrounded by gentle slopes of soft sand and mud and small boats often use the area as a mooring. From its northern tip at Stone Point there are great views of the mouth of Hamford Water and across Pennyhole Bay to the tall gantries of the container port of Harwich. It is an important breeding site for little terns and

Great Oakley

N

Pewit Island

Pennyhole Bay

New Island

Oakley Creek

Garnham's Island

Stone Point

Hamford Water

Stone Marsh

Landermere Creek

Skipper's Island

Horsey Island

The Naze

Honey Island

Kirby Creek

Landermere Wharf

Landermere

The Wade

Hedge-end Island

Walton-on-the-Naze

Walton Backwaters group

off limits during the breeding season. The best way to reach the island is via the varied coastal walk from The Naze Centre, starting either along the clifftops or, at lower tides, along the beach at the base of the red cliffs of London Clay, which are a fossil-hunters paradise. From here it is straightforward to follow the sand spit north-west to the island. Walk below the high-tide mark from May to mid-August to avoid the ground nesting birds. Return via the same route or continue around the sea wall then alongside the Walton Channel to make a longer, circular route.

Horsey Island

ACCESS NO PUBLIC ACCESS; VIEW FROM MAINLAND PATH

The largest island in the Hamford Water National Nature Reserve, the surrounding maze of creeks and marshland to the west of The Naze is immortalised in the novel *Secret Water* by Arthur Ransome, in which Horsey was referred to as Swallow Island. The island has a high point of seven metres. It is mostly farmed, with a farmhouse and associated buildings; private holiday accommodation is available in Island Cottage. Many rare seabirds overwinter here, particularly brent geese. Access is along a tidal causeway, known as Island Road, from Kirby-le-Soken on the mainland.
www.holidaylettings.co.uk/rentals/frinton-on-sea/138182

Hedge-end Island

ACCESS KAYAK; PADDLEBOARD; TIDAL WALK; VIEW FROM MAINLAND PATH

An uninhabited marshland island at the eastern edge of the Walton Channel, best viewed from the coast path along the western edge of The Naze. The island has a high point of less than

five metres; the waters around the island are very popular with yachts. For the adventurous, it can be reached from Horsey Island at low tide, outside of the bird breeding season, by crossing the mudflats.

Skipper's Island

ACCESS NO PUBLIC ACCESS; VIEW FROM MAINLAND PATH

The island is the hidden gem of the Hamford Water National Nature Reserve. It is home to many special species of flora and fauna; of particular note is the Fisher's estuarine moth. The island is the last stronghold for this moth (which is endemic to North Essex and Kent), and this is only possible because the island is also one of the last places that hog's fennel grows which is essential to its caterpillar stage. Skipper's Island is designated as an Environmentally Sensitive Area, National Nature Reserve, Ramsar site, Site of Special Scientific Interest and a Special Protection Area. Made up of three islands, Lodge, North and Herony (which all have high points of less than five metres), each teems with wildlife. The grassland paths and thickets were previously maintained by the island's warden Ray Marsh, who lovingly recorded every species here over sixty years. Since his retirement in 2019, nature has completely taken over. No landing is permitted on the island but a high-tide kayak trip around its outer edge gives plenty of insights into what a special place this is. A convenient launch spot is Titchmarsh Marina; the island can also be readily seen from the coast path, walking north from Kirby-le-Soken.

Honey Island

ACCESS KAYAK; PADDLEBOARD

In the middle of Kirby Creek, between Horsey Island and Skipper's Island, this marshland island is the only one in Hamford Water that remains an island even at high tide, even though

1 Horsey Island 2 Havergate Island, barn owl 3 Havergate Island, avocet 4 Skipper's Island

its high point is less than five metres. Arthur Ransome, in *Secret Water*, named it Bridget Island after one of the characters. Today it can be circumnavigated by kayak or paddleboard and it is an important site for birds. A convenient launch spot is Titchmarsh Marina.

Other islands in the Walton Backwaters

Several other islands that sit barely above the water will be encountered in any exploration of the Backwater's islands by boat or kayak. The most northerly, **Pewit Island**, lies to the east of Oakley Creek, and with no sea defences it is more an area of low-lying marshland. Immediately to the south, **New Island** is very similar in character and is known as Peewitland in Arthur Ransome's *Secret Water*. Heading west across Oakley Creek, **Garnham's Island** is a cluster of marshland areas, known as Blackberry Island in *Secret Water*.

Havergate Island

ACCESS LOCAL BOAT TRIP; NO DOGS
This small island in the River Ore, which has a high point of less than five metres, is famous for its amazing birdlife including avocets, terns and spoonbills. In autumn and winter the island provides a haven for large numbers of ducks and wading birds. It is the only island in Suffolk and sits at the confluence of the River Ore and Butley River near Orford. It is managed by the RSPB and consists of six salt water lagoons, salt marsh and shingle. Access is by boat trips from Orford Quay on certain dates and times only (prior booking is required). It is possible to view the island from the mainland on a circular walk along the banks of the Ore and Butley between

Orford and Butley village, including a river crossing via ferry at Gedgrave.
www.rspb.org.uk/reserves-and-events/reserves-a-z/havergate-island
www.aldeandore.org/index.php/butley-ferry-2

Chedgrave Island

ACCESS ROAD BRIDGE
Nestled in the Norfolk Broads between the River Yare, River Waveney and New Cut, this island, which has a high point of less than five metres, consists of marsh pastures that form part of Pettingell's Level. An eighteen-kilometre walk goes around the perimeter of the island. The Pettingell family have lived on the island for at least two centuries and their house is situated on the marsh beside the dyke on the western bank of the River Waveney; it is marked on Ordnance Survey maps as Seven Mile House, because it is seven miles from Great Yarmouth. This is a true wilderness walk in the Broads. Start at St Olaves Bridge (roadside parking); food is available at the sixteenth-century Bell Inn at nearby St Olaves.
www.islandeering.com

Scolt Head Island

ACCESS TIDAL CROSSING; SEASONAL FERRY
An island paradise with salt marsh, mudflats, warm pools and tidal creeks on its south coast and the pounding waves of its North Sea along the extensive sand dunes and shingle of the northern shore. Owned by the National Trust, it is an internationally important site for birdlife, especially the five species of tern that breed here. The high point of the island is in sand dunes and reaches seven metres. The island is uninhabited; the two buildings at the western end and at Hut Marsh are for birdwatchers only.

1 Scolt Head Island, the island ferry

Getting here is part of the fun. At low tide it is possible to walk and wade from Burnham Overy Staithe, initially across salt marsh and then the sands of Overy Cockle Strand to reach the main picnic beach. Alternatively, there is a seasonal ferry from the village quay that runs 1.5 hours before and after high water. The western tip is not accessible from April until August due to nesting terns.

www.burnhamoveryboathouse.co.uk/ferry

Wade around the island

There are a number of options for this walk depending on the level of adventure you're after and confidence in reading tides. The full circumnavigation is definitely for those who love mud and splashing around in water. The walk starts at Burnham Overy Staithe; you'll cross two tidal creeks to get to the island then wade along the main channel, Norton Creek, around the southern length of Scolt Head Island to return alongside the dunes of the northern shore. Most of the creeks will be water-filled even at low tide but are easy to wade through at ankle to knee height. There are plenty of warm pools to bathe in on the way. The full route continues to the western tip (out of bounds due to nesting terns from April to August) before returning along the northern shore with its wild sand dunes and shingle. A shorter route cuts to the northern shore via Hut Marsh. A further option is to walk to the island, follow its northern shore, cut through to the southern shore via Butcher's Beach, wade Norton Creek at low tide and return to Burnham Overy Staithe along the Norfolk Coast Path.

www.islandeering.com

Picnic on a wild beach

The eastern end of the island is the perfect place for a picnic on the sweep of golden sand below the high, marram-topped dunes. At high tide the sun-warmed mud and sand make the water here the perfect temperature for swimming, and on sunny days it is a fun-filled destination for flotillas of brightly coloured boats of every description landing their occupants for a picnic and swim.

There are surprisingly few islands in the North of England, making those we do have very special. Many of them are protected bird reserves with large populations of puffins and other seabirds, rarities or spectacular migrations. Others are places of spiritual retreat or destinations for physical challenge with tidal crossings across some of Britain's most notorious sands. There is plenty of mind-blowing history, as well as the opportunity to walk on Spurn Head, the most recently formed island in England. There are some quirky islands too; where else can you realistically expect to meet a king and a royal family?

NORTH EAST & NORTH WEST COASTS

Opposite Farne Islands **Overleaf** Hilbre Island

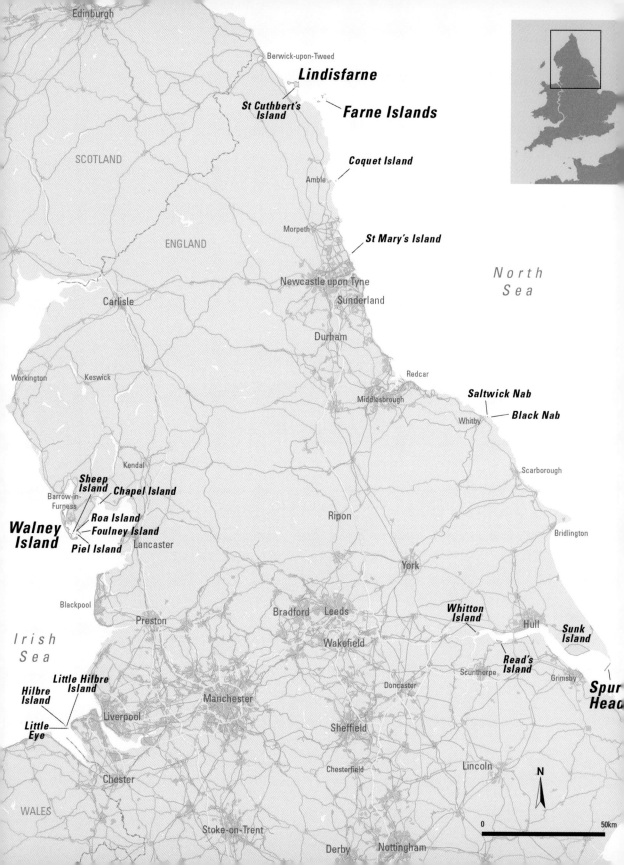

Whitton Island

ACCESS VIEW FROM MAINLAND PATH

At the western end of the Humber Estuary, this uninhabited, wild island is part of the Humber Wild Fowl Refuge. Once a sandbank until changing tides turned it into an island in recent years (it has a high point of less than five metres), it straddles the county boundary between East Yorkshire and Lincolnshire. Owned by Associated British Ports, in 2017 the RSPB signed a fifty-year lease to manage it as a nature reserve. The lagoon and several ponds were made by the RSPB to improve the habitat for wetland birds. Birdwatchers flock to the nearby mainland banks to watch bearded tits, avocets, pink-footed geese, spoonbill, marsh harriers and turnstone amongst the many other species that thrive here. There is no direct access to the island but it can be closely approached on the embankment either side of Weighton Lock, reached on foot from Broomfleet via part of the Trans Pennine Trail; cyclists may use route 65 of the National Cycle Network via Broomfleet which also has a train station.

Read's Island

ACCESS VIEW FROM MAINLAND PATH

Almost in the shadow of the Humber Bridge, the ever-shifting sands of this island are a birdwatcher's paradise and, according to local myth, hold a dark story. Throughout history, the island (which has a high point of less than five metres) has been at the mercy of the flows of this great river, each shifting channel changing the island's shape and mass. Situated just outside the Ferriby Sluice, about fifty metres into the Humber Estuary, it was originally a sandbank known as 'Old Warp'. The island was 'reclaimed' by scuttling a ship and using its structure to protect the southern shore, before it was extended further through a process known as warping. Once owned by the Humber Conservancy Board it was rented

out for a variety of uses from developing new strains of sheep and cattle to storing explosives used to blow up dangerous wrecks on the Humber and a drop-off point for smugglers. Although tranquil today, legend has it that a vagabond set up home here and scraped a living as a ferryman. At that time, many local people went missing in mysterious circumstances. Acting on information from his passengers, the authorities raided his island shack and discovered piles of skeletons and bones. They arrested him for cannibalism, but at his trial legend has it that he transformed into a howling werewolf – so be wary of visiting on a full moon. Today Read's Island is an important RSPB reserve, managed and renowned for the high numbers of breeding avocets. The island and its birdlife can be seen from the embankment at Ferriby Sluice.

Sunk Island

ACCESS ROAD BRIDGE

This island is about as flat as it gets, reaching a high point of less than five metres, with huge skies and the only trees lining a few straight roads. Owned by the Crown Estate, it lies to the north of the Humber Estuary on a bend in the river. Starting life as a sandbank, silt accumulated here and outer banks were constructed to keep the water out so that the reclaimed land could be used as pasture. During World War I, a fort was built here and today the settlement consists of a church, a few houses and a few farms. An island by virtue of the Winestead Drain and North Channel delineating the north of the island, one access point is along the lane leading from Ottringham. After crossing the channel, the lane passes through emptiness for two kilometres before reaching the red-brick church, which acts as a heritage centre, and a couple of houses that make up the community of Sunk Island. The lane continues west to Stone Creek on the Humber, once a centre for commercial shrimp and prawn fishing, today the moorings for a small number of leisure craft. Across the estuary the industrial silhouette of Immingham lies in a stark contrast and its vast ships can be seen ploughing through the Humber. A two-kilometre walk south-east of Stone Creek, along West Bank, leads to a small woodland with some very well-preserved remains of an anti-aircraft gun station.

Spurn Head

ACCESS TIDAL CROSSING; NO DOGS
Often known as Yorkshire's very own Land's End, this island makes for one of the most striking features of Britain's coastline. It's a curving spit, essentially a series of sand and shingle banks held together by marram grass and sea buckthorn, that stretches for five kilometres across the Humber Estuary. In some places the spit is only fifty metres wide; the high point of the island reaches fourteen metres. A high tidal surge in 2013 washed away the road connection, leaving it as Yorkshire's newest island, and one of the most recently made islands in Britain. Owned by the Yorkshire Wildlife Trust since its purchase from the Ministry of Defence in the 1950s, this National Nature Reserve is a haven for migrant birds, lizards, roe deer and numerous species of insects. Famed for birding and a fabulous walk along its entire length, it is a slice of wild heaven on the doorstep of Hull. Spurn Bird Observatory in the nearby village of Kilnsea offers hostel-type accommodation and there are a couple of small motorhome sites close to the village. The Crown and Anchor is a popular spot to sit and watch the tides and sunsets and compare notes after a day's birding or walking. The cedar-clad, award-winning Discovery Centre run by the Yorkshire Wildlife Trust has a cafe and a gift shop.

Birdwatching
With big skies, remoteness and a wonderful mix of habitats, it is often cited as one of the best areas for birding in mainland Britain.

Across habitats and seasons it is possible to see anything from little terns and avocets to woodcocks, rails, finches and buntings. Scarcities vary from red-backed shrike, scarlet rosefinch and barred warbler to Siberian accentor, masked shrike and pine buntings. One of the great spectacles here is the thousands of common swifts that fly past during midsummer. Information on the latest sightings is available in two centres – the Yorkshire Wildlife Trust's Discovery Centre on Spurn Road and Spurn Bird Observatory in the village of Kilnsea. For beginners, the Yorkshire Wildlife Trust run 'Bespoke Birding' trips where you can join an expert on an exclusive tour of Spurn National Nature Reserve and nearby Kilnsea Wetlands on foot and aboard the Spurn Safari vehicle, an ex-army Unimog.

Walk or cycle along Spurn Head
The best way to experience the unique and ever-changing landscapes and spectacular wildlife of Spurn Head is to walk or cycle the island's length at low tide. Start in Kilnsea village; once in the reserve, follow the road to the washed-out beach section at low tide to reach the island itself. Here the sandy path passes through the dunes with some great views across the Humber. A pair of lighthouses, situated close to each other towards the southern end of the point, mark the end of a long history of lights here. Around eight of their predecessors were swept away by storms. The black-and-white-striped lighthouse, known as Spurn Point, was built with extra lamps making the Spurn Point Low on the beach to its west redundant – with subsequent use as an explosive store and water tower before it was deserted. Due to improvements in navigation, Spurn Point was then discontinued in 1985 and today public tours are available through Yorkshire Wildlife Trust. Further south, the Royal National Lifeboat Institution (RNLI) Lifeboat Station was built in 1810, with cottages for the lifeboat crew added a few years later. It is the only station in the UK, other than

119

1 Black Nab, with the wreck of the *Admiral Von Tromp*

one in London on the Thames, which has full-time staff. Beyond the station, small tracks lead through the low woodland and brush past the concrete ruins of two World War I artillery batteries to reach Spurn Point. It is a wonderfully wild and dynamic place with the sights and sounds of turbulent waters all around. The huge container ships that ply the waters of the Humber, to and from the giant ports of Hull, Immingham and Grimsby, feel almost within touching distance.

Black Nab and Saltwick Nab

ACCESS TIDAL CROSSING

Saltwick Bay, just two kilometres east of Whitby, has two small islets, some incredible geology and the very real chance of finding rare fossils. Black Nab and Saltwick Nab are islets off promontories at either end of the bay. The high point of the group is less than ten metres. The bay itself is beautiful, with sand and plenty of rockpools to explore; it is accessible via the steep steps from Whitby Holiday Park. It makes a great walking destination from Whitby, along the Cleveland Way, which passes Dracula's Whitby Abbey, Whitby Harbour and the fabulous North Yorkshire coastline. Access to the islets and stone shelves is possible for

one hour either side of low tide; take care at the base of the cliffs as rockfalls are common. Saltwick Bay Cafe is in the holiday park.

Historic alum quarries

Alum quarries were established on both promontories of Saltwick Bay for subsequent use in the textile industry. The earliest quarry, operational from 1649 to 1791, was cut into the cliffs to the south-west of Saltwick Nab and is a Scheduled Monument. Steeping pits and cisterns for the first processing stages of the mineral, along with other associated buildings on its terrace and a slipway on the foreshore that was once part of the harbour facilities, can be seen from the beach or viewed above from the coast path. There are a series of rutways used to guide horse-drawn waggons across the intertidal area running parallel to each side of the promontory.

Fossil and jet hunting

Saltwick Bay is a renowned site for the discovery of ammonites, fossilised reptiles, shells and jet, the gemstone which Whitby is most famous for. Most discoveries are made along the foreshore while reptile fossils can be found in the cliff face about one metre above the beach level. Over the centuries Saltwick Bay has yielded many amazing fossil finds including a nearly complete skeleton of a Jurassic marine crocodile. Hammering the bedrock is not permitted.

Sunrise and sunset

Saltwick Bay is one of the few places in Britain that you can watch the sun rise and set across the sea from the same spot on the same day. This rare occurrence happens between late May and late July, so it also makes it a perfect spot to celebrate summer solstice. It is a favourite with photographers who, at sunrise, use the reflections of the pools and the wreckage of the *Admiral Von Tromp* fishing trawler in the foreground of stunning, artistic shots of Black Nab; at sunset they pick out the whale-shaped silhouette of Saltwick Nab.

St Mary's Island

ACCESS TIDAL CAUSEWAY

Just a few hundred metres offshore, across a tidal causeway, this much visited island remains a haven for wildlife and offers spectacular views of the rugged coastline. Managed by North Tyneside Council, the lighthouse and former keepers' cottages are operated as a visitor's centre. The surrounding nature reserve contains rockpools, clifftop grassland, a beach and newly created wetland habitat. A viewing area and hide on the seaward side of the lighthouse is a good place to watch grey seals haul themselves out of the water; harbour porpoises or white-beaked dolphins might also make an appearance. Birdlife is prolific in all seasons and includes resident species as well as those on their summer or winter migrations. Visitors paying a small entrance fee can climb the 137 steps to the top of the lighthouse for the most spectacular views of the coastline. Other exhibits explain the history of the lighthouse and give an insight into the wildlife of St Mary's Nature Reserve. Access to the island, which has a high point of around five metres, is across a low-tide causeway. There is a small gift shop on site with drinks machine and basic refreshments. *https://my.northtyneside.gov.uk/category/635/st-marys-lighthouse*

Coquet Island

ACCESS NON-LANDING BOAT TRIP; KAYAK

Lying less than two kilometres off the coast at Amble, this bird reserve is the summer home to over thirty-five thousand seabirds. Fulmars, black-legged kittiwakes, eider ducks, terns and oystercatchers all nest here but the island is of special significance because it supports ninety per cent of the UK's roseate tern population – one of the country's rarest nesting seabirds. The island is also well known for its eighteen thousand pairs of puffins. It has a distinctive lighthouse whose first keeper was the brother of the Victorian heroine Grace Darling. The island, which has a high point of less than five metres, is owned by the Duke of Northumberland and managed by the RSPB. It is not possible to land here but wildlife boat trips from Amble approach very close to the island.

Farne Islands

ACCESS BOAT TRIP; NO DOGS

A true wildlife spectacle, these rugged islands are home to around forty-three thousand pairs of puffins and are one of the top grey seal pupping sites in England, with more than two thousand pups born every autumn. The fifteen to twenty islands (the exact number depends on the level of the tide) in this archipelago are scattered between two and seven kilometres from the mainland and are classified as the Inner Group and Outer Group, separated by Staple Sound. Made of sloping, resistant dolerite outcrops they characteristically have steep vertical cliffs on their south coasts that are surrounded by hardy sea stacks with gentle beaches to their north. The earliest recorded inhabitants of the Farne Islands were religious recluses living in hermitages. St Aiden then lived here, followed by St Cuthbert, who died here after he left Lindisfarne for the solitude of these islands. Cuthbert introduced special laws in AD 676 protecting the eider ducks and other

1 St Mary's Island   **2** Farne Islands, puffins   **3** Farne Islands, guillemots   **4** Farne Islands, arrival on Inner Farne

seabirds nesting here; these are thought to be the earliest bird-protection laws anywhere in the world. The main islands of the Inner Group are **Inner Farne**, **Knoxes Reef**, **East Wideopen** and **West Wideopen** (all joined together on very low tides) and the more isolated **Megstone**. The main islands in the Outer Group are **Staple Island**, **Brownsman**, **North Wamses**, **South Wamses**, **Big Harcar** and **Longstone**. The high point of the group, measuring nineteen metres, is on Inner Farne. The sea around the islands is a popular dive spot with shipwrecks and underwater life that includes seals and diving seabirds. Boat trips from Seahouses land on Inner Farne, Staple Island and Longstone only.

Inner Farne

ACCESS BOAT TRIP; NO DOGS

Inner Farne is home to dive-bombing terns, the medieval Chapel of St Cuthbert, an early nineteenth-century lighthouse and an information centre. The puffins are very popular on this island and are easily spotted as they waddle to and from their burrows. Arctic terns nest close to the path and dive-bomb visitors who approach them. One record-breaking Arctic tern migrated from the Farne Islands to Melbourne, Australia – a sea journey over twenty-two thousand kilometres made just three months from fledging. It remains one of the longest known distances travelled by any bird. The prominent white streak on the

cliff facing the mainland is often thought to be bird droppings but it is the result of chalk deposits from the many years of spent calcium carbide from the lighthouse being thrown down the cliff. This compound was used to generate acetylene, the fuel for the light prior to electricity. The only inhabitants of the Farne Islands are the National Trust rangers who live in Pele Tower for nine months of the year and welcome visitors from the tourist boats. Inner Farne is home to puffins, shags, guillemots, Arctic terns and many other birds.

Staple Island

ACCESS BOAT TRIP; NO DOGS

Staple Island offers unrivalled close-up views of the more than 10,000 pairs of puffins that breed here and has more of a sense of adventure and freedom than the other islands. Boat trips land here during the breeding season only (1 May until 31 July). A footpath leads directly from the boat to the puffins on the cliff faces of The Pinnacles, isolated rock stacks off the north-east of Staple Island. The only building is the ruins of the base of the old lighthouse.

Longstone

ACCESS BOAT TRIP; NO DOGS

Longstone Lighthouse was once the home to Victorian heroine Grace Darling, whose father was the light's keeper. In the early hours of 7 September 1838, Darling spotted the wreck and survivors of the *Forfarshire* on Big Harcar, a low, rocky island nearby. Together with her father they took a rowing boat 1.5 kilometres across heavy seas to rescue four men and the lone surviving woman. A second sortie rescued four more. She became the nation's heroine and along with her father received a medal and a large financial reward. Her actions remain in British folklore today. Visitors to the lighthouse can view Grace's tiny bedroom from where she first spotted the survivors clinging to the rocks.

Lindisfarne / Holy Island

ACCESS TIDAL CROSSING (ROAD AND PATH)

One of the most spiritual places on British shores and once its cradle of Christianity, this island remains an atmospheric and soul-nourishing destination for pilgrims, nature lovers and day trippers alike. It has a mind-blowing history that stretches back to Anglo-Saxon Britain when Irish missionary Aidan from Iona founded the monastery on Lindisfarne with the aim of converting pagans to Christianity. A subsequent bishop, Cuthbert, who went on to become a saint, spurred a cult that led to the writing of the eighth-century Lindisfarne Gospels in the island's monastery. It became one of the world's most precious books. With such riches on the island, pagan Vikings chose Lindisfarne for their first raid of Britain and Ireland, which was the beginning of almost 300 years of destruction and occupation that dramatically shaped English history. Today, standing amongst the ruins of Lindisfarne Priory is a very thought-provoking experience. The other significant building on the island is the iconic and much visited Lindisfarne Castle, its fabulous architecture looked after and restored by the National Trust. Rising from the sheer rock face, which is the high point of the island at twenty-three metres, and dominating the tip of the island, it was originally built to defend the harbour sheltering English ships during battles with Scotland. Aside from the island's historical pedigree, there is an incredible array of wildlife within the tidal mudflats, salt marshes and dunes of the Lindisfarne National Nature Reserve. There is a range of food and accommodation on the island, which is accessed by a tidal road causeway as well as the Pilgrim's Way across the sands. Check the safe crossing times before you travel to the island. *https://holyislandcrossingtimes. northumberland.gov.uk*

Lindisfarne Priory ruins and St Mary's Church

Built on the site of the original monastery that was the centre of Christian teaching in Anglo-Saxon times, the twelfth-century priory remains a significant destination for modern-day pilgrims. The seventh-century monk and bishop St Cuthbert lived on the site briefly before moving to St Cuthbert's Island. Gaze up at the 'rainbow arch', one of the priory's most dramatic features, as you wander the richly decorated ruins that are the birthplace of the Lindisfarne Gospels. The Priory is managed by English Heritage (admission charge). Close by, the Saxon-era St Mary's Church (free entry) forms part of the priory complex. Its peace and tranquillity can be enjoyed inside where there is also plenty of information about the saints who established and lived at the priory. The church is home to the impressive large wooden sculpture called The Journey. Carved from seven elm trees, it depicts the carrying of St Cuthbert's coffin from Lindisfarne to Durham following the Viking raids.

Getrude Jekyll Garden

Garden designer, writer and artist Gertrude Jekyll created a small walled garden just north of Lindisfarne Castle in 1911. She was a friend and colleague of Edwin Lutyens, who had transformed the castle into a holiday home for Edward Hudson, who was the founder of *Country Life* magazine. Using the site of the vegetable plot that once fed the castle's soldiers, Jekyll designed a walled garden with a riot of colour and scent in the summer. Restored by the National Trust to its original design in 2003, it once again offers visitors a wonderful and tranquil oasis; the garden was awarded *Countryfile* magazine's Garden of the Year award in 2019. Free admission.

Deserted north shore

Stretching from Snook Point to Emmanuel Head along the island's north coast this vast expanse of wild coastal beauty, with wind-blown sand dunes and views across to Berwick-upon-Tweed and the domed Cheviot, is one of Britain's most stunning yet rarely visited beaches. At its eastern end, seals haul out on the rocks of the Back Skerrs and Snipe Point and a number of sandy paths wind inland through marram-topped dunes. Castlehead with its crenelated formations, ledges and caves and Coves Haven are two fine secluded coves to explore while the vantage point of Emmanuel Head offers far-reaching views to the Farne Islands and Bamburgh Castle.

Walk in the footsteps of pilgrims

Crossing the shining, tidal grey mud and sand of St Cuthbert's Way offers the most authentic way of reaching this island. Leaving the causeway just after crossing South Low, it stretches for just under four kilometres to reach the island. The whole route is defined by marker poles and refuges on tall stilts that offer protection to those who may have misjudged the tide. Closer to the island, the walk will likely be accompanied by the haunting wails of the seals hauled out on the sandbanks at low tide.

Walk around the island

This unofficial sixteen-kilometre route on footpaths, beaches and dunes explores the little visited corners of this otherwise busy island. It includes a walk alongside Lindisfarne Causeway, the extensive and beautiful dunes of the western peninsula and the wilds of the northern shore. It then follows the well-trodden coast path at the eastern end of the island past Lindisfarne Castle, then on to the harbour and Lindisfarne Priory. Short diversions inland are possible throughout the route to experience everything this spiritual island has to offer. *www.islandeering.com*

Holy Island coffee

Nestled in a walled garden in the village is Pilgrims Coffee House; this unique island roastery produces its own delicious blends with names like Daily Bread and Holy Grail, not to mention excellent cakes including their own version of flapjack known as Cuthbert cake.

St Cuthbert's Island

ACCESS TIDAL CROSSING

This small island, which has a high point of six metres, lies just offshore from Lindisfarne Priory and is where St Cuthbert lived as a hermit for a short time. Legend has it that the monks used to shout across to him on the island so he later sailed to nearby Inner Farne to find greater solitude. A large cross has been placed on the island and can be visited at low tide. Its rockpools are full of crabs, anemones, starfish, sponges and more.

Walney Island

ACCESS ROAD BRIDGE; NO DOGS IN NATURE RESERVE

An island of contrasts sitting in the shadow of the Lakeland Fells. Its northern and southern ends are special places for nature: one has views of the mountains, the other across the wide expanse of Morecambe Bay. The whole of its west coast is a sand and shingle beach while its east coast varies between salt marsh and the regimented rows of houses of Vickerstown, built to house the shipbuilding employees of the Barrow-in-Furness submarine yard across the Walney Channel. The island has a high point of twenty-one metres. The rural village of Biggar is also situated on the east coast and is home to the excellent and rustic Queens Arms, which makes for a perfect spot for a pint of their microbrewed beer and a chat with the friendly locals. A circumnavigation of the island forms part of the England Coast Path, with other activities on the island including windsurfing and kitesurfing, particularly around Earnse Bay, which annually hosts one of the rounds of the British Kitesurfing Championship. Perhaps the island's biggest claim to fame is as the fictional island of Sodor in *The Railway Series* books by the Reverend W. Awdry, later adapted into the television series *Thomas the Tank Engine and Friends*. The main access is via Jubilee Bridge, although for the adventurous, the narrow and shallow channel to the north of the bridge is passable on foot at low tide on stepping stones known locally as Widow's Crossing. There are a range of cafes and restaurants, self-catering accommodation in Walney Lighthouse and South End Caravan Park close to the reserve.

Round the island walk

Some of Cumbria's most spectacular coastline on the England Coast Path can be found on Walney Island. The twenty-six-kilometre circular coastal walk is full of glorious beaches, dunes and salt marshes, wonderful wildlife and dramatic views. Starting at Earnse Point on the west coast, the coastal walk heads north to round the northern tip of the island and then continues south along the east coast. During the sensitive bird breeding season, the England Coast Path that skirts the island's airfield can be followed to avoid the bird reserve. The route then passes through Vickerstown on streets and lanes before heading alongside the road south to Biggar with an optional loop to visit the salt marsh just south of Biggar, reaching the South End Caravan Park and then the South Walney Nature Reserve beyond. Here, there are great views of the other Furness Islands. The route then follows the entire west coast back to Earnse Point where the sense of wilderness is complete.
www.islandeering.com

Natterjack toads and 'dive bomb alley'

The spits at the island's northern and southern tips are both nature reserves, consisting of salt marsh, shingle, sand dunes and brackish ponds. South Walney Nature Reserve, managed by the Cumbria Wildlife Trust, is especially important to a wide number of migrating birds and is home to the Walney Bird Observatory, as well as a large colony of seals. During the breeding season it is known as 'dive bomb alley' on account of it being the biggest gullery in Europe with around seventeen thousand pairs of lesser black-backed gulls and herring gulls, who protect their young if threatened. The North Walney National Nature Reserve, managed by Natural England, is a landscape dominated by sand dunes, salt marsh and wet areas which provides the perfect habitat for the rare natterjack toad; its distinctive yellow stripe on its back sets it apart from its common toad relatives. Their loud rasping calls can be heard over a kilometre away on a still night. Other rarities include the Walney geranium, found only on this island, dune helleborine, seaside century, yellow horned-poppies, viper's-bugloss, coralroot orchid and variegated horsetail. Flocks of eider ducks can be readily spotted in both reserves.

Foulney Island

ACCESS TIDAL CROSSING; NO DOGS

Formed entirely of pebbles that were brought from the Lake District to the coast by glaciers during the last ice age, the southern tip of Foulney Island juts into the wild expanse of Morecambe Bay with great views across to Roa Island and Piel Island beyond. In the summer it hosts a nationally important colony of breeding little and arctic terns, along with many other species; it is managed as a bird reserve by the Cumbria Wildlife Trust whose warden lives on the island in a caravan in the summer months; otherwise, the island remains uninhabited. The only other humans you may see are cocklers far away in Morecambe Bay, fishermen and the occasional windsurfer. Here sea kale, sea campion and yellow horned-poppy grow amongst the shingle and sea purslane, while sea lavender and glasswort thrive in the salt marsh. Connected to the mainland via a tidal, Victorian-built rock causeway, the highest point is no more than three metres above the high tide level and most of the island can be underwater on the highest spring tides. Access to Foulney Island lies halfway along the causeway between Rampside and Roa Island, on the eastern side. No dogs are allowed on the island; avoid the nesting grounds at Slitch Ridge during the breeding season. The closest facilities are on Roa Island; the Concle Inn is a good waterside pub in Rampside.

Roa Island

ACCESS ROAD

At the southernmost point of the Furness Peninsula this tiny island, which has a high point of less than five metres, offers plenty of interest. Its road causeway was originally built in 1846 to support the Furness Railway line

making it, along with a deep-water pier from where steamers sailed to Fleetwood, a small transportation hub. Today the only remnants of the railway are the square stone sleepers along the sides of the causeway. With a population of around 100, Roa Island has plenty to offer with a vibrant yacht club with its own nanobrewery, a cafe and the departure point for the small ferry to Piel Island. There are several buildings of note including Trinity Terrace, a row of terraced houses built to provide accommodation for the ten Trinity House pilots; the Watch Tower, a former Customs and Excise House; and a large RNLI lifeboat station, open to visitors when manned. For experienced swimmers it is possible to swim around the whole island at high water. At low water the beach along the south coast is a great place to look for crabs, starfish, brittle stars, butterfish and sea spiders, to name a few of the species that live here.

Piel Island

ACCESS FERRY; TIDAL CROSSING

With an entertaining inn, a beach, lake, great wildlife, medieval castle ruins and a short boat trip or walk from the mainland, Piel Island is a near perfect island to visit. The views are extraordinary and stretch from Barrow-in-Furness to the Old Man of Coniston in the Lake District and along the vast stretch of the Fylde coastline to Blackpool Tower. Piel Island has a long and interesting history and was once of considerable importance in the local area both because of its links to Furness Abbey and as a major deep water harbour. Its fourteenth-century motte-and-bailey castle was likely to have been used as a fortified warehouse built by monks under the Abbot of Furness to keep cargoes safe from pirates and other raiders. It didn't just keep the pirates out though; it also kept the King's customs men at a distance and

it was widely known at the time that, under the ownership of Furness Abbey, it was active in the smuggling business. Today, the romantic ruins are cared for by English Heritage. The island, which has a high point of ten metres, is a haven for wildlife with many different species of seabird, along with other species found in the pond at the centre of the island. The Ship Inn offers camping, self-catering accommodation, food and beer. A small ferry departs from Roa Island (April to September; T: 07798 794 550).

Tidal walk to Piel Island

For those confident in navigation and reading tide times, the ultimate way to arrive here is to walk across the tidal sands from Walney Island. The emptiness of the vast sands offers a real wilderness experience. Depart from Snab Point, taking an east-north-east route, initially past grassy, uninhabited **Sheep Island** which once had a small isolation hospital for sailors. Continue on this bearing then arc between Coup Scar and Haws Scar to access Piel Island on the clear slipway at its northern tip. Once on the island, a one-kilometre circumnavigation around the island on the easy paths is well worth doing to see the highlights and enjoy the views.
www.islandeering.com

Good knight at the Ship Inn

The Ship Inn offers a unique island experience where you'll be served by the island's royal family and, if you time your visit well, can take part in a knighting ceremony. This tradition is thought to be a nod to when Colonel Martin Schwartz and his German mercenaries landed on the island in 1487 as part of an attempt by Lambert Simnel to seize the English Crown. Simnel claimed that he was the Earl of Warwick and therefore was the rightful King of England – he ended up a prisoner of Henry VII. To commemorate this pretender to the throne every new landlord here is made the King of Piel in a proclamation ceremony that involves him sitting on a wooden throne, wearing a ceremonial helmet and a sword, with large quantities of beer poured over him. The boozy 'knighting' ceremony is not for the faint-hearted. For those that want to throw themselves into the event, the rustic campsite is only a short crawl away.

Chapel Island

ACCESS TIDAL CROSSING

This limestone outcrop in the middle of the Leven Estuary hovers above the quicksands and racing tides of Morecambe Bay and makes for an adventurous destination. The five-kilometre walk from Canal Foot enters the channels of the River Leven, where you can catch flatfish with your feet, then crosses the sands of Morecambe Bay. The channels and position of the sinking sands often change and so the use of a guide is highly recommended. The island itself, which has a high point of less than five metres, is a tangle of undergrowth, but the soft sands that surround it are glorious. There are extensive views of the seaside town of Morecambe, the nuclear plant at Heysham, Blackpool Tower and the peaks of the South Lakes. The southern end of the island is a reserve for a number of the nation's most southerly breeding eider ducks. Accommodation and food are available at the Bay Horse Hotel, Canal Foot.
www.guideoversands.co.uk
www.islandeering.com

Hilbre Island, Little Hilbre Island and Little Eye

ACCESS TIDAL CROSSING

This string of islands in a tiny archipelago in the Dee Estuary has magnificent views of the English and Welsh coastlines; they are accessed

1 Chapel Island, Canal Foot   **2** Hilbre Island

by an exciting tidal crossing across the vast sands of Liverpool Bay. Stacked with wildlife, the area is one of the ten most important sites in Europe for overwintering birds, with a nursery for terns in the summer and a large colony of seals. Uninhabited Hilbre Island, which has the high point of the group at sixteen metres, has a cluster of interesting buildings and some beautiful geological features all around its coastline, including a large cave and red

sandstone cliffs that have been dubbed Wirral's Ayers Rock. The eight-kilometre round trip, possible two hours either side of low tide, starts from West Kirby and heads around the back of Little Eye, then over the top of Little Hilbre Island before reaching Hilbre Island itself. West Kirby offers a full range of food and accommodation; the very popular West Kirby Tap offers a great selection of real ales and ciders.
www.islandeering.com

The islands of North and Mid Wales are some of the most varied in the British Isles. Stacked with ancient history, wild coastlines and incredible wildlife, some are homes and places of work while others are wildlife reserves and places of pilgrimage. Anglesey is the largest island in Wales and, together with Holy Island, the most populated. Their dramatic coastlines are full of geological wonders, beaches to play on and amazing wildlife to watch. The other islands in this region are mostly sanctuaries for wildlife and people alike. The ancient holy isle of Bardsey Island, just off the Llŷn Peninsula, is now as famous for its bird and marine life as it is for its Arthurian legends and remains a place for pilgrimage and peace. Cei Ballast, one of the newest islands in Wales, sits secretly within a few metres of Porthmadog. Its deep, sun-warmed emerald pools are incredible for swimming and diving. The islands of Wales hold plenty of drama too and the precipitous tidal headland of Ynys Lochtyn will challenge even the most sure-footed.

NORTH & MID WALES

Opposite Ynys Gifftan, sun-warmed tidal pools   **Overleaf** Ynys Seiriol / Puffin Island

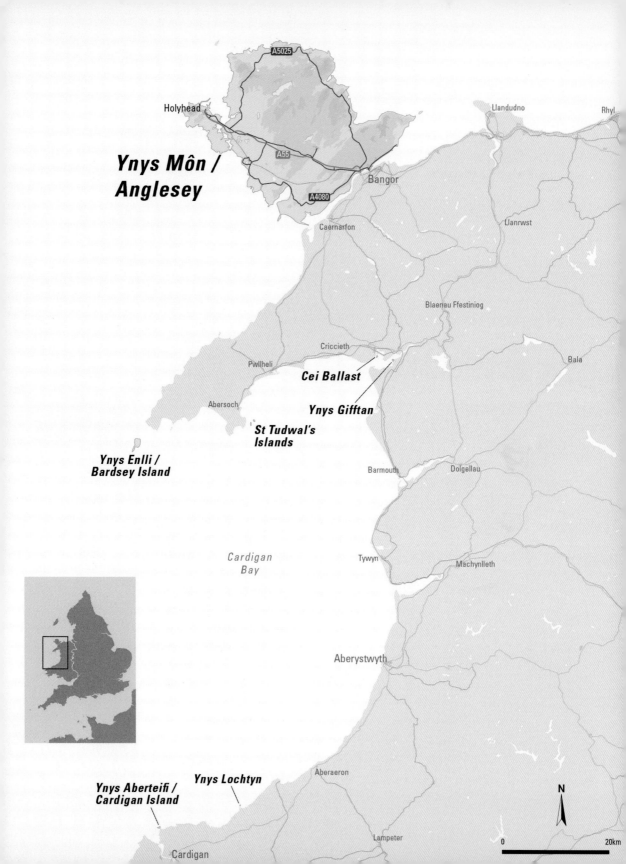

Holyhead

A5025

Ynys Môn /
Anglesey

A55

Bangor

A4080

Caernarfon

Llandudno

Rhyl

Llanrwst

Blaenau Ffestiniog

Bala

Criccieth

Pwllheli

Cei Ballast

Ynys Gifftan

Abersoch

St Tudwal's
Islands

Ynys Enlli /
Bardsey Island

Barmouth

Dolgellau

Cardigan
Bay

Tywyn

Machynlleth

Aberystwyth

Ynys Aberteifi /
Cardigan Island

Ynys Lochtyn

Aberaeron

Lampeter

Cardigan

N

0   20km

Ynys Môn / Anglesey

ACCESS ROAD BRIDGE; RAIL; PLANE

Mam Cymru, 'Mother of Wales', is the largest island in Wales and England with its own set of fascinating tiny satellite islands, a stunning coastline, idyllic villages and Wales' greatest concentration of ancient sites. Separated from the mainland by the Menai Strait, it remains a stronghold of Welsh language and culture and lies in the shadow of the mountains of Snowdonia. A land of druids and saints, it holds some of Wales' finest chambered cairns and passages including Barclodiad y Gawres, the largest Neolithic tomb in Wales, and Bryn Celli Ddu, where you can join Druids and celebrate the summer solstice. There are also hidden holy wells and possibly the oldest Christian remains in Wales, close to Penmon Priory. The charming harbour town of Beaumaris boasts a castle, which is part of a World Heritage Site and feted as the most technically perfect in Britain. More recent remains on the island include the impressively located ruins of Porth Wen Brickworks and the surreal, colourful moonscape of the copper mine at Parys Mountain – once the largest in the world. There are fabulous wild beaches at Newborough Warren, Aberffraw and Dulas which are perfect for all sorts of outdoor activities, and bird hotspots at Cemlyn Bay amongst many others. A 200-kilometre coast path around the whole island boasts some of the best scenery in Wales, while the extensive network of lanes and cycleways make cycling here a joy. The island, which has a high point of 178 metres, has every type of accommodation and can be reached easily from the mainland.

Isle of Anglesey Coastal Path

This 200-kilometre path along some of the best coastal scenery in Wales passes through wide sandy bays and estuaries, hidden coves, dramatic cliffs, sand dunes, salt marsh, mudflats and forests, and also gives access to the many smaller islands off Anglesey's coast. The official start point is St Cybi's Church, Holy Island, from where it heads along the harbour front then uphill to enjoy the incredible views from the summit of Holyhead Mountain before descending to view the precariously located lighthouse on the tiny island of South Stack. Before leaving Holy Island, the path passes the sea arches at Bwa Gwyn and St Gwenfaen's Well near Rhoscolyn then heads inland to Four Mile Bridge to cross to Anglesey's south-west coast. Highlights here include the beaches of Rhosneigr, with **Ynys Groes** (Cross Island), a low-tide, grassy islet about three hundred metres from the village, and **Ynys Feirig**, three small interconnected tidal rocky islets with an important tern colony. Other points of interest include the large estuary and village of Aberffraw and the dunes and forest of Newborough Warren before the route heads north-east up the Menai Strait. North of Menai Bridge, Beaumaris is the gateway to the remote coastline leading to Penmon Point and beyond to the fantastic sands of Red Wharf Bay. Continuing towards the north coast, between the fishing village of Moelfre and the old copper port of Amlwch there is plenty of natural beauty in the wild sandflats of Traeth Dulas. The north coast highlights include the ternary of Cemlyn Nature Reserve, Porth Wen Brickworks, the wilds of Carmel Head and the islet of Ynys y Fydlyn before returning to Holy Island.
www.visitanglesey.co.uk/en/about-anglesey/ isle-of-anglesey-coastal-path

Nant y Pandy Nature Reserve

Just a stone's throw away from the streets of Llangefni, this is one of nature's hidden gems. Also known as the Dingle Local Nature Reserve, this steep-sided gorge is covered in ancient woodland, ferns and mosses with tranquil walks alongside the babbling Afon Cefni. The reserve is home to a variety of wildlife including kingfishers, moorhens, woodpeckers, foxes, bats and dragonflies. The wet areas are home to newts, while lizards, adders, bank voles and wood mice live in the drier spots; eight

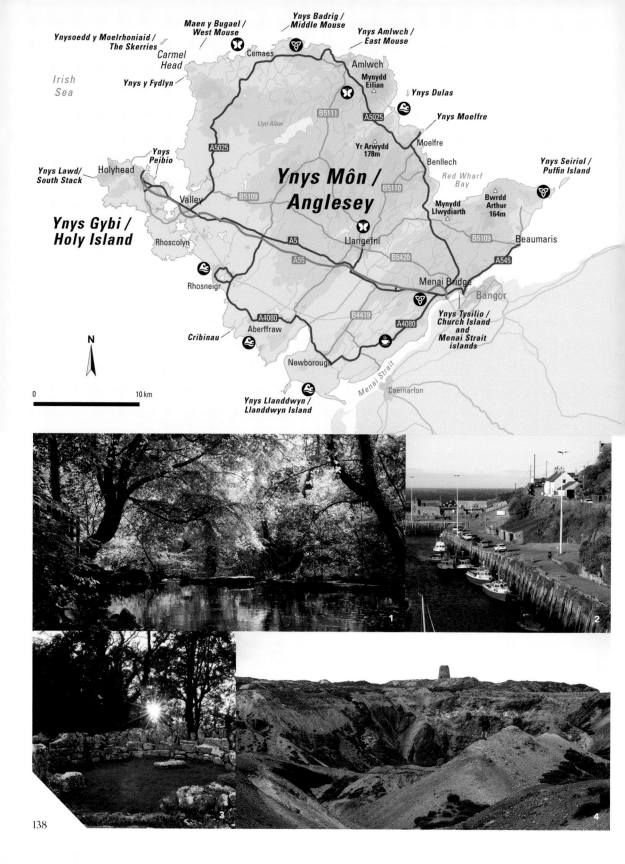

species of bat can be spotted at dusk. Much of the ancient woodland is a carpet of bluebells and wood anemones in the spring. The local community have built a series of wooden boardwalks that wind their way along the river and its deep pools, with sculptures, benches and picnic tables to stop and enjoy. A ten-kilometre walk through the Dingle and around the Cefni Reservoir is a great way to see one of the loveliest inland areas in Anglesey; a weekly Parkrun also takes place in the reserve. *www.anglesey.gov.uk/en/Residents/ Countryside/Dingle-Nant-y-Pandy-Nature-Reserve-Llangefni.aspx*

Mynydd Parys – Wales' own Grand Canyon

Otherworldly is the only way to describe this geological 'extravaganza' – material has been scooped out of the mountainside by metal mining activity here since the Bronze Age. Gazing across the Great Opencast, a vast one-kilometre hollow, the coloured rock layers of red, orange, pink, brown, purple, black, green, yellow and grey that paint the landscape are mesmerising. Copper ore was discovered here in the late 1760s and large-scale mining ensued with such abundance that the nearby port of Amlwch dominated the world copper market for a decade; the copper even coated Royal Navy warships at the Battle of Trafalgar in 1805. Today, six million tonnes of the metal are thought to remain beneath the old mine workings. The Parys Mountain Windmill, which can be seen for miles around, once pumped water out of the mineshafts and today provides a great vantage point to look across to the Carneddau Mountains and distant views of Snowdonia, or to shelter form the elements in this exposed spot. The dramatic stony landscape appears barren but it supports a variety of wildlife including birds such as skylark, meadow pipit and chough. Plants that can tolerate high concentrations of copper and zinc are also able to survive here. The area has

distant views of Snowdonia with the peak of Snowdon (Yr Wyddfa) visible on clear days. There are a number of walks to explore the landscape and the relics of industrial history, including the floor of the mine where small cave entrances can be found as well as a level walk around the top of the Great Opencast and its viewing area. *www.copperkingdom.co.uk/mynydd-parys-mountain*

Penmon Priory and Penmon Point

Penmon's history stretches back to the sixth century when a monastery was established here by St Seiriol. All that remains of this era are stone walls, thought to be part of St Seiriol's Church, which could be the oldest remaining Christian building in Wales, and the enchanting holy well, with reputed healing properties. Penmon Priory, the ruins of which can be seen today, was built on the site in the thirteenth century when it became part of the Augustinian order. Inside, an impressive medieval stone cross is on display. Close to the priory, the huge seventeenth-century Penmon Dovecote, likely built to house pigeons for their meat and eggs, marks the start of an unmarked track that leads down to the shingle beach and substantial remains of Flagstaff Quarry which provided the mortar for Liverpool docks. Penmon Point can be reached along the toll road from the priory, or via the Isle of Anglesey Coastal Path. It is wild and rugged with the Trwyn Du Lighthouse perched on a rocky outcrop at the east end of the pebble beach and the seabird-packed Puffin Island beyond. During the day, dolphins and porpoise may be spotted hunting for fish in the tidal race just offshore and seals haul out on the rocks around the point. At night, in the right conditions, the northern lights can be seen off the point. A seasonal spectacle is to watch the blue glow in the water of bioluminescent algae that emit light when disturbed. The beach is good for sea angling and rockpooling. The Pilot House Cafe just above the beach is a great pit stop.

---

1 Ynys Môn / Anglesey, Nant y Pandy Nature Reserve **2** Ynys Môn / Anglesey, Amlwch Harbour
3 Ynys Môn / Anglesey, Din Lligwy **4** Ynys Môn / Anglesey, Mynydd Parys

Family-friendly beaches

Anglesey has such a variety of beaches that there is something here for everyone. Family favourites include Benllech Beach on the east coast with its clear Blue Flag waters and fine golden sands that at low tide stretch for miles, leaving plenty of space for swimming, building sandcastles, windsurfing and fishing as well as rockpooling. Families also love the excellent sandy beach, backed by forest and extensive dunes, at Newborough Warren, with Aberffraw Bay another unspoilt sandy beach nearby. Close to Moelfre on the east coast, Traeth Lligwy is backed by low sand dunes giving it a wild and elemental feel. Enjoyed by families, it is also good for windsurfing, kitesurfing and surfing with a range of facilities including toilets, car parks and a shop. Slightly further north Traeth Dulas is a long, secret sandy beach adjacent to the wonderful wild sandflats of the Dulas Estuary where kids can run wild. Between Traeth Dulas and Traeth Lligwy, the wide sand and shingle beach of Traeth yr Ora offers a wonderful hidden gem. Another family favourite and equally popular with kitesurfers, windsurfers, canoeists, surfers and paddleboarders is Rhosneigr's Traeth Crigyll, a fine expanse of golden sand with easy access from the village, with great low-tide rockpooling where the Afon Crigyll flows into the sea. The slipway also allows easy beach access making it a good spot for launching small boats.

Menai mussels and oysters

The fertile Menai Strait produces around half of the UK's entire crop of mussels as well as some mighty fine oysters. Menai Oysters & Mussels is worth visiting to stock up on the freshest shellfish around (collection on Sundays and Wednesdays). If you meet the marine biologist owner, he's full of fascinating mussel factoids. Did you know that a ton of mussels will produce seventeen tons of mud a year? The algae-rich waters impart a special sweet flavour to these rope-grown molluscs that are hand-harvested with the welfare of other wildlife in mind, making this product as honest as it is delicious.

There is also a good campsite for tents and motorhomes on the farm.
www.menaioysters.co.uk

Get active at Newborough Warren

One of the largest and best dune systems in Britain, this is a great destination for anyone seeking nature, wild beaches, walking, cycling or water sports. The dunes, coastal marshes and sandy and rocky shores have been shaped over thousands of years by the wind and sea and are fringed by Corsican pine trees planted to stabilise the shifting sand dunes. The Cefni Estuary and the pools behind the Pen Cob embankment are a sanctuary for birds and wildlife and there are views across the estuary over an expanse of coastal marsh, open sand and sea that reach as far as Snowdonia and the Llŷn Peninsula. The Isle of Anglesey Coastal Path traverses the reserve, throughout which there is an extensive network of footpaths and waymarked trails including the seven-kilometre Saint, Sand and Sea Trail out to Llanddwyn Island. The shorter 1.5-kilometre Nature and Animal Puzzle Trail is great for families; the Red Squirrel Trail does what it says on the tin. There are also waymarked family-friendly cycle trails on the forest roads. Runners have the opportunity of taking on part of the challenging route used in the 2011 Commonwealth Mountain and Ultra Distance Running Championships. There is even a Trim Trail with eleven exercise stations amongst the inspiring woods as well as an orienteering course suited to both the beginner and the more experienced.

Walk to the high point of Anglesey

Yr Arwydd is the highest point on the island of Anglesey at 178 metres; it has fabulous views across to the peaks of Snowdonia and the north coast of Anglesey. The walk starts from Brynrefail, a small hamlet between Amlwch and Moelfre, and takes the footpath south-west for a steady ramble to the summit, through terrain that changes from pine forest to heathland, with a small lake and a number of springs.

1 Ynys Môn / Anglesey, Menai Suspension Bridge

Bridges and suspension bridge walk

This six-kilometre circular walk, which is part of the much longer Isle of Anglesey Coastal Path, offers extraordinary views of the Menai Strait and the whirlpools of The Swellies between Pont Britannia and the Menai Suspension Bridge. Start in the Coed Cyrnol car park (grid reference: SH 554719) then head west on the footpath downhill towards Church Island, and follow Belgian Promenade, which was named after the Belgian refugees who built it during World War I, to reach the bridge. Cross the impressive Menai Suspension Bridge, which was designed by Thomas Telford, to reach mainland Wales. Head west to the Treborth Botanic Garden to enjoy the large areas of woodland, rock gardens, orchard and wild flower meadows that reach down to the shore, which, along with its cafe, make for a good stop to explore. Continue west to Pont Britannia, designed and built by the noted railway engineer Robert Stephenson, cross back on to Anglesey, then leave the A5 to return along the coast path back to the Menai Suspension Bridge.

Walks around Aberffraw village

The charming village of Aberffraw was the capital of the Kingdom of Gwynedd in the early Middle Ages and at one point was the most important political centre in medieval Wales. With shops and an excellent tea room at the Llys Llewelyn Heritage Centre it is a great place to start several spectacular walks and explore the nearby island of Cribinau. A favourite is the walk to the wild, expansive, dune-backed beach of Traeth Mawr; alternatively you can swim down the sandy creek from Aberffraw village at high tide. The hidden beach of Porth Twyn-mawr, to the south of the main beach, can be reached by a walk along the foreshore; it is almost inaccessible by other means.

Explore Porth Wen Brickworks

Spectacularly located at the bottom of cliffs with a ruined harbour, Victorian brickwork buildings, beehive kilns and a remote beach for a sheltered swim, this is a treasure trove for explorers. Once used to make fire bricks from locally quarried quartzite to line steel-

1

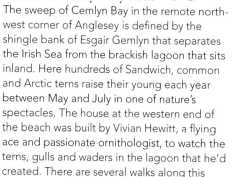

making furnaces, the work stopped in the early twentieth century. Today, most of the buildings and much of the equipment remain on the site and this Scheduled Monument is now a romantic ruin. You can spend hours poking around the quarries, crushing house, moulding and drying sheds, kilns, engine and boiler houses, chimneys, warehouses and a quay. In the right conditions it is also possible to swim from the white pebble beach through the rock arch.

Watch the Cemlyn Bay terns

The sweep of Cemlyn Bay in the remote north-west corner of Anglesey is defined by the shingle bank of Esgair Gemlyn that separates the Irish Sea from the brackish lagoon that sits inland. Here hundreds of Sandwich, common and Arctic terns raise their young each year between May and July in one of nature's spectacles. The house at the western end of the beach was built by Vivian Hewitt, a flying ace and passionate ornithologist, to watch the terns, gulls and waders in the lagoon that he'd created. There are several walks along this stretch of coast including options to see the ancient gneiss of Carmel Head and to Trwyn Cemlyn, both with the chance of spotting bottlenose dolphins from the clifftops.
www.nationaltrust.org.uk/cemlyn

Explore ancient tombs and villages

Barclodiad y Gawres tomb above Porth Trecastell is the largest Neolithic tomb in Wales. This atmospheric tomb was constructed at the same time as the Egyptian pyramids and Stonehenge and built as a grave for the local community. The exterior can be viewed at any time; the interior can be viewed on open days. It is worth making the effort to explore inside to see the passageway, cross-shaped chamber, etched zigzags and spiral patterns. Such megalithic art is also found at Bryn Celli Ddu, south-west of Menai Bridge. One of the best-preserved passage tombs in Wales, it is set within its own stone circle. Free entrance is through a tall stone slit to find the pillar within

the octagonal chamber, and the carved pattern stone beyond. Druids greet the summer solstice when shafts of light shine directly down the tomb's passageway to illuminate the chamber within. Just inland from Moelfre, there is a three-in-one opportunity to visit Neolithic, medieval and Roman ruins all within a few hundred metres of each other. First up, the ruins of the twelfth-century Old Lligwy Chapel on a lonely hillside overlooking Lligwy Bay with views across to the Isle of Man on a clear day. Further to the south-west the ruins of Din Lligwy walled village form a Romano-British site, the stone foundations of which make for a wonderfully atmospheric spot surrounded by woods. Close by, a Neolithic burial chamber offers further interest.
*www.cadw.gov.wales/visit/places-to-visit/
barclodiad-y-gawres-burial-chamber*

Ynys Tysilio / Church Island

ACCESS FOOTPATH
A small, hidden island in the Menai Strait that sits tranquilly to the side of the whirlpools and eddies of The Swellies, just south of the town of Menai Bridge. The main feature of the island is the fifteenth-century St Tysilio's Church that resembles a charm on a bracelet along with its churchyard and ancient yews. A Grade II listed war memorial sits on the high point of the island, which reaches less than five metres. A small path circumnavigates the island, offering wonderful views of both the Menai Suspension Bridge and Pont Britannia as well as the nearby islets. At low tide the surrounding mudbanks are a haven for birdwatchers with little egrets, oystercatchers, curlew and terns; in springtime the island is painted yellow with primroses. Accessed by a short causeway that leads from the Isle of Anglesey Coastal Path from Belgian Promenade, it is accessible on all but the highest spring tides.

Other islands in the Menai Strait

ACCESS NOT PERMITTED; VIEW FROM MAINLAND PATH
There are several private tidal islands in the Menai Strait that can be readily viewed from the Isle of Anglesey Coastal Path on a fabulous waterside walk between Pont Britannia and the town of Menai Bridge. Between the two bridges, **Ynys Gored Goch** is a private island with a white house in the middle of the strait whose residents once made their living from fish caught in traps built on the island. Wild and uninhabited, **Ynys Benlas** and **Ynys Welltog**, a breeding site for greylag geese, oystercatchers and herons and a great place to watch little egrets, can be easily seen from Ynys Tysilio. North of Menai Suspension Bridge, **Ynys Faelog** is privately owned. **Ynys Gaint**, linked by a short bridge to the town of Menai Bridge, was once a small military base in the 1960s, then a well-loved summer camp for cadets before today's private ownership of the island, with just a few buildings remaining for the use of cadets. **Ynys Castell** is a beautifully located private holiday let and was used as one of the main sets for the BBC's crime drama *Hidden*. The furthest north of the Menai islands, **Ynys y Bîg**, is wooded with a 1930s house, its own harbour and boathouse. All the islands have a high point of less than five metres.

Ynys Llanddwyn / Llanddwyn Island

ACCESS TIDAL CROSSING
A stunning island in all seasons, whether walking the glistening white-shell paths and swimming in pristine secluded coves or watching winter storms from its shores. This uninhabited rocky peninsula is surrounded by the sands of the bays of Llanddwyn and Malltraeth and backed by the incredibly beautiful dunes of Newborough Warren. There are magnificent views across to the mountains of Snowdonia and every aspect of this island is full of adventure and natural beauty. Associated with St Dwynwen, the Welsh patron saint of lovers whose saint's day is 25 January when love spoons and cards are exchanged, her legend lives on today. The island, which has a high point of fifteen metres, is accessible on all but the highest spring tides from the Isle of Anglesey Coastal Path.

Romantic ruins of St Dwynwen's Church
On the spine of the island the ruins of sixteenth-century St Dwynwen's Church sit on the site of the fifth-century convent she founded and where her body is said to be buried. A Celtic and a plain cross, erected in her memory, can be seen on the skyline to the south. According to accounts of her life, Dwynwen was in love with Maelon Dafodrill. However, when she rejected his advances, he stormed off spreading rumours and gossip to besmirch her reputation as he went. Heartbroken, Dwynwen swore that she would never love again and prayed to God to cure her of her love. God granted her wish and released Maelon, whom he had temporarily frozen into a block of ice, and Dwynwen took the veil and founded her church on the island.

Discover amazing geology
The rocks of Porth Twr Bach, below the Twr Mawr Lighthouse at the south-west tip of the island, are an amazingly colourful mix of dark green lava, rose pink quartzite, purple manganese-rich shales, blue-black dolerite and honey-coloured limestone. The northern end of the island is the best place to see pillow lava which is formed when underwater eruptions produce massive amounts of hot, molten basalt, rich in iron and magnesium. The lava extrudes through from the mantle, with the consistency of toothpaste, into cold sea water. This rapid cooling resulted in the separate pillows that can be seen today between the tip of the island and Newborough Forest. These, along with the other geological highlights

1 Ynys Llanddwyn / Llanddwyn Island, rock hopping the west coast   **2** Ynys Llanddwyn / Llanddwyn Island
3 Ynys Llanddwyn / Llanddwyn Island, Celtic cross from the church ruins   **4** Ynys Llanddwyn / Llanddwyn Island, Pilots Cove

of the area, contribute to the island being part of a UNESCO Global Geopark. The lighthouse is also a good point to view the large cormorant colony of **Ynys yr Adar**, around 100 metres offshore to the west.

Circumnavigate the island on shell paths

Once on the island, an unmarked walking circuit on shell paths is accessed via elaborately carved wooden gates decorated with swirling Celtic designs. Edged with sea holly and thrift, the path winds down to secluded sand and shingle coves, with short deviations inland to explore the sites linked to the rich history and legends of the island.

Pilots Cove and cottages

At the island's south-east tip, across the stone cob, the daymark identifies the entrance to Pilots Cove, the site of the old lifeboat station and Pilots Cottages. These single-story whitewashed cottages were once home to the men who guided ships between Caernarfon Docks and the open sea, and whose roles doubled up as lifeboatmen and lighthouse keepers. The cottages now house a fascinating museum depicting what life was like for the previous inhabitants as well as a small interpretation centre for the surrounding geology. The small cannon located outside was the main way of summoning the lifeboat crew.

145

St Dwynwen's Well   ✪ ✪

This hidden freshwater well, located high on a cliff edge, remains a destination for people who wish to divine the identity of future partners or to test whether existing love will last. Its pure waters cascade over moss-covered rocks into a narrow steep-sided bay below. A short scramble down the rocks reveals a small cave that extends a few metres back into the cliffs, its walls displaying the vibrant reds and purples of the Cambrian rocks.

Secluded swims   ✪ ✪ ✪

Depending on the prevailing wind and sea conditions, it is possible to find a sheltered swimming spot in one of the island's coves. On the west coast, low tide reveals idyllic pools and swims in large rock gardens. The east coast has more tiny bays and coves. There are also plenty of opportunities to snorkel for crab and lobster amongst the kelp beds.

Cribinau

ACCESS TIDAL CROSSING

This tiny remote island near Aberffraw has perched upon it one of the most recognisable churches in Anglesey. The medieval Grade II listed St Cwyfan's Church, popularly known as The Church in the Sea, is still fully consecrated and holds several services every year with the sea and mountains of Snowdonia as a backdrop. The church is thought to be dedicated to St Kevin, who founded the monastery across the sea at Glendalough in County Wicklow, Ireland. The area around the island is excellent for rockpooling and the sunsets here are spectacular. The island, which has a high point of less than five metres, is encircled by an oval-shaped sea wall, built in the late 1800s to protect it from sea erosion. Reached either from the Isle of Anglesey Coastal Path or the small lane down to Porth Cwyfan, a short walk across the beach leads to the tidal causeway then up a set of stone steps cut into the flank of the sea wall.

1

Ynys y Fydlyn

ACCESS TIDAL CROSSING; SCRAMBLE
Remote with steep cliffs, sea caves and a sea arch to swim through at high tide, this adventurous island is accessed via a tombolo from a small rocky cove. The island is split with the larger part to the west; both can be accessed via a short, easy scramble from their southern sides. The island has a high point of less than twenty-five metres. A large sea cave just north of the island on the mainland is also good to explore. Inland, there is a small freshwater lake, enclosed by woodland, that was formed by sea action creating the shingle bar and blocking the inlet. The island can be reached by walking the spectacular stretch of the Isle of Anglesey Coastal Path between Church Bay and Carmel Head, where the towering cliffs and incredible views across to the mountains of Ireland and The Skerries off Anglesey's north-west coast can also be admired. A more direct approach starts at a car park (grid reference: SH 303914), from where there is a one-kilometre walk across sheep-grazed grass through a secluded wooded valley to the beach.

Ynys Amlwch, Ynys Badrig and Maen y Bugael / East Mouse, Middle Mouse and West Mouse

ACCESS NON-LANDING BOAT TRIP; VIEW FROM MAINLAND PATH
This scattered chain of islands is uninhabited but popular with wildlife watchers and divers and can be approached by a chartered boat from Holyhead Marina. The islands can also be seen from the Isle of Anglesey Coastal Path. East Mouse is the site of the wreck of the *SS Dakota* which sank off the island in 1877 with all 218 lives saved. Middle Mouse, which has the highest point of the group at sixteen metres, is the northernmost point of Wales and is a favoured place for cormorants, guillemots and razorbills. West Mouse is located in an area of notoriously strong tides so there are at least three shipwrecks here that attract divers.

Ynys Dulas

ACCESS KAYAK; VIEW FROM MAINLAND PATH
This small rocky island within Dulas Bay, which has a high point of less than five metres, has a prominent cylindrical cone-shaped stone rescue tower that once stored food and provided shelter for shipwrecked seamen. Today it is a popular spot for seals and roosting cormorants. A small sandy beach emerges at low tide. Surrounded by strong water flows, it is possible for the advanced sea kayaker with knowledge of local waters to access the island. It can also be clearly seen from Traeth Dulas, and from along the nearby Isle of Anglesey Coastal Path.

Ynys Moelfre

ACCESS TIDAL CROSSING; SWIM; KAYAK
This island, which has a high point of ten metres, sits around 200 metres across the shallow channel of Y Swnt from the charming fishing village of Moelfre. Gulls, terns, gannets and fulmars can be found and it is home to a colony of seals. Y Swnt is only waist-deep on many low tides and on extreme spring tides it is possible to wade from Moelfre Beach across to the island and remain relatively dry.

Ynys Seiriol / Puffin Island

ACCESS NON-LANDING BOAT TRIP
Less than one kilometre off Penmon Point at the north-east entrance of the Menai Strait is the ninth largest island off the Welsh coast; the island has a high point of fifty-eight metres. It was once home to the sixth-century saint St Seiriol; the remains of his monastery are still visible on the top of the island today. Ynys Seiriol is privately owned by the Baron Hill Estate and is an important bird sanctuary. Its great cormorant colony of over 750 pairs is one of the largest in the British Isles. Between April and July common guillemots, razorbills, kittiwakes and the occasional puffin nest on the island – the latter suffered a heavy loss after a rat infestation in the late nineteenth century. Fulmar and eider duck also breed here, while shags are on the island all year round along with resident Atlantic grey seals. Tour boats from the pier in Beaumaris run non-landing wildlife trips around the island.

Ynysoedd y Moelrhoniaid / The Skerries

ACCESS NON-LANDING BOAT TRIP; KAYAK; VIEW FROM MAINLAND PATH

This group of sparsely vegetated rocky islets is located three kilometres offshore from Carmel Head. They can be seen from most of the north-west coast of Anglesey, along with The Skerries Lighthouse which sits on the island's highpoint of fifteen metres. The islets are an important breeding site for seabirds, especially the Arctic tern and the roseate tern along with the puffin, kittiwake, common tern and gulls. An RSPB warden lives on the island during the tern breeding season. It is a coveted destination for divers to explore the numerous shipwrecks in the vicinity. The individual islets are accessible from one another at low tide and by small bridges. Non-landing tour boats from Holyhead Marina approach the island to spot the wildlife and experienced kayakers can make the serious trip from Cemlyn Bay. All are asked to avoid disturbing nesting birds from May until August.

Ynys Gybi / Holy Island

ACCESS ROAD BRIDGE; FERRY

With a dramatic coastline, impossibly located lighthouses, powerful tidal races and spectacular bird life, this is an outdoor paradise. Separated from the west coast of Anglesey by the narrow Cymyran Strait, the western side of the island is taken up mainly by Holyhead Mountain, the highest peak in the county of Anglesey at 220 metres, with the two tiny islands of North Stack and South Stack at its base. Most of the coastline is dramatically rocky, with sea caves and arches to explore, but there are larger sand beaches at Trearddur Bay and Penrhos Coastal Park. The main centre, Holyhead, the largest town in Anglesey county, is built around St Cybi's Church and today is mostly known as being a busy ferry port which incorporates **Ynys Halen / Salt Island**, accessible only to port workers and passengers and named after its previous use as a factory that extracted salt from seawater. Holyhead's strong sea heritage is seen through the extensive harbour area, breakwater and promenades. It is called 'Holy' because of the high concentration of standing stones, burial chambers and other religious sites here. Joined to Anglesey by two road links, the Cob Causeway between Valley and Holyhead and Four Mile Bridge, it is readily accessible by car and there are frequent trains from Welsh and English cities. Holy Island is also well served by buses from Anglesey and beyond. There is a full range of accommodation, including campsites and larger group accommodation.

Holyhead Breakwater Country Park

Just a few kilometres west of Holyhead's town centre, this hidden gem of a park is set in a dramatic location in the old quarries between Holyhead Mountain and the Irish Sea. Once the source of stone used to construct Holyhead Breakwater, it then housed brickworks that made the special brick used in smelting furnaces before closing in the early 1970s. The country park opened in 1990. The brick kiln chimney, axles from the crushers and a fog signal cannon once used on North Stack are part of this fascinating outdoor museum with further information available on site. The park has its own well-stocked lake, around which the nature trail, along with the many other paths, are great places to spot birds. Chough and peregrine falcon are frequently seen and heard enjoying the updrafts from the quarry walls. The gorse and bramble attract willow warblers, stonechats, wheatears and linnets, and little owls frequent the reserve. The surrounding heathland areas are a haven for insects; look out for the silver studded

1 Ynys Gybi / Holy Island, Bwa Gwyn   **2** Ynys Gybi / Holy Island, Holyhead Breakwater Country Park
3 Ynys Gybi / Holy Island, Holyhead Breakwater Country Park   **4** Ynys Gybi / Holy Island, Holyhead Mountain summit

blue butterfly and moths such as the ruby tiger, cinnabar, buff-tip and silver Y. There are also many different types of orchids here such as bee, marsh and common spotted. From the vantage point of the cliffs it is possible to spot harbour porpoises, grey seals and both Risso's and common dolphins below. The park is the start of many fabulous walks; it offers orienteering trails and has a visitor centre and cafe. *www.anglesey.gov.uk/en/Residents/Countryside/Holyhead-Breakwater-Country-Park.aspx*

Holyhead Mountain and South Stack walk

This circular walk combines a superb section of the coast path and some modest but rough mountain terrain. Despite its relatively low 220-metre summit, Holyhead Mountain has a true mountain feel. Start at Holyhead Breakwater Country Park. Immediately head up the rock steps carved out of the hillside on to the Isle of Anglesey Coastal Path for great views over Holyhead Harbour and two hidden rocky bays below. The large ferries to Ireland can be seen slipping in and out of the harbour beyond the breakwater and several kilometres

out to sea The Skerries can be spotted on a clear day. Continue uphill past the old magazine hut, once used as part of the quarry to store explosives and dynamite, until you arrive at the foghorn station at **Ynys Arw / North Stack**, now a private house. The views from here are staggering, with precipitous sea cliffs diving into swirling seas below. Directly beneath the stack is an enormous sea cave where grey seal pups can be spotted in the autumn. Head south along the coastal footpath towards Holyhead Mountain to find the steep rocky track towards the summit. Pass the Iron Age hill fort of Caer y Tŵr, whose walls are made of naturally occurring rocky outcrops and extensive stone ramparts that the Romans were thought to have built a watchtower within. At the trig point there are 360-degree views over Holyhead Harbour, the Carneddau Mountains and Snowdon (Yr Wyddfa). From the summit, descend through a rocky landscape to reach a wide path leading to South Stack. Look out for choughs, gulls, the odd puffin and peregrine, thousands of guillemots and razorbills and the occasional porpoise. Continue to the small tourist car park above Ellin's Tower. To return, take the path that heads north-north-east from the road, then veers increasingly east towards the radio stations and skirts the southern base of Holyhead Mountain. Head into the fields with medieval field boundaries and follow the track between old drystone walls to reach the lane and the houses of the hamlet of Gorlan then return via a path to the country park.
www.islandeering.com

Walk the length of Holyhead Breakwater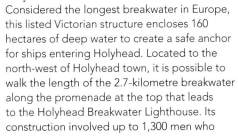

Considered the longest breakwater in Europe, this listed Victorian structure encloses 160 hectares of deep water to create a safe anchor for ships entering Holyhead. Located to the north-west of Holyhead town, it is possible to walk the length of the 2.7-kilometre breakwater along the promenade at the top that leads to the Holyhead Breakwater Lighthouse. Its construction involved up to 1,300 men who

initially raised a mound from the sea and then encased this in ten-tonne blocks of limestone. Underwater, divers in submarine bells created the foundations using picks and blasting using gunpowder in watertight pipes. It took twenty-eight years to build and required over seven million tonnes of limestone from the quarry on Holyhead Mountain. Today it is a very popular walking and fishing spot.

South Stack Cliffs Nature Reserve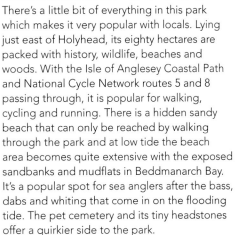

This wonderful reserve is made up of heathland and farmland set on a stretch of dramatic sea cliffs which face the islet of South Stack. In spring thousands of guillemots, razorbills, kittiwake, fulmars and puffins breed on the iconic cliffs, making it a seabird spectacle readily accessed from the reserve's car park. Around ten pairs of the rare chough can be seen swooping along the cliffs all year round. The reserve's heathland is part of the largest area of maritime heath in North Wales and supports the wonderfully named endemic plant, the spatulate fleawort, along with the silver-studded blue butterfly, adders and common lizards.
www.rspb.org.uk/reserves-and-events/ reserves-a-z/south-stack-cliffs

Penrhos Coastal Park

There's a little bit of everything in this park which makes it very popular with locals. Lying just east of Holyhead, its eighty hectares are packed with history, wildlife, beaches and woods. With the Isle of Anglesey Coastal Path and National Cycle Network routes 5 and 8 passing through, it is popular for walking, cycling and running. There is a hidden sandy beach that can only be reached by walking through the park and at low tide the beach area becomes quite extensive with the exposed sandbanks and mudflats in Beddmanarch Bay. It's a popular spot for sea anglers after the bass, dabs and whiting that come in on the flooding tide. The pet cemetery and its tiny headstones offer a quirkier side to the park.

St Cybi's Church and  William Morris windows

St Cybi, the son of a sixth-century Cornish king, became a priest in North Wales, where the King of Gwynedd gave him an old Roman naval fort in which to base his religious community. It is one of the few examples of a three-walled fort, with the fourth wall being the sea. Today, Holyhead's town centre is built around the now Gothic St Cybi's Church with its interesting medieval carvings and beautiful stained-glass windows. The William Morris Tree of Life window is a major tourist attraction. Commissioned by a Muslim family for a Christian building, the window is unique in not depicting people or animals. Instead, the entire window is given to the Tree of Life which fills the glass with rich green foliage and pomegranates in pink and deep orange.

Borthwen Beach, Rhoscolyn

Borthwen is a pretty, sandy crescent located on the southern shore of Holy Island, with views across the Irish Sea to the Llŷn Peninsula. Backed by sand dunes, there are also a few little rocky islets along the length of the beach. This is a great family beach with its shallow sloping sands and abundance of rockpools and is a popular launch point for sea kayaks and other boat users. It is a good starting point to explore the dramatic, rocky coastline along the Isle of Anglesey Coastal Path. There are numerous inlets and coves and many small offshore islands, including **Ynysoedd Gwylanod** upon which the Rhoscolyn Beacon stands – a popular destination for sea kayakers along with the rock-hopping nearer the beach. The beach is reached by a very narrow lane and there is a small car park with toilets and cold showers.

Spectacular sea arches

A pair of striking natural arches are located a short, dramatic walk along the cliff tops west of Rhoscolyn. The superb Bwa Gwyn, the white arch, is comprised of fractured quartzitic rocks (grid reference: SH 259 762). It is possible to swim through the arch and also explore the adjacent sea cave accessed by a short but easy scramble. A small land bridge from the surrounding cliff gives access to the top of the arch where a grindstone once used to extract china clay from the quarry can still be seen. A short walk to the north leads to another natural arch, Bwa Du, the black arch. Both can be reached via the coast path.

St Gwenfaen's Well

The ruins of this early medieval holy well house are nestled in a small hollow overlooking the cliffs of Porth Gwalch to the west of Rhoscolyn (grid reference: SH 259 754). Old stone walls still delineate two small rooms that sit a metre or so below the surrounding landscape. Stone steps lead down to an antechamber with four corner seats and a small well chamber from which the spring rises. Water flows into a second pool outside of the building which has steps into it for bathing. The church of St Gwenfaen, the only church in Wales dedicated to her, is in the village of Rhoscolyn. Gwenfaen's legend is that she was chased by Druids and escaped by climbing the rock stack off Rhoscolyn Head. The tide came in and she was carried away by angels; Porth Saint was thus named. She was known for curing mental illness and an offering of two white quartz pebbles into the water of the well is said to cure such problems. The well is blessed every year on, or near, St Gwenfaen's Day (4 November) after Holy Communion in the nearby church. The well is located alongside the coast path between Borthwen Beach and Bwa Gwyn.

Ynys Lawd / South Stack

ACCESS FOOTBRIDGE

Spectacularly located to the west of Holyhead, this small rocky island (which has a high point of forty-one metres) is home to one of Wales' most iconic sights – the South Stack Lighthouse. It acts as a waymark for coastal traffic and a landmark and orientation light for vessels crossing the Irish Sea between the ports of Holyhead, Dublin and Liverpool. Visitors can experience the majesty of the surrounding sea cliffs by descending the 400 steps to the thirty-metre-long metal footbridge that spans the turbulent sea and treacherous rocks below to reach the island. Prior to the footbridge, the only means of crossing to the island was via a wicker basket suspended from a hemp rope over the swirling sea. The lighthouse tour is worthwhile, especially to learn more about the unique lives of the keepers.
www.trinityhouse.co.uk/lighthouse-visitor-centres/south-stack-lighthouse-visitor-centre

Ynys Peibio

ACCESS TIDAL CROSSING

This very small, grass-covered, tidal island has a high point of less than five metres and is around fifty metres from the beach to the south-east of the port at Holyhead. Its small square tower is thought to have been an old navigational aid for Holyhead Harbour. It is easy to access from the Môrawelon housing estate and from the Isle of Anglesey Coastal Path and involves a very short walk across a pebble beach.

1

Ynys Enlli / Bardsey Island

ACCESS BOAT; NO DOGS

Just off the Llŷn Peninsula its English name means 'Island of the Bards' and its Welsh name means 'Island in the Currents', which gives a sense of its rich cultural and natural heritage. This ancient holy island is unique in combining a National Nature Reserve with farming and fishing such that it is the only working island in Wales, other than Anglesey and Holy Island. Here, peace is absolute with no cars or mains electricity. The island has a high point of 167 metres. The coastline is stunning and rich in bird, marine and plant life. The island has deep spiritual connections and is known as the final resting place of 20,000 saints with many believing that Merlin, of Arthurian legend, is buried here. Tŷ Pellaf Farm, a short walk from the harbour, sells delicious honey from the island's bees and has a small craft shop that operates on an honesty basis and a cafe, where cafetières of coffee and pots of tea are freshly brewed in the farmhouse kitchen. There are twelve properties on the island, each of which is Grade II listed – one is leased to the farm, one to the Bardsey Bird and Field Observatory and one as a private letting. The other nine properties are let out by the Bardsey Island Trust as holiday lettings. These range from a five-bedroom farmhouse, to converted lofts and one small traditional cottage. *www.bardsey.org/book*

Walk to the island's high point, Mynydd Enlli

The mountain rises up from Tŷ Pellaf's farmhouse door, its slopes bearing the traces of Bardsey's long history of habitation, including the remains of hut circles close to the ridge that date back more than 3,000 years. Its east cliffs are home to around 20,000 pairs of Manx shearwaters, and puffins. Once on the summit ridge there are great views across to the Llŷn Peninsula and the hills beyond, while the descent offers a bird's-eye view of the ruins of St Mary's Abbey below.

Ancient ruins of St Mary's Abbey

St Cadfan is thought to have established a monastery on Bardsey in the sixth century, and the island supported around 2,500 monks. Bardsey was deemed so holy that in the twelfth century the Pope proclaimed that three pilgrimages to Ynys Enlli was equal to one to Rome. Refounded as the Augustinian Abbey of St Mary in the thirteenth century, it attracted pilgrims until the Dissolution of the Monasteries in the sixteenth century. Today, only its original bell tower remains. The Celtic cross amidst the ruins commemorates the many saints reputed to be buried here.

Unique boat trip

A visit to the island starts with the unusual embarkation process for the island's boat. The craft is hauled out on to the small rocky cove of Porth Meudwy on the Llŷn Peninsula to board on dry land and then towed back into the sea by a rusting tractor. This well-practiced manoeuvre is executed perfectly by Colin Evans, a Bardsey native, larger-than-life character and fount of all island knowledge. He will inform and entertain you for the whole journey through some of the most dangerous tides in Europe. Arrival at the island's slipway is usually heralded by the eerie wails of the hundred or so seals hauled out nearby on their favourite beach, Henllwyn.

Abundance of wildlife

Bardsey is renowned for its wildlife and is a great place to spot choughs, grey seals, puffins and Manx shearwaters. Around 310 species of birds have been recorded here, including the rare hoopoe, by virtue of the island's position on its principle migration route. A small interpretation centre in the Bardsey Bird and Field Observatory in Cristin gives plenty of information. Wildlife hides on the north coast are a great place to spot the colony of up to 200 Atlantic grey seals in the rocky bays of the island. Risso's dolphins

1 Ynys Enlli / Bardsey Island **2** Cei Ballast, views across Afon Glaslyn

and harbour porpoises are also regularly spotted here. The plant life is equally impressive with blue carpets of spring squill along the coast path, dense tufts of thrift and thyme and the heady scents of bell heather. Lichens are amongst the most notable of plants here with over 350 species.

Take a pilgrimage to Bardsey Island

The North Wales Pilgrim's Way is a spectacular 219-kilometre waymarked walking route from Basingwerk Abbey, near Holywell, to Aberdaron then on to Bardsey Island. It follows old routes and footpaths across a stunning variety of farmland, moorland, mountain and shoreline and harks back to centuries ago when pilgrims in their thousands arrived on Bardsey Island drawn by stories of the special peace that can be found there. An annual pilgrimage is organised along the full length of the route for a fortnight every year.
www.pilgrims-way-north-wales.org

Walk the island's coastal circuit

A straightforward seven-kilometre route that incorporates the island's high point and all the key sites of the island's myths and legends.

There are the evocative ruins of St Mary's Abbey, a chance to spot dolphins off the north coast and a crossing of the narrow isthmus, with the possibility of bathing in the right conditions at Porth Solfach. The deep gullies and inlets of the southern tip are great to peer into and discover their rich marine life.
www.islandeering.com

Taste a Bardsey apple

For those that associate Bardsey with Avalon, the mythical isle where the wounded King Arthur was taken, the discovery of an aged apple tree here was significant. Avalon means 'place of apples' and it is believed that there was some sort of early greenhouse here where apples could grow, protected from the prevailing winds. A famous old, gnarled apple tree was discovered growing on the south-facing side of one of the island houses. Both the tree and its pink-streaked, lemon-scented fruit were pronounced unique. Today, only the roots of that original tree survive and the Bardsey apple is cultivated commercially and is delicious to taste.

St Tudwal's Islands

ACCESS NOT PERMITTED; NON-LANDING BOAT TRIP; KAYAK

This small archipelago lying south-east of Abersoch consists of **St Tudwal's Island East** and **St Tudwal's Island West**. The east island, which has the remains of a priory, was owned by author Carla Lane until her death in 2016 and the west island, with St Tudwal's Lighthouse and the high point of the group at forty-three metres, is owned by adventurer Bear Grylls who has converted it into a holiday home. The islands are known for their seal population and pleasure cruises out to them leave from Abersoch.

Cei Ballast

ACCESS TIDAL CROSSING

One of Britain's newest islands built of rock picked up from all over the globe. Getting here is quite an adventure but worth it to bathe in the beautiful pools. Cei Ballast sits in almost complete secrecy in the northern reaches of the Afon Glaslyn, just a few hundred metres from the bustling town of Porthmadog. Low-lying (the high point of the island reaches six metres) and covered in scrub, this man-made island was formed around 200 years ago from the discarded ballast carried by ships returning from delivering the highly prized slate from the Ffestiniog quarries. The island's unique, colourful foreshore is a mix of chalk, red granite, brick, limestone, industrial slag, flint and the occasional piece of pottery. At low tide the southern tip of the island has a superb tidal pool which is an incredible place to swim when sun on the surrounding sandbanks has warmed the water. The island can be accessed at low tide by dropping down on to the sands from the Cob, the stone embankment that carries the steam trains of the Ffestiniog Railway. Once on the sands, the short route to the island involves crossing the tidal stream before heading into the samphire beds and cockle-filled sands. *www.islandeering.com*

Ynys Gifftan

ACCESS TIDAL CROSSING

This island sits in one of the most natural places in Cardigan Bay, surrounded by vast tidal sands, wild salt marsh and the mountains of Snowdonia. The outline of the ruins of Harlech Castle and the pastel-coloured domes and spire of Italianate Portmeirion just across the river blend perfectly with the landscape. Bequeathed to the current Baron Harlech's ancestors by Queen Anne in the early eighteenth century, the island has now been uninhabited for several years. The ruins of the old stone farmhouse and outbuildings are hidden within the bracken, gorse and elder that covers the island. The island, which has a high point of thirty-nine metres, is accessed by footpath from Talsarnau, through salt marsh then across the tidal tributaries of the Afon Dwyryd. At the island's southern tip the deep, emerald-green pools are refreshed daily by the tide and heated by the summer sun. Floating, swimming or diving into these remote pools from the surrounding rock ledges is one of life's greatest pleasures.
www.islandeering.com

Ynys Lochtyn

ACCESS TIDAL CROSSING

A dramatic and iconic tidal headland that offers those with a head for heights a wealth of adventure and a very good chance of spotting Europe's largest pod of bottlenose dolphins. Between the seaside villages of Llangrannog and New Quay this wild island, which has a high point of twenty-eight metres, can only be accessed by a precipitous path down the vertiginous sea cliffs. Once on the rocks below with their verdant rockpools and small beaches, the route continues through a sea cave, on to a large ledge then up a grass path on to the island itself. This must only be attempted at low tide. The view back to the cliff's colourful layers of shale, gritstone and sandstone are rarely seen and from the island's plateau the whole sweep of Cardigan Bay can be enjoyed with views north as far as the Llŷn Peninsula. For the climber, the island's cliffs offer some aptly named routes – *Lochtyn Syndrome*, *Fish Fingers* and *Piano Tuna*.
www.islandeering.com

Ynys Aberteifi / Cardigan Island

ACCESS NOT PERMITTED; NON-LANDING BOAT TRIP

Under 200 metres from the Welsh coastline north of the town of Cardigan, this uninhabited island, owned by the Wildlife Trust of South & West Wales, is managed for wildlife. Birds such as guillemots, razorbills, cormorants, shags, fulmars and a variety of gulls all nest on the island, while bottlenose dolphins, harbour porpoise and Atlantic grey seals may be seen in the surrounding sea. The island has a high point of fifty-two metres. Non-landing wildlife boat trips operate from Patch Beach, south of Gwbert. The island can also be approached on the superb all-day mega-fauna surveys in Cardigan Bay operated by the wildlife trust, where you are highly likely to encounter a staggering array of wildlife.
www.welshwildlife.org/visitor-centres/ cardigan-bay-marine-wildlife-centre/boat-trips

Pembrokeshire and the Gower are two legendary stretches of coastline in the UK with wild and rugged landscapes, extraordinary beaches and coves, historic fishing villages and the smallest city in Britain, St Davids. Tiny rocky islands are strung along the coast here like a protective necklace. Many were once inhabited as mainland promontories, before the pounding waves created these islands, and the footprint of those ancient dwellings and villages can still be seen today nestled amongst the windblown turf. A night spent on Skokholm Island, watching the Manx shearwaters return to their burrows and seeing the Milky Way in its full glory, is an experience that will stay with you forever. There are few islands for the casual tourist here though, except the wonderful holy island of Caldey. Many require a boat trip, walk or easy scramble to reach – others can be viewed by walking the stunning Pembrokeshire Coast Path and Wales Coast Path.

SOUTH WEST WALES

Opposite Middle Head, with **Mumbles Head** beyond　**Overleaf** St Margaret's Island

Cardigan
Bay

Cardigan

Newcastle Emlyn

Ynys Onnen **Ynys Meicel**
Carreg Onnen
Pen Brush
Ynys Ddu
Ynys y Ddinas
Ynys Deullyn
Ynys-fach **Ynys y Castell**

Fishguard

St Davids

**Ynys Dewi /
Ramsey Island**

Ynys Gwelltog **Gewni**
Ynys Bery **Ynys Cantwr**

Solva

Carmarthen

Llandeilo

St Brides Bay

Haverfordwest

**Ynys Gwales /
Grassholm Island**

**Ynys Sgomer /
Skomer Island**

Narberth

Milford Haven

**Ynys Sgogwm /
Skokholm Island**

Dale

**Gateholm
Island** **Islands
of Angle**

Angle

Pembroke

Saundersfoot

Tenby

**Ynys Catrin /
St Catherine's Island**

**Ynys Bŷr/
Caldey Island**

Burry Holms

**St Margaret's
Island**

Carmarthen
Bay

Rhossili

Llanelli

Swansea

Mumbles *Swansea
Bay*

Port Ta

**Pen Pyrod /
Worms Head**

**Middle
Head** **Mumbles
Head**

N

0   15km

1

2

3

164

Islands between Strumble Head and Pwll Deri

ACCESS VIEW FROM MAINLAND PATH

One highlight of the Pembrokeshire Coast Path is the view across to Strumble Head and the three tiny rocky islands of **Ynys Meicel**, **Ynys Onnen** and **Carreg Onnen**. The Strumble Head Lighthouse sits on the high point of Ynys Meicel (at thirty-four metres) and is used as a waypoint for many transatlantic flights. The small, gated suspension bridge that stretches above the swirling waters is the main route to the island for Trinity House staff but is not open to the public. At low tide, the dry causeway to the island can be spotted below. On the mainland, slightly to the north-east, the sturdy World War II lookout is one of Europe's most important wild-life watching observatories and was officially opened in 1988 by Bill Oddie. In calm seas you have a good chance of spotting whales, dolphins, basking sharks and even sunfish. The Sea Trust often run wildlife watching events for the public.
www.seatrust.org.uk

For walkers, the stretch of the Pembroke-shire Coast Path between Strumble Head and Pwll Deri is truly spectacular and the best way of viewing further islets. South from Strumble Head, **Pen Brush** can be viewed from the steep cliffs with a short detour from the coast path. Further south, just beyond the spectacular Porth Maenmelyn, the group of islets to the west of Garn Fawr include **Ynys Ddu** and **Ynys y Ddinas**; the latter can be approached on a footpath from the main coast path for a closer look. The youth hostel at Pwll Deri is a good base for these islands.
www.yha.org.uk/hostel/yha-pwll-deri

Ynys y Castell

ACCESS TIDAL CROSSING

A craggy islet at the mouth of family-friendly Abercastle Bay, Ynys y Castell is a fun island to reach at low tide along a wide, rock causeway. A promontory fort crowns the island's high point of twenty-six metres, and an indentation south of the enclosure is the 'Grave of Sampson's Finger'. The plateau is covered in a thick blanket of tussock grass. Access to the island is by a short, easy rock scramble and a steep path from the south-west side. There's a great view from the top of the long, narrow picturesque inlet dotted with kayakers and boats of every sort. It is also fun to swim in the sheltered waters around the south of the island and explore the sea cave. To the north-west of Ynys y Castell, **Ynys Deullyn** sits just a few metres off the Pembrokeshire Coast Path. It can be reached by a moderate, slippery scramble at low tide after dropping down to sea level from the nearby mainland cliffs. A further island to explore, four kilometres south-west of Ynys Deullyn along this stretch of coast path, is **Ynys-fach**. For the committed island bagger, it is possible to scramble down the mainland cliffs on to the island at low tide. The island can also be readily viewed on a circular walk from the tiny, picturesque fishing hamlet of Porthgain.

Ynys Dewi / Ramsey Island

ACCESS BOAT

Across the notorious tidal flows of Ramsey Sound, this RSPB-owned island that sits off St Davids Head is famed for its wildlife. The prolific seals and birdlife along with the potential of spotting dolphins and porpoise are always a draw but the small population of red deer,

1 Ynys Meicel **2** Ynys Dewi / Ramsey Island, seals **3** Ynys y Castell, tidal causeway

transported to the island in a net suspended beneath an RAF helicopter in the 1970s, and five white Welsh mountain ponies that thrive here might be more of a surprise. With farmland and a hill in the north, heathland in the south and some of the highest cliffs in Wales to the west (the high point of the island reaches 136 metres) the views from every aspect of this island are spectacular. Uninhabited except for the island's wardens, it is accessed by boat from St Justinian's Lifeboat Station. Tea, coffee and basic snacks are available at the farmhouse.

Admire the ferocity of The Bitches

Getting to Ramsey across the tidal flow of The Bitches is an experience in itself. This reef of jagged rocks creates different heights of water on either side at certain states of the tide. On rough days there are big whirlpools, eddies and spectacularly chaotic water, while calmer days offer the opportunity to watch numerous porpoises feeding in the waters.

Walk the island circuit and traverse the three peaks

This seven-kilometre walk includes the island's three heather-clad peaks of Carnllundain, the highest at 136 metres, Foel Fawr in the south and Carnysgubor in the north, where there are excellent views of the jagged teeth of the islets and the lighthouse of the **Bishops and Clerks**, 2.5 kilometres to the west.
www.islandeering.com

Spot hundreds of seal pups

The cove of Aber Mawr is home to one of the largest breeding colonies of Atlantic grey seals in Britain. Their numbers peak in late August through to November when up to 1,000 come to the island to breed. An average of 600 pups are born here every year. Towards the south end of the cliffs above the beach is a small wooden observatory where wildlife researchers study the colony and are sometimes available to tell you more about their work.

Birdlife of Ogof Glyma

The caves and cliffs of the west coast are a big draw for birdwatchers. From spring to early summer they are one of the premier sites in Wales to see nesting choughs. Other breeding birds on these cliffs include ravens, peregrines, gulls, Manx shearwaters, razorbills, kittiwakes, shags and guillemots.

Ramsey's smaller islands

ACCESS VIEW FROM MAINLAND PATH

Off Ramsey's dramatic southern tip lie three steep-sided islands: the tidal **Ynys Gwelltog** and **Ynys Cantwr** and the larger **Ynys Bery** (which has the high point of the group at seventy-one metres). The most spectacular views of these islands can be seen from the small hill of Foel Fawr at the southern tip of Ramsey Island. Ynys Cantwr translates to Chanter's Island and it is said that St Justinian, a hermit who sought sanctuary and had a chapel on Ramsey, would send priests in need of punishment to the cave there. Tied to a large rock, they were obliged to chant their penance over a period of two high tides. Their survival was proof of God's forgiveness but in reality few lived to tell the tale, which St Justinian put down to their not having chanted zealously enough. At some point the monks rebelled against such an extreme regime and cut off St Justinian's head. Kittiwakes now rest in the cave.

Gewni

ACCESS VIEW FROM MAINLAND PATH; KAYAK

An island with a stunning sea arch that is spectacularly located at the base of the steep cliffs at the mouth of the estuary of the River Solva. The village and harbour of Solva is considered to be one of the jewels of the Pembrokeshire Coast and at high tide the harbour area is often compared to a Norwegian fjord. The island,

1 Ynys Sgomer / Skomer Island, ferry at Martin's Haven

which has a high point of thirty-five metres, can be viewed from a much-loved and beautiful section of the Pembrokeshire Coast Path between Solva and St Davids. On calm days experienced kayakers will be able to land on the island and kayak or swim through the sea arch.

Ynys Sgomer / Skomer Island

ACCESS BOAT

Only one kilometre off the coast of Pembrokeshire, this is an island of exposed headlands, dramatic sea stacks, and sheltered bays that is famed for its extraordinary wildlife. Together with Skokholm Island, it is the seasonal home to half the world's population of Manx shearwaters and the largest colony of puffin in southern Britain. It is also home to the unique Skomer vole, three species of stick insect, glow-worms and slow-worms with plenty of offshore life that includes dolphins and porpoise, which are often spotted on the boat trip across Jack

Sound, along with good views of **Midland Isle**. Overnight self-catering accommodation in the island's Old Farm is very popular and guests are offered a nightly bird log and talks from conservation experts. The island has a high point of seventy-nine metres. Boats sail to Skomer from Martin's Haven every day (weather dependent) except Monday from April to September.
www.welshwildlife.org/skomer-skokholm/skomer

Overnight wildlife spectacular

Between April and September, the stretch of coast around Skomer Head hosts the largest colony of Manx Shearwaters in the world. The birds hunt out to sea during the day, returning to the island at dusk to feed their chicks. After fledging, the remarkable young birds migrate to the coasts of Brazil and Argentina remaining at sea for around five years before returning to breed within a few metres of the burrow in which they were born. The starry night skies are incredible here, as is the peace of having this island almost to yourself.

Seashore foraging with the wardens

Normally the public don't have access to the beaches on Skomer to minimise disturbance to wildlife, but during the summer the wardens often organise seashore foraging events on the beach at North Haven. Look under rocks on the beach to spot shore clingfish, also known as Cornish lumpsuckers. Their pelvic fins have fused together to form suckers which help them to remain stuck to the rocks on exposed shores. They are also covered in a layer of mucus which keeps them hydrated when out of the water. Other species include the broad-clawed porcelain crab, by-the-wind sailors, compass jellyfish, barnacles, limpets, topshells, dog whelk, anemones, shannies, blennies and common shore crab.

Springtime bluebell walks

An island without trees doesn't immediately jump to mind as having one of the best bluebell walks in Wales, but during the springtime Skomer is covered in a display of these beautiful flowers so vast that the whole island turns violet-blue. The atypical open habitat of the island greatly enhances their visual impact, with the added bonus of being able to spot puffins, rabbits and short-eared owls at the same time.

Bird cities of The Wick

This spectacular, deep inlet along the island's south coast has dramatic cliff faces where razorbills build single nests in crevices while guillemots construct seabird cities that echo with their kazoo-like calls. Inland from the cliffs thousands of puffins nest in the grassy banks between April and July before leaving to overwinter in the Atlantic Ocean.

Iron Age round house

The archaeology of Skomer is exceptionally well preserved. Across the island the remains of boulder-built boundaries, neat stone walls and the footings of round houses reveal how the island was extensively farmed in the Iron Age and Romano-British times. A prominent standing stone, the Harold Stone, and other megaliths on the island suggest Neolithic and early Bronze Age occupation. Of particular note is the Iron Age or Romano-British round house at The Wick, close to the main viewing point for the puffins. Visitors can walk into the footings of the round house through its well-defined doorway and imagine what life might once have been like.

Walk the coastal circuit

This seven-kilometre trail around the outside edge of the island is the best way of seeing the wildlife and the staggering views from every corner. Starting at North Haven, an easy path leads past The Neck and through the flower-filled South Stream Valley to the southern tip of the island. From here there are excellent views across to the cormorant-studded sea stacks of the **Mew Stone**; Grassholm Island and Skokholm Island can be seen to the west and south respectively. Rounding the headland to reach The Wick, the path then continues to Skomer Head. On the north coast, seals haul out on the skerries at the eastern end of the Garland Stone while gannets dive for fish in the rich waters. Here the path turns inland, past prehistoric burial cairns and an iris-filled marshy area, towards the Old Farm at the centre of the island before returning to North Haven. *www.islandeering.com*

Ynys Gwales / Grassholm Island

ACCESS NON-LANDING BOAT TRIP

This tiny white speck of land is around twelve kilometres west of Skomer Island; it is uninhabited other than 39,000 pairs of breeding northern gannets, the only gannet colony in Wales and third largest in the UK after St Kilda and Bass Rock. This westernmost point in Wales, which has a high point of forty-two metres, comes alive in early spring when around ten per cent of the world's population of gannets return to the island. The air is filled

1 Ynys Sgomer / Skomer Island, Manx shearwater chick **2** Ynys Gwales / Grassholm Island, gannets

with males returning with nesting materials, keen to establish territory ready to attract a female. A single egg is laid in April and chicks begin to hatch in early June. The chicks are then fed by both parents for three months until they are fully grown and ready to leave the island in late August and throughout September. It is an outstanding seabird spectacle, unrivalled anywhere in Wales for this species. Grassholm is an RSPB reserve with a strict 'no landing' policy, but boat trips that approach the island are available. Often porpoise and bottlenose dolphins are spotted in the seas around the island.

Ynys Sgogwm / Skokholm Island

ACCESS BOAT

Lying in the Celtic Sea four kilometres off the south-west coast of Pembrokeshire, Skokholm has a real sense of remoteness with its tall sandstone cliffs and wild landscape surrounded by seas packed with porpoises, dolphins and Atlantic grey seals. In spring and summer tens of thousands of nesting seabirds return here to their island home. The island has a high

point of fifty-six metres. Day visitors are not permitted, only those booked into the island's accommodation, so there are never more than twenty-six people on the island. Owners, the Wildlife Trust of South & West Wales, claim 'that's ten acres of space for every visitor'. It makes a perfect retreat for birdwatchers, artists, walkers, photographers and anyone seeking a relaxing getaway. If you're not staying on the island, non-landing boat trips are available which sail around the bases of the island's cliffs.

Live off-grid ⌂ ✖

Quieter and smaller than Skomer, Skokholm Island is a wild and beautiful place to stay. Off-grid style accommodation is available for limited numbers for a short time each year. There are a mix of single, twin and double rooms in the renovated cowsheds, cottage and the warden's old quarters. Visitors can choose either three, four or seven night stays, with a self-catering kitchen, no showers or heating and a small shop selling basic food. Every night there is a bird log where visitors can share what they have seen. You can wander the island to your heart's content, visit several wildlife hides or chill out in the library. On clear nights, those who like astronomy will be treated to a view of the Milky Way.

Birds galore

The high cliffs and isolated nature of the island make it a haven for breeding seabirds. In spring and summer huge populations of seabirds descend, including around 5,000 puffins returning to their burrows, while the cliffs and ledges are decorated with thousands of razorbills and guillemots and up to 100 pairs of fulmars. Together with Skomer, it is also home to the largest concentration of Manx shearwaters in the world, with an estimated 45,000 breeding pairs on this island alone. Around 5,000 storm petrels join them in returning to their burrows to feed their chicks in the nightly spectacle throughout the summer. Night walks with infra-red equipment to see the birds for those staying overnight are a once-in-a-lifetime experience and visitors can also help with the nightly bird ringing projects. Skokholm is also perfectly situated to attract passage migrants and in spring and autumn warblers, flycatchers, pipits and thrushes amongst many others may be seen. Skokholm is the site of the UK's first ever bird observatory built in 1933 by the pioneering ornithologist Ronald Lockley.

Sunsets from Skokholm Lighthouse

A magnificent lighthouse stands at the south-west tip of Skokholm. Now home to the wardens as well as visiting researchers, it forms a triangle of protection for ships around Milford Haven along with the lighthouses at South Bishop and the Smalls. The views from the top are incredible, particularly watching the vibrant colours of a Pembrokeshire sunset.

Gateholm Island

ACCESS TIDAL CROSSING

This dramatic rocky tidal island has a scramble on to the plateau for stunning views and the remains of prehistoric settlements and an Iron Age fort. At the western end of the vast and beautiful expanse of Marloes Sands, Gateholm's dramatic old red sandstone cliffs rise to a plateau forty metres high. Most of the summit area has evidence of a settlement consisting of over 100 rectangular hut structures organised into rows with courtyards; there is also a rampart and gate to control access at the island's north-west tip. Not only has Gateholm appeared on Channel 4's *Time Team*, it was used in the filming of the 2011 film *Snow White and the Huntsman*, where a computer-generated castle was superimposed on the rugged island in post-production. Access to this National Trust-owned island is not for the faint-hearted. It can be reached from the Pembrokeshire Coast Path; a steep, narrow path first heads down the cliff on to the beach and

boulders at low tide. The beach at Albion Sands is a wonderful, secluded swimming spot. Walk past the Gateholm Stack and continue south along the north-east edge of the island to reach the obvious wide grass and rock gully to climb to the plateau.

Islands of Angle

ACCESS VIEW FROM MAINLAND PATH

The stretch of stunning Pembrokeshire coastline from the charming village of Angle, on the Milford Haven Waterway, around the headland to Castles Bay, on the south-west tip of the Angle Peninsula, is home to three islands. Only one of the islands is accessible but all can all be enjoyed from the coast path. **Thorn Island**, off the north-west tip of the peninsula, is a rocky islet dominated by a military fort built to defend Milford Haven in the mid-nineteenth century from French naval attack. It was converted into a hotel in 1947 and has since been bought and sold several times. Today's owner is renovating it with the intention of transforming it into a 'party pad'. At the western tip of the peninsula, tidal **Rat Island** is not possible to access down the steep cliffs but the ruins of a medieval blockhouse is of interest on the adjacent mainland. Further south, beyond Castles Bay, **Sheep Island** can be accessed via a tricky scramble across a loose arête and then a low-tide col. The remains of an Iron Age enclosure have been discovered with ramparts across the neck of the promontory dividing it from the mainland. The high point of the group is thirty metres.

Ynys Bŷr / Caldey Island

ACCESS SMALL FERRY

Less than four kilometres south of Tenby, this holy island owned by the Cistercian monks of Caldey Abbey is a haven of peace and tranquillity with sandy beaches and hidden coves, woodland, wildlife and fabulous views. Caldey has a fascinating history stretching back to when the first Celtic monastery was built here in the sixth century. Today it is home to around forty permanent residents and a varying number of Trappist monks who farm and sell their produce, including delicious chocolate and fudge. Three caves – Nanna's Cave, Potter's Cave and Ogof-yr-Ychen – have been discovered on the island and excavated to unearth human bones, tools and shells, dating back to the Neolithic, Bronze Age and Romano-British periods. The island, which has a high point of sixty metres, has its own postage stamps and its own monetary unit named after the local fish, the dab. There is a colonial-style tea shop on the green. Boats leave from Tenby from Easter until October, every day except Sunday.

Take a spiritual retreat

St Philomena's is a retreat house for organised groups and individuals wishing to spend a few days of quiet and reflection, particularly those who would like to attend some of the monastic services and experience more fully the spiritual life of the island. Guests live and eat communally and take part in some household chores. There are also a few rooms in the Monastic Guesthouse for men interested in making a retreat for a few days, worshipping with the monks, eating with them in their Refectory and assisting with various daily tasks. *www.caldeyislandwales.com/philomenas-retreat-house*

St Illtyd's Church and the Old Priory

Atmospheric St Illtyd's Church, linked to a twelfth-century priory, is still a consecrated church and is thought to be the oldest church in Britain still used for Catholic worship. It is noted for its floor of pebbles from the nearby beach, its impossibly twisted spire and the sixth-century Ogham Stone that has been carved with the ancient Ogham script which originated in Ireland.

Temptation
in the chocolate factory

Just beyond the Old Priory the chocolate-making room, more like a large kitchen, is where the 'Abbot's Kitchen' chocolate bars are hand-made and wrapped in their luxurious gold foil. Visitors can buy chocolate and fudge and glimpse the process from a small viewing and sales area, as well as smell the rich heavenly scent of these sweet delights. This is also the only place where you can buy Caldey fudge.

Caldey Abbey

A working monastery with the Cistercian, or Trappist, monks. The current Italianate building was constructed in 1910 and is the home of a varying number of monks who follow the Rule of St Benedict with vows of poverty, chastity and obedience. Devoting their lives to the service of God, they live to an austere set of rules set to a demanding timetable of prayer, study and work. They attend seven services a day, the first at 3.15 a.m., and observe a twelve-hour silence from 7.00 p.m. The monks farm alongside the other forty or so islanders and produce a range of home-grown items including tomatoes, chocolate, ice cream, milk, butter, clotted cream and yoghurt. They eat communally in the Refectory, an imposing oak-panelled hall with timbered roof, and a cloister for contemplation is set around a central garden. Monastery tours are available for men and the church service is open to all.

St David's Church

On a small hill just outside the island's main settlement is the medieval stone chapel of St David, the parish church of Caldey. It is worth a visit to see its impressive round-arched Norman door and the unique stained-glass windows – the Fish window and Tree of Life window. The church courtyard contains simple graves of monks and islanders marked with weathered wooden crosses.

Priory Bay

Adjacent to the landing quay, this wide, golden sandy beach backed by low dunes is a tempting place to spend your whole time on the island. Never busy and generally considered safe for swimming with just a short walk to the nearby village – it doesn't get more perfect than this.

Scramble down to Drinkim Bay

Drinkim is a small sandy cove on the eastern side of the island. The beach is backed by high cliffs and a gap in the rocks on the northern side leads to the smaller cove of Little Drinkim. Under dry conditions the sand at this beach makes a squeaky sound when walked on. There is no official path to it and access requires a scramble down a very steep path which descends a small gully at the back of the beach. Several ropes have been fixed alongside the path as aids. Swimming is not advised here due to strong currents offshore.

Caldey Lighthouse

Built in 1829, the light had the dual purpose of helping coastal traffic trading limestone and coal to Mid and North Wales as well as helping the North American traffic identify the Bristol Channel and avoid confusion with the English Channel. The superb views on a clear day extend east to Worms Head on the Gower Peninsula; west to St Govan's Head along the Pembrokeshire Coast; south to Lundy; and north to the Preseli Hills. Below, at the base of the cliffs, is a popular spot for basking seals.

Caldey Island walks

With so many places of interest, tranquil wooded paths, spectacular coastline, beaches to swim and glorious views from every angle, taking a walk around the island is the best way to experience this island to the full. At only 2.4 kilometres long and 1.6 kilometres wide, most of the island's paths can easily be covered in half a day. Maps are available on the island showing the permissive paths and the areas private to the monks.

St Margaret's Island

ACCESS VIEW FROM CALDEY ISLAND COAST PATH
Adjoining the north-west tip of Caldey Island, this small rocky tidal islet is home to the UK's largest colony of cormorants as well as cliff-nesting guillemots, razorbills, great black-backed, lesser black-backed and herring gulls. Its spectacular vertical western cliffs are the southern outcrop of the famous South Pembrokeshire Syncline. The southern slopes are shattered and eroded, and there are several high sea stacks to the south of the island. There are signs of past quarry workings and the ruins of houses and a medieval chapel. The islet, which has a high point of forty metres, can be readily viewed from the north-west coastline of Caldey Island but crossing the low tide isthmus to the island is discouraged due to safety and the sensitive nature of this bird reserve.

Ynys Catrin / St Catherine's Island

ACCESS TIDAL CROSSING
This small tidal island is linked to Tenby and is dominated by the ruins of a fort that is undergoing renovation, which makes it all the more fascinating and engaging to visit. Getting to this island is an adventure in itself with a short tidal beach crossing, lots of steps, a bridge and a few more steps before reaching the World War II gun emplacement. Visitors

are rewarded with 360-degree views around Carmarthen Bay and the best view of Tenby. The main gun-deck of this Palmerston military fort is the centre of the attraction where visitors can enjoy a host of events including regular film showings, illustrated talks and theme events such as Titanic evenings where guests have to 'scramble for the lifeboats'; there is also ballroom dancing on the 'promenade deck'. The island was used as a film location for 2016's 'Final Problem' episode of BBC's *Sherlock*, which cemented it as a venue for atmosphere and innovation in entertainment. Formed from an outcrop of limestone and with a high point of thirty metres, the island is riddled with tidal caves.

Burry Holms

ACCESS TIDAL CROSSING

Stand on top of this tidal island at the northern end of Rhossili Bay and wonder what life was like around 9,000 years ago when the sea was nineteen kilometres away, the views were across expansive plains and the island was a basecamp for Mesolithic hunters. The island subsequently became an Iron Age hillfort, which can still be seen today, and then a medieval monastery. On a clear day you can see Caldey Island to the west and in spring and summer it is covered by flowers such as thrift and sea campion. The island, which has a high point of thirty metres, is popular with surfers and walkers enjoying the Wales Coast Path or circular walks through the dunes from Broughton.

1 Pen Pyrod / Worms Head   **2** Pen Pyrod / Worms Head, tidal causeway   **3** Pen Pyrod / Worms Head, Rhossili Bay
4 Pen Pyrod / Worms Head, Devil's Bridge   **5** Pen Pyrod / Worms Head, Inner Head   **6** Mumbles Head, view from Middle Head

Pen Pyrod / Worms Head

ACCESS TIDAL CROSSING

The most westerly point of the Gower Peninsula, Worms Head offers many natural wonders. Together with adjacent Rhossili Bay and the idyllic village of Rhossili, it was part of the first designated Area of Outstanding Natural Beauty in the UK. The island is joined to the mainland by a rocky tidal causeway and is divided into three parts, each accessed by clambering over low-lying rocky sections which makes for quite an adventurous walk and easy scramble. The first section is the steep-sided, forty-seven-metre-high, flat-topped Inner Head. Next is Middle Head, which is split in two by Devil's Bridge, a spectacular natural rock arch. The rocky, fifty-six-metre summit of the spiral-shaped Outer Head, which from a distance looks more to be the preserve of mountaineers, can be reached by a steep but easy scramble, making a spectacular finale. From Rhossili village leave the coast path to descend the causeway below the Lookout Station. The large board outside displays the safe crossing times; there is also a siren to warn stragglers of the incoming tide.

www.islandeering.com

Middle Head and Mumbles Head

ACCESS TIDAL CROSSING

Mumbles Head is a rocky headland on the south-western side of Swansea Bay and is dominated by the unusual, octagonal Mumbles Lighthouse built on top of a Victorian fort, initially built to deter a French invasion. The island has a collection of fascinating ruins including the lighthouse keeper's cottage, engine house, searchlight installations and gun emplacements. There are fabulous views back to the village of Mumbles, the pier and the whole of Swansea Bay. Access is from the characterful resort of Mumbles with its quirky shops, galleries and eateries. Take the steps down from the pier on to the small beach and at low tide head across the rocks to Middle Head. Cross its plateau to the rocks on the east coast from where you can walk across on a low spring tide to the concrete steps that ascend Mumbles Head. Middle Head has the high point of the group at twenty-eight metres.

With the second largest tidal range in the world, after the Canadian Bay of Fundy, the islands of the Bristol Channel experience up to fourteen metres height difference between high and low water twice daily. The largest islands here are Steep Holm and Flat Holm which, together with the promontory of Brean Down, are limestone extensions of the Mendip Hills. Both important nature reserves, they also have some incredible histories to discover and views of the English and Welsh coastlines to savour. Inland, Alney Island offers the opportunity to experience the spectacular Severn tidal bore on the doorstep of the city of Gloucester and Spike Island is rich in the seafaring history of Bristol.

SOUTH EAST WALES
& THE BRISTOL CHANNEL

Opposite Spike Island, looking out from Underfall Yard   **Overleaf** Steep Holm, landing beach

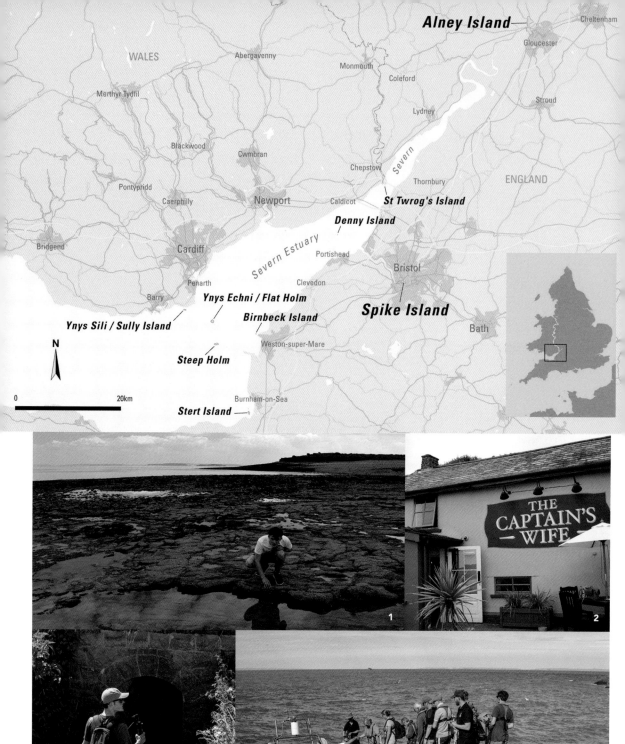

Ynys Sili / Sully Island

ACCESS TIDAL CROSSING

Cross the seabed of one of the second highest tidal ranges in the world to discover this hidden beauty just a short distance from Cardiff. Once a haven for pirates, including Alfredo de Marisco, known as the 'Night Hawk', it was well known in the Middle Ages for its involvement in smuggling activity. Its location 300 metres from the mainland makes it a perfect vantage point to appreciate the vastness and power of the Bristol Channel. The best way to experience the island is the two-kilometre walk from the nearby Captain's Wife pub on the mainland. Go along the causeway then follow the foreshore of the north and west coasts before ascending to the island's high point of twenty-one metres. From here follow the grass path at the top of the cliffs of the south coast. The views from the north coast extend west to Barry Island, north to the striking orange cliffs of mainland Swanbridge and the cliffs of Lavernock Point. On the south coast, the overhanging red and cream sandstone that overlays ancient grey limestone is made for a geology field trip. From here there are expansive views across to Exmoor and Brean Down in Somerset, while in the foreground are the distinctive shapes of Flat Holm and Steep Holm. Safe passage to the island is indicated by a traffic light system installed by the RNLI at the head of the causeway; it is generally open three hours either side of low tide. *www.islandeering.com*

Ynys Echni / Flat Holm

ACCESS BOAT TRIP; NO DOGS

Lying in the Bristol Channel, around four kilometres from the Welsh coast, this is an island that many Cardiff locals spend a lifetime looking at but few venture across the water to visit. Managed by Cardiff Council, it is a significant nature reserve cared for by wardens and volunteers. Its gentle, grassy slope rises from the exposed rocky shore of the west to the cliffs in the east. The interior is open, flat and windswept; the island has a high point of thirty-two metres. Natural forces are not the only ones to have shaped the island's character, though. Augustinian monks, radio geniuses, Victorian gunners and the diseased have occupied it over the last 800 years and have all left their mark. Boat trips from Cardiff, timings dependent on weather and tides, give around three hours on the island. Some operators also offer longer trips, as well as overnighters. Arrival on the island starts with a welcome from the wardens and an orientation talk. You can then join one of the tours or wander freely to explore by yourself.

RIB ride to the island

Setting off from Cardiff's Mermaid Quay, with the vast lock gates of the Cardiff Bay Barrage far above your head, there is a certain apprehension at leaving the safety of the calm lagoon to enter the treacherous brown waters of the Bristol Channel. As the RIB powers towards this distant speck of rock, the island features slowly reveal themselves.

Bunkers, barracks and bug-busting hospitals

Any visit here starts at the old barracks, once the quarters of the gunners stationed here as part of the Victorian strategic coastal defence system. Close by, the impressive, tiled catchment area and underground storage tank is testament to the ingenuity of the Victorians who developed it as the island's water source. To the south, the lighthouse stands on the island's high point; its associated battery has a Moncrieff pit that housed a platform-mounted cannon that would be lowered down below

1 Ynys Sili / Sully Island, rockpooling on the causeway   2 Ynys Sili / Sully Island, refreshments on the way to the island
3 Ynys Echni / Flat Holm, military bunkers   4 Ynys Echni / Flat Holm, RIB ride from Cardiff

ground after it was fired to protect it. The tunnels and rooms here are interesting to explore. Inland from the fossilised beach on the west coast, a dilapidated building marks the site of the Victorian-era isolation hospital where ships would drop off crew and passengers suspected of carrying cholera to stop it spreading to the ports of Bristol and Cardiff. The last patient to die here was the victim of bubonic plague. Nearby, a silver plaque commemorates the first wireless transmission across open water that Guglielmo Marconi sent from Flat Holm to Lavernock Point on the south coast of Wales.

Spot the rare wild leek

The extremely rare, purple-flowered wild leek that stands 1.5 metres tall is found in sheltered spots around the island. It only occurs in small populations in Cornwall, Somerset and Wales and flowers from June to September. The wardens ask you not to touch them.

Gulls galore

There are around 300 pairs of herring gulls that nest here, and over 3,000 pairs of lesser black-backed gulls that generally nest inland on the plateau of the island. Flat Holm's only breeding pair of great black-backed gull, Britain's largest gull, choose Castle Rock to nest in the north of the island. During breeding season the island becomes a frenzy of noise with many of the buildings occupied by birds and their chicks. Visitors that stray too close may be dive-bombed.

Largest pub garden in Wales

The Gull and Leek pub is a fine place to finish a trip to the island. Stocked with bottled beer, cider and wine, its usual winter regulars are the island's sheep, but in the summer it comes to life with daytime visitors having a quick tipple before they depart for Cardiff. The beer garden uniquely comprises the whole island.

Stay overnight

Staying on this wild island at night with only the wildlife, stars and twinkling lights strung along the coastline of the Bristol Channel for company is a wonderful way to appreciate its incredible location. Cardiff Harbour Authority offers organised wellness retreats on the island. Two-day stays involve yoga, reiki, reflexology and meditation sessions with vegan food and drink. Dormitory accommodation is available in the farmhouse field centre or camping in the farmhouse paddocks; the Grade II listed Fog Horn Cottage has been converted into a self-catering cottage, offering more stylish accommodation.

Walk around the island

A two-kilometre walk around the edge of the island reveals a striking shoreline with rock outcrops, caves and rock beaches (some areas may be out of bounds during nesting season). There are plenty of opportunities to deviate inland and explore all of the historic sites on the way. www.islandeering.com

Denny Island

ACCESS VIEW FROM MAINLAND PATH

This small rocky island lies in the middle of the Bristol Channel, three kilometres north of Portishead and roughly halfway between Avonmouth and Redwick, Newport. It lies at the south end of Bedwin Sands, a large area of sandbanks also known as the Welsh Grounds which are exposed at low tide. The boundary between England and Wales runs along the southern foreshore of the island, which is located in Monmouthshire for administrative purposes. Strong tidal currents and the danger of quicksand on a rising tide make the island almost impossible to land on and it remains a roost for seabirds. Small colonies of cormorants and great black-backed gulls and a few pairs of rock pipits nest on the island. The island, which has a high point of ten metres, can be seen in the distance from the Wales Coast Path near Redwick.

St Twrog's Island

ACCESS TIDAL CROSSING

This low-level (the high point is less than five metres) tidal island lies at the western end of the Severn Road Bridge, off Beachley Point. The ruins of a chapel balance precariously amongst sparse grassland above the high tide line. A number of theories propose the purpose of this building, ranging from warning people off the rocks where the Wye and Severn meet to a marker for the crossing point of the river to an island hermitage. The chapel possibly dates from the thirteenth century and has an early Gothic style. Benedictine monks probably gave services on the island, making it a popular destination for pilgrims in the fourteenth century but its popularity is thought to have declined with rising sea levels. Access is possible for around two hours either side of low tide, by walking across seaweed covered rocks.

Alney Island

ACCESS FOOTBRIDGE

This island, which has a high point of ten metres, is located on the banks of the tidal River Severn and less than a kilometre from Gloucester city centre. The island is mostly a quiet nature reserve of riverside meadows, but is one of the best places to see the spectacular phenomenon of the Severn bore. The best place to watch it, especially if it's forecast as a three star or greater event, is in the south of the island at Lower Parting, where the tidal Severn splits into two channels. For centuries the island was the lowest river crossing point from England to Wales and so is steeped in heritage and connected to many long-distance paths including the Severn Way, Gloucestershire Way, Three Choirs Way, Glevum Way and Wysis Way. There are also plenty of other waymarked cycle paths and footpaths throughout, including a full circular route of the island. The island is directly accessed from Gloucester Docks.

www.thesevernbore.co.uk
www.islandeering.com

Spike Island

ACCESS BRIDGES; FERRY

Spike Island, once the site of working quays, shipyards and warehousing, is a vibrant city-centre harbour area with its historic buildings now filled with lively cafes, restaurants and museums. Adjoining Bristol city centre, it comprises a strip of land between the Floating Harbour to the north and the tidal New Cut of the River Avon to the south, from the dock entrance to the west and to Bathurst Basin in the east. Attractions include the M Shed, which is the museum of Bristol, located in a former dockside transit shed. Also, Isambard Kingdom Brunel's *SS Great Britain* and the historic boatyard and visitors centre of Underfall Yard are great places to experience more of Bristol's seafaring heritage. Spike Island, which has a high point of five metres, can be easily reached on foot or bus from Bristol city centre; Bristol Ferry Boats provide services from various points along Bristol's historic waterways and a ferry also crosses the harbour and leaves from opposite *SS Great Britain*.

Circular walk around the island

This fabulous five-kilometre walk is the best way to see much of the vibrant city's maritime and trading history. Starting from Prince Street Bridge, the route follows the walkway parallel to the Floating Harbour and along the old tracks of the Bristol Harbour Railway, passing the M Shed and other historic dockyard buildings to Brunel Square where it cuts inland to avoid the *SS Great Britain* exhibition. Here, Banksy's *Girl with the Pierced Eardrum* can be seen on the clock tower of the Dockside Studios. It appeared in 2014 and is a take on Johannes Vermeer's famous painting, *Girl with a Pearl Earring*. In Banksy's version the girl's earring is replaced with an outdoor security alarm. Nearby, the Orchard Inn has been serving cider since 1834 and is a real Bristol institution. At Bristol Marina the route continues through the historic Underfall Yard, which retains its rich maritime vibe, and on to Cumberland Basin to reach the western point of the island beyond Brunel's Swing Bridge. From here there are great views upriver to the Clifton Suspension Bridge. The return route is along the tidal New Cut on the south side of the island. *www.islandeering.com*

Paddleboard in the city harbour

This is a more adventurous way to see the island and its surroundings from a completely different perspective. It is a unique experience to paddle alongside *The Matthew*, a modern reconstruction of the ship that John Cabot sailed to Newfoundland in 1497. You also get a closer look at *SS Great Britain* and appreciate the cranes and scale of the large dockside buildings and the whole historic enterprise from the water. Hire boards or join an organised paddleboard adventure. *www.supbristol.com*

Birnbeck Island

ACCESS TIDAL CROSSING

At the north end of Weston-super-Mare, this is the only island in Britain linked to the mainland by a pier. The Grade II* listed pier opened in 1867 and was popular with locals, tourists and those departing on the steamers that once plied the waters of the Bristol Channel. A fire in 1897 led to the replacement buildings seen today. These included Mutoscopes, a shooting gallery, a merry-go-round and a theatre of wonder. During World War II the pier was taken over by the Admiralty for secret weapon research then reopened after the war, this time in competition from the town's Grand Pier which ultimately led to its demise. The pier, gothic toll house and pierhead buildings have been closed since 1994 and remain derelict. Access to the island, which has a high point of ten metres, is at low tide only; walk along the natural stone causeway north of the pier, then around the outside of the island's perimeter fence. Keep to the foreshore; all buildings are unsafe.

Steep Holm

ACCESS BOAT TRIP

Tens of thousands of visitors to the Somerset coast see Steep Holm on the horizon, yet few ever make the journey to discover this extraordinary uninhabited, wildlife and history-packed gem. Its limestone flanks rise steeply from the Bristol Channel to reach a high point of seventy-eight metres, eight kilometres west of Weston-super-Mare. Managed by the devoted trustees of the Kenneth Allsop Memorial Trust, set up in the memory of the broadcaster and environmentalist, it is an important nature reserve and showcases an array of military history. First settled in the Iron Age, later the island had a Roman lookout post and an Augustinian priory; its strategic position finally led to its fortification from Victorian times through to the world wars. Today, Steep Holm is packed with underground ammunition stores, signal stations, watchtowers and gun batteries – many of which are located precariously down the cliffs. Wildlife has colonised the old buildings with around 2,000 gulls nesting between April and August; the rare Mediterranean wild peony thrives on the island and muntjac deer and giant slow worms are readily spotted by the eagle-eyed. There are

incredible views throughout of the English and Welsh coastlines along the Bristol Channel. Boats to the island depart from Weston-super-Mare and Cardiff; on arrival access to the island's plateau is via a steep path from the beach. There is a visitor centre in the barracks building with an exhibition, hot and cold drinks, beer and home-made cakes.
www.steepholm.online

Circular walk around the island

All of the island's military highlights and wildlife can be experienced on this two-kilometre walk with panoramic views of Somerset, the Welsh Coast, the Quantock Hills and the whole of the Bristol Channel. The route stays on the island's plateau with an optional descent to South Landing to rock hop around the cliff base to East Beach and Goose Neck Spit at low tide (accessible only outside of bird nesting season). Starting at the landing point, the route climbs Zig Zag Path, past the ruins of Cliff Cottage and the ruins of an inn to the island's plateau, then heads directly to the Barracks Visitor Centre for refreshments. It continues to Split Rock Battery, Rudder Rock Battery and the Searchlight Post that sits on dramatic sea arches. Along the north coast the path ascends steeply to Summit Battery and on to Laboratory Battery and Tombstone Battery to Garden Battery.
www.islandeering.com

Searching for the culvert spider

These large spiders, described scientifically as long-jawed orb-weaving spiders, suspend their eggs in large white 'cotton-wool' sacks from the ceilings of the underground ammunition stores. They hang eerily and silently and can be picked up by torchlight. The adult spiders shy away from the light, but young spiders are attracted to it. They are shiny, satin black and are one of the largest spiders found in the UK with adults having a leg span of around five centimetres and a body length of fifteen millimetres. Despite their fearsome look they are known as 'gentle giants'.

Stert Island

ACCESS NOT PERMITTED; VIEW FROM MAINLAND PATH
This low-lying (the high point is eight metres), uninhabited island in the Bristol Channel, opposite Burnham-on-Sea, is part of the Bridgewater Bay National Nature Reserve. Stert Island was formed in the late eighteenth century when it broke off from the mainland's Steart Peninsula. The island is noted for its birds, including spotted redshank and whimbrel, which have a major night roost on the island.

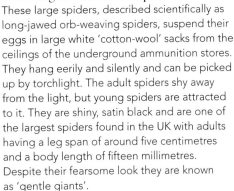

In the warm Gulf of St-Malo, closer to France than the UK, the islands of Jersey, Guernsey, Sark, Herm and Alderney are more than the sum of British and French cultures. They are proudly independent, self-governing British Crown Dependencies with an allegiance to the Queen, that are distinctly different yet vaguely familiar at the same time. They all have spectacular coastlines, a huge range of outdoor activities, bucolic lanes and old-world charm. With more sunshine and milder winters than the UK, along with great local food including an amazing array of succulent seafood, they are popular destinations served by the two vibrant and upmarket towns of St Helier and St Peter Port. Life hasn't always been so blissful here though and it has often been the front line with Europe, as evidenced by the numerous castles and fortifications that dot the coastlines, with poignant museums telling stories of the islanders' resilience during World War II when this archipelago was the only territory within the British Isles occupied by the Germans.

CHANNEL ISLANDS

Opposite Les Etacs, gannet colony   **Overleaf** Herm, Belvoir Bay

English Channel

Burhou

Les Etacs

St Anne

Raz Island

Alderney

Les Houmets

Rat's Island

Herm

Lihou

St Peter Port

Jethou

Crevichon

Brecqhou

Sark

Guernsey

Écréhou

Jersey

La Corbière

St Brelade

St Helier

L'Île au Guerdain

L'Islet / Elizabeth Castle

Icho Tower

La Motte

Seymour Tower

Minquiers
21km (13 miles)
due south of Jersey

N

0   10km

Guernsey

ACCESS FERRY; PLANE

The second largest of the Channel Islands, Guernsey is resolutely British, yet it feels Mediterranean. From pretty St Peter Port with its glittering, cosmopolitan marina, leafy, cobbled streets and lush botanic gardens to the coastline's gloriously expansive golden beaches, hidden coves and clifftops dotted with World War II fortifications, there is plenty to explore. It is part of the Bailiwick of Guernsey along with sister islands of Alderney, Sark, Herm, Jethou and Lihou and many small islets and rocks. A centre for tourism and international finance, its famous icon is the Guernsey cow, prized for its rich creamy milk. There are activities galore on the island with a coast path, waymarked cycle routes, sea swimming and every water sport imaginable. Easy to get to with frequent ferries arriving from Portsmouth, Poole and St-Malo; regular flights arrive from a range of UK and European destinations. Guernsey is the hub for inter-island transport with frequent services to Jersey, Alderney, Sark and Herm. The high point of the island is at Guernsey Airport and reaches 107 metres. A full range of accommodation is available.

Walks around St Peter Port

Often feted as having one of the prettiest harbours in Europe, a ramble through its flower-filled lanes and steep cobbled streets is a great introduction to the island and there are plenty of great pit stops along the way. Along the seafront, the Liberation Monument at St Julian's Pier marks the main arrival point for ferries. Nearby, Victoria Pier and the old harbour and warehouses still retain many original features and are full of good eateries. At the southern end of the seafront, Castle Cornet provides a spectacular backdrop to the town and with its museums, gardens, theatre productions and musical events is a popular attraction. Close by, Hauteville House, once home to French writer Victor Hugo during his exile from France and where he wrote *Les Misérables*, gives a wonderful insight into his character through the extravagantly decorated rooms. Walking from Town Church to Hugo's house, look out for the plaque dedicated to three women who lost their lives after being accused of witchcraft, once a common practice in the island. Within the town, Fresh Friday Market (Market Square; Fridays, 8.30 a.m.– 2.30 p.m.) is a good place to pick up delicious local food. Beautiful parks and gardens line the town's high points with Les Cotils Gardens, Cambridge Park and restored Victorian Candie Gardens offering some great panoramas over the harbour and beyond to the neighbouring islands. The views can be best appreciated from the top of Victoria Tower. Built to commemorate a visit paid to the island in 1846 by Queen Victoria and Prince Albert, Victor Hugo carved his initials and that of his mistress here, the place they would secretly meet.

Beaches, swimming and water sports

Guernsey is famous for its great array of secluded coves and beaches with crystal clear waters that are perfect for swimming, relaxing and every kind of water sport. On the north coast the large sandy beaches are popular with visitors and locals alike and include Vazon Bay and Portinfer for surfers, bodyboarders and kitesurfers. Similarly, Pembroke and L'Ancresse bays have thriving water sports communities with excellent windsurfing, surfing, sailing and sea kayaking. High-tide swimming is popular near the small natural fishing harbour of Bordeaux, which has two sandy beaches, as well as the hidden gem of Port Grat near the Rousse Tower. 'The Island' at Port Soif Bay, with pink granite rocks and sheltered by large sand dunes, also has good current-free swimming. The best way to finish the day along the north coast is to tuck into fish and chips on the sea wall at sunset at Cobo Bay where the pink quartz in the granite rocks enhances the beautiful sunset colours.

On the east coast, within walking distance of St Peter Port, Havelet Bay is a great spot for

N

0   2km

La Grande
Havre Bay

Les Houme

Vale

Cobo
Bay   Cobo

St Sampson

Guernsey

Vazon
Bay   Castel

Lihou

Perelle
Bay

St Peter Port

Jeth

Rocquaine
Bay

Pezeries
Point

St Pierre
du Bois

St Martin

St Martin's Point

Moye Point

Saints
Bay

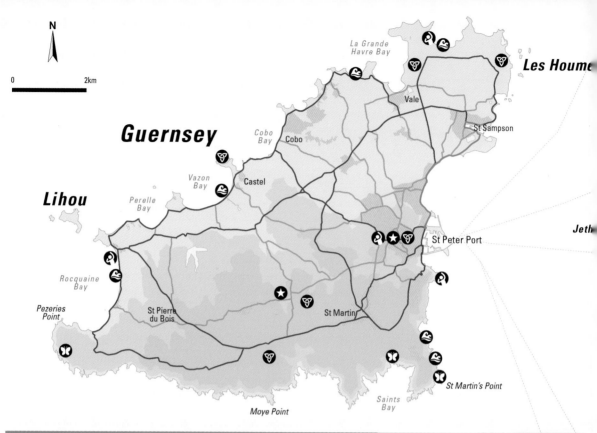

views of Cornet Rock and its castle and a swim in any one of the four Victorian pools of La Vallette Bathing Pools. Further south, a beautiful cliff path leads to Fermain Bay, a rare pebbly beach. The walk down the hill to reach the bay offers breathtaking cliff views. Nearby, a little path and steps lead down to Bec du Nez, a lovely quaint fishing harbour. Further south, the very secluded rocky cove of Marble Bay makes for a beautiful swim in gentle waters surrounded by tall cliffs and stunning views across to Sark and Herm. Guernsey's west coast has L'Eree, a popular beach with gently sloping golden sands and a generally sheltered spot for swimming. The snorkeling here is good too with teeming rockpools to explore. Close by, the L'Eree Headland Nature Reserve has spectacular views over the surrounding coast.

Guernsey's south coast offers something very different as the bays are often located at the bottom of cliffs and are not as readily accessible. They are a haven for nature-lovers, sea kayakers and for coasteering. Starting towards the east, there are many gorgeous bays around St Martin. Petit Port is breathtaking with its steep steps down to a spectacular beach and Moulin Huet is a sandy bay and a perfect swimming spot with fantastic rockpooling at low tide. The beautiful, clear blue cove at Saints Bay is a perfect place to swim. There is also wild Le Jaonnet Bay with sweeping cliffs and steep steps leading down to the blue waters of this incredible bay as well as Petit Bôt, another sheltered sandy bay, surrounded by impressive high cliffs and a waterfall, and great swimming and rockpooling.

Occupation museums

The German occupation during World War II left a legacy of heavy fortification which is visible today on the island; some excellent museums tell Guernsey's wartime stories and give plenty of insight into what life was life on the island during this period.

The German Military Underground Hospital, hewn out of rock by slave labourers during the occupation, is the largest World War II structure in the Channel Islands with around 7,000 square metres of tunnels. It was large enough to house 500 patients and included an operating theatre, X-ray room, dispensary, laboratory and staff quarters, as well as a cinema, central heating plant and kitchen. The hospital was only used in 1944 for German casualties of the D-Day invasion.
www.germanundergroundhospital.co.uk

The German Occupation Museum, housed in an extended cottage in the south of the island, offers a compelling insight into island life between 1940 and 1945. With various items of weaponry, German propaganda-filled local newspaper cuttings and an exhibit on the relationship between a local woman and a German officer, the highlight is the iconic Enigma machine used to send encrypted messages to U-boats in the English Channel.
www.germanoccupationmuseum.co.uk

La Vallette Underground Military Museum, at the southern end of St Peter Port, is a series of tunnels where U-Boat fuel was stored that now houses occupation memorabilia and exhibits.
www.visitguernsey.com/see-and-do/things-to-do/la-vallette-underground-military-museum

German Naval Signals HQ was established in two hotels before being moved to a safer location in purpose-built bunkers in the grounds of La Collinette Hotel. It was responsible for all radio traffic to and from Germany and the other islands during the occupation, using the Enigma machines that were being decoded at Bletchley Park. Soldiers from the British Royal Signals used this headquarters to send messages to England after the liberation of the island by *HMS Bulldog* in 1945, the same vessel that captured the German Enigma machine in 1941 which helped the British break important Enigma messages.
www.visitguernsey.com/see-and-do/things-to-do/german-naval-signals-hq

---

1 Guernsey, St Peter Port   **2** Guernsey, subtropical plants   **3** Guernsey, Fermain Bay

Explore Fort Hommet

Fortifications have been on the Vazon Bay headland since the seventeenth century; later additions include a Martello tower, Victorian-era fortifications and bunkers and gun emplacements constructed by occupying German forces in World War II. This is an interesting place to explore with two levels and great views across the bay. It is home to the Shrine of the Sacred Heart, a World War II bunker transformed by Hubert Le Galloudec from a place of war into a place of peace and beauty using local seashells to depict stories of the *Bible* and Christian symbols. The area surrounding Fort Hommet is great for a walk, and the fort is easily accessible on the coast path leading from Vazon Bay.

Pick a festival

Guernsey hosts festivals on themes from walking and literature to folk and rock music and regattas. One that's unique to Jersey and Guernsey is Liberation Day, which commemorates their freedom from German occupation.

Discover ancient history

Guernsey has more than its fair share of megalithic sites including dolmens, menhirs and pagan sites. The most impressive sites are the dolmens, or burial chambers, and probably the best of these is Dehus Dolmen, 700 metres north of Bordeaux Harbour. This is a large, accessible, multi-chambered tomb beneath a grass mound with standing stones around the edge. Towards the back of the tomb there is a faint image of a bearded face, known as Le Gardien du Tombeau, carved on to one of the ceiling stones. The island's largest megalithic site is the eighteen-metre-long Stone Age tomb of La Varde on L'Ancresse Common. Other notable structures on the common include Les Fouaillages which, at around 6,000 years old, is one of the oldest monuments in Europe. Close to the L'Eree Headland, Le Creux ès Faïes is a large Neolithic tomb which legend says is the entrance to the fairy world. Le Trepied, on La

Rocques Headland, is a Stone Age passage grave thought to be a meeting place used by witches in the seventeenth century. The island also has a number of standing stones, the most notable of which is La Gran'mère du Chimquière, which sits outside the entrance to St Martin's churchyard. Around 4,000 years old, the stone has been carved with a female face and figure. Locally, it is reputed to be a source of fertility.

Squeeze into Little Chapel

Situated in the Les Vauxbelets Valley, in the village of St Andrew near the heart of the island, Little Chapel is thought to be the smallest functioning chapel in Europe and the world's smallest consecrated church. It can fit about eight people. The current structure is the third version built by Brother Déodat who created the first structure in 1914, as a miniature version of the grotto and basilica at Lourdes. The original, measuring 2.7 by 1.4 metres, was demolished soon after building, as it received so much criticism from the locals. The second version, measuring 2.7 by 1.8 metres, was demolished after the Bishop of Portsmouth visited in 1923 and could not fit through the door. Brother Déodat then demolished his creation again and started to build a third, but died never seeing the finished chapel, which now measures 4.9 by 2.7 metres. The Little Chapel is decorated with seashells, pebbles and broken china and is mentioned in the plot of *The Guernsey Literary and Potato Peel Pie Society*, by Mary Ann Shaffer and Annie Barrows.

Walk the coast path

The sixty-two-kilometre unofficial coast path, part of the longer Channel Island Way, is a walk along country lanes, woodland pathways, wild coastal cliffs, hidden coves and sandy bays. Along the way there are ancient churches, Napoleonic watchtowers and German fortifications as well as some great pit stops. The walk can be completed as a whole or there are shorter walks that take in the highlights of the island's coast. One such walk from

Fermain Bay to secluded Marble Bay can be completed as a circular walk from St Peter Port. It passes wild headlands, plunging cliffs and deep-cut coves along a wooded section of the coast path. It continues past rocky outcrops and tidal pools to St Martin's Point then on to Jerbourg Point and the Pea Stacks, six large stacks at the tip of the headland. Other highlights include the coastal section between Petit Port Bay and Saints Bay Harbour, where there are opportunities to climb down to more secluded coves as well as enjoy the spectacular views from Moulin Huet Bay, which inspired Pierre-Auguste Renoir to paint the scene. The Pleinmont Peninsula, in the south-west of Guernsey, is also dramatic with many lookouts and fortifications. Over 150 species of bird have been recorded here, making it one of the best places for birdwatching on the island. Most of the north coast entails walking alongside the road or on wide sandy beaches, passing the causeway leading to Lihou on the way.

Cycle around the island

An unofficial forty-nine-kilometre road route around the whole island starts and finishes in St Peter Port. It heads north along a cycle lane most of the way to St Sampson, beyond which

travel is on Guernsey's country lanes to reach the main coastal road at L'Islet. The route along the north and west coast passes some of the best bays Guernsey has to offer, including Port Grat, Cobo, Port Soif, Vazon and Rocquaine, before finally reaching Portelet Beach – there are numerous fortifications along the way if you want to break the tempo of this fast, flat stretch of road. Turning south with a short, steep climb over Pleinmont, the route along the south coast uses mostly quiet lanes with the occasional stretch on the main road. The highlight is an exciting descent in to Petit Bôt Bay and the requisite steep ascent the other side before joining the main road back in to St Peter Port. *www.islandeering.com*

Circumnavigate the island with one bus ticket

Bus numbers 91 and 92, which are named The Guernsey Vaeux, do a complete circuit of the island via St Peter Port and the airport with stop-offs at all the major attractions along the coast. All single journeys (excluding going all the way round the island) cost £1 per person; travel passes are available.

Cycle the Ruettes Tranquilles

These routes take you through some of the island's most scenic and peaceful areas in the parishes of Castel, Forest, St Andrew, St Martin, St Saviour, St Sampson and Vale. Priority is given to pedestrians, cyclists and horse riders, and the lanes have a recommended speed limit of fifteen miles per hour for motor vehicles. They wind through fields, woodland and the glasshouses where salads were once grown, and down to small bays, great beaches and places of interest. There are numerous 'hedge veg' stalls where locals sell fresh produce from their gardens or smallholdings using an honesty box system. The western and northern coasts offer flatter terrain, while the valleys in the south of the island offer more of a challenge. *www.gov.gg/cycling*

Lihou

ACCESS TIDAL CROSSING

An adventure away from the more mainland feel of Guernsey, this tiny island (with a high point of twenty-three metres) sits off the north-west coast across a tidal causeway. The island and its surrounds form an important marine reserve packed with fabulous creatures above and below the water. The two islets, **Lihoumel** and **Lissroy**, are important seabird breeding sites and are roped off during the breeding season. Inland, rare plants such as sand crocus, dwarf pansy and sand quillwort make it a destination for plant hunters. This tiny windswept island has a rich history; in the twelfth century it was home to a Benedictine priory, the haunting ruins of which are passed on a short circular walk around the island. The island is managed by the States of Guernsey and Lihou Charitable Trust. Lihou House, which was built in the 1960s to replace a previous building which collapsed after being used for target practice by German artillery in World War II, is used mainly for school trips and ecotourism. The 800-metre cobbled causeway from L'Eree to Lihou is only exposed on low spring tides and isn't accessible every day. There is plenty to see in the vicinity of the causeway on Guernsey if you can't cross to Lihou, such as L'Eree German bunker, the legendary entrance to the fairy kingdom at Le Creux ès Faïes and the views of Fort Saumarez. *www.gov.gg/lihou*

Swim in Venus pool

Hidden off the island's western tip the famous Venus Pool, a natural low-tide rockpool, is deep enough to jump into and long enough for a swim. Unless there are residents in Lihou House you are likely to have this wild experience all to yourself.

Rockpooling along the causeway

At low tide the rockpools teem with shore crabs, edible crabs, porcelain crabs, velvet crabs and hermit crabs. Squat lobsters, shrimps and prawns thrive amongst limpets, winkles, top shells, dog whelks, starfish and anemones. Together with over 200 species of seaweed of every shape, size and colour, some not found on any other Channel Island, a veritable array of birds with curlews, oystercatchers, egrets and redshanks can be spotted feasting on this seafood platter.

1 Sark, island transport   **2** Sark, dark sky island   **3** Sark, La Coupée

Les Houmets

ACCESS TIDAL CROSSING; RESTRICTIONS ON HOUMET PARADIS (MAY–JULY)

These wild, uninhabited islands on the north-east coast of Guernsey (which have a high point of under ten metres) are accessible at low tide from the beaches between Millette Bay and Petils Bay. The most northerly of the group, **Homptolle**, is used for gathering ormer, the Channel Island name for abalone. Mostly covered in thrift, it is home to a large colony of common terns in breeding season. Further south, **Houmet Paradis**, once used for fish gutting and drying on stands, is a grass-covered island of granite outcrops and shingle storm beaches managed by the National Trust of Guernsey as a nature reserve. There is an adventurous geocache to find on the island and it is a special destination for nature lovers. Access is only during low spring tides across a shingle causeway, with some restrictions during nesting season. The most southerly islet, tiny **Houmet Benest**, is 180 metres from the shore and has an eighteenth-century gun battery once used to defend against the French. The German occupiers added another, then the British another after the Germans left. There are several shipwrecks close by. It is covered in grass and brambles and is rich in flora.

Sark

ACCESS SMALL FERRY

Quirky and timeless, its coastline is packed with caves and swimming spots and the night sky spangled with stars. Sark bills itself as a 'world apart' and sometimes it does feel like it's in a bit of a time warp as there are no cars and the only transport is by bike, tractor or horse-drawn cart. It has its own parliament and it was one of Europe's last feudal states. Although most visitors come here to relax, there is plenty of outdoor adventure along the steep cliffs, coves, gullies and caves and there are some excellent beaches to explore including Dixcart Bay, Port du Moulin and La Coupée along with plenty of places for wild swimming such as Le Creux Harbour and the famous natural Venus Pool and Adonis Pool. There are sporting and cultural festivals throughout the year that range from SarkFest to sheep and lawnmower racing. The second smallest inhabited island of the Channel Islands, it has a high point of 109 metres and offers a range of accommodation including campsites. It is accessed by a regular one-hour boat ride from Guernsey or less frequent services from Jersey.

www.sarkshipping.gg

www.manche-iles.com/en

Walk the coast path

Unmarked, yet easy to follow, this seventeen-kilometre full island circuit along the cliff tops of the plateaus of Sark and Little Sark passes through farmland and spectacular headlands with optional descents to explore the many beaches, caves and other points of interest and with plenty of excellent pit stops on the way. Starting at Le Creux Harbour, the route immediately climbs on to the wild clifftops, with optional descents to Derrible and Dixcart bays to enjoy the arch, caves and beaches. The route continues across La Coupée to Little Sark. Here, the derelict ventilation chimneys of the copper mines of Port Gorey can be explored on the way back from the Venus Pool. Back on Greater Sark a myriad of paths lead across the wildflower-filled Gouliot Headland before turning inland past the island stores and various cafes and restaurants as well as the iconic tree-lined Rue de Rade and La Seigneurie. The coast around the north of the island near Eperquerie Landing is full of caves, bathing pools and great scrambles before heading south along the eastern coast past the lighthouse at Point Robert to return to the harbour.
www.islandeering.com

La Coupée

Greater Sark and Little Sark are joined by La Coupée, a steep-sided three-metre-wide walkway with an eighty-metre drop down to Sark's most extensive sand beach, La Grande Greve.

Explore Eperquerie Landing and Boutique Caves

The northern tip of Greater Sark is a fabulous place to scramble, explore the caves, find the various shallow bathing pools or simply picnic on the common to enjoy the fabulous views of the surrounding Channel Islands. On the west coast, Boutique Caves offer a variety of tunnels, shallow pools to bathe in and wet and dry caves to explore at low tide with beautiful light throughout. Reached via a rocky scramble from the common, it is not for the faint-hearted. On the east coast, Eperquerie Landing offers good rocks to bathe amongst and a small paddling pool for children. It is also possible to explore the north end of Sark, Bec du Nez, at low tide by descending into the gulley dividing La Grune from the main island by way of some concrete steps and a little scramble.

Swim in Venus Pool

At the southern tip of Little Sark, protected by the overhanging granite rocks, this hidden gem makes for an idyllic swim; it is usable for around 2.5 hours either side of low tide on calmer days. Its turquoise waters are so clear that the large rocks at the bottom appear to be just below the surface, rather than several metres below. From La Sablonnerie Hotel, walk across Gorey Common and head towards the small island of **L'Etac** and scramble down the cliffs to reach the pool.

Swim in the Adonis Pool

Even more beautiful than the Venus Pool, but accessible only to the adventurous few, this five-metre-deep natural pool on the south-west tip of Little Sark is filled with crystal clear water and every kind of seaweed imaginable. Plunging in and bathing is swimming perfection. On an ebbing tide it is also possible to swim across to the islet of **Moie de la Bretagne** opposite, which can also be walked to on the lowest of spring tides. To get there, take the path that leads south-west from La Sablonnerie Hotel to the Adonis Headland. On the coast, looking left, you can see the rocky bay of Rouge Caneau; on the right is the islet of Moie de la Bretagne. Between the islet and the mainland there is a large, detached rock within which the Adonis Pool can be spotted sixty metres below, surrounded by other smaller pools within the rock. A deep gully needs to be crossed via the large boulder that helps bridge the gap, ideally attempted two hours either side of low tide.

Star gazing

With little light pollution and no cars or street lights, Sark became the world's first dark sky island, an honour taken seriously by the islanders who cover their torches at night with red cellophane to reduce light pollution. Comets, meteor showers and bright constellations dazzle in the dark sky and this is one of the few places in the UK where you can still see the Milky Way in its full glory. La Coupée is the best summer viewing site for Scorpius,

Sagittarius, Lyra and Cygnus. The darkest skies are visible between September and April, and for two hours after sunset. Visitors can borrow telescopes from the Sark Astronomy Society. Alternatively, Sark Observatory, located near the church and accommodating up to eight people at a time, has an indoor screen showing views from the telescope.
www.sastros.sark.gg

Gouliot Caves and headland

On the west coast of Sark, opposite Brecqhou, this headland holds a mind-blowing array of natural wonders. Above ground, wild flowers, including the rare sand crocus, bloom in the spring meadows, while the beautiful, accessible sea caves below are carpeted with sea anemones, sponges, soft corals and sea squirts. Water surges through this network of caverns on all but the lowest of tides and, laden with plankton, nourishes the rich marine life that colourfully adorns every available surface. The uniqueness of the caves, along with the wealth of marine life they support and the variety of flora above, led to the site being declared a Wetland of International Importance. The inner passages can only be reached on the lowest of spring tides. Access is from Gouliot Headland, directly opposite Brecqhou; follow the broad grassy path west from La Vaurocque and descend towards the headland. Just before the path starts to head out on to the headland, take the path to the right along the top of a sea gorge to your right. Where this path ends on the promontory turn left, and after a few metres the chimney entrance of the cave can be spotted. Descend into the main cavern, the Chimney, from where the other caves can be then explored. Take a torch.

Window in the Rock and Port du Moulin

For some of the most spectacular views of Sark's coastline the Window in the Rock, a man-made opening cut into the sheer cliff face, can be visited on the way down to Port du Moulin. The beach is encircled by sea arches and weirdly shaped rocks that jut out of the water at low tide. The three granite columns of Les Autelets rise to the right of the bay. After La Seigneurie, bear left on to a road and a track winding along the cliff (signposted *Window and Bay*).

La Seigneurie Gardens

The official home of Sark's feudal lord is still a private residence, but its lovely gardens are open to the public. One of the most historic buildings in Sark, its granite walls and woodland protect a beautiful garden brimming with colour and tranquillity. A central path navigates past the rose, vegetable and sensory gardens and glasshouses of this island jewel. You can also get lost in the maze and visit the chapel to discover the enchanting history of Sark's Seigneurs and the Seigneurie itself as well as the history of the island.
www.laseigneuriegardens.com

Coasteering and sea kayaking

Sark is possibly one of the best coasteering locations in the UK – you can don a wetsuit and explore incredible caves and cavern systems such as the Victor Hugo's Cave, Cathedral Cave, Boutique Caves, Derrible Head Caverns and the famed Gouliot Caves. The coastline of Sark offers a range of experiences for families as well as adrenaline junkies. With sea-level traverses, rock hopping, cliff jumping, gully swimming, swell riding and sea cave exploration, you can experience Sark's wonderful environment via its aquatic nature trail and abundance of wildlife. With huge tidal flows and the inaccessibility of some of Sark's coastline, sea kayaking will take you to places few people have been such as Secret, Red and Pigeon caves, Convanche Chasm, Dixcart Souffleur and Derrible Creux to name a few with a fabulous array of marine life and birdlife to spot on the way. Equipment hire and guiding are available on the island.

Herm

ACCESS SMALL FERRY

The smallest of the publicly accessible Channel Islands and only five kilometres east of Guernsey, Herm is a popular destination. With six astounding beaches, no cars, and a hotel where there are no radios, clocks or TVs, it is a perfect place to relax. Its history stretches back to monks, smugglers, quarrymen, Prussian Princesses and occupying Germans, all who have left their mark. With fabulous dunes, white sand beaches, a large flower-filled common, Neolithic tombs, wild cliff paths and winding inland lanes, there is plenty to explore. The island has a high point of sixty-five metres. Owned by the States of Guernsey, its current tenants aim to retain the identity of the island while keeping it open for the enjoyment of all. At the harbour you'll find the Mermaid Tavern, a shop and the upmarket White House Hotel. There is a range of self-catering options on the island. A frequent, seasonal boat service leaves St Peter Port, Guernsey, for the twenty-minute trip to Herm.
www.traveltrident.com

Walk idyllic lanes to Manor Village

The inland grass tracks lined with pink dog roses, honeysuckle, fuchsias and foxgloves lead ultimately to the centre of the island and Manor Village, a lovely stone hamlet with a chapel, farm and power station. St Tugual's Chapel has fine stained-glass windows featuring scenes including Guernsey cows boarding Noah's Ark and Jesus talking to the fishermen at Herm Harbour. The other buildings are a mix of islanders' homes and self-catering holiday accommodation.

Walk the coast path

This laid back six-kilometre walk starts as soon as you step foot on Herm Harbour. Heading south, there are wonderful views of the islands of Jethou and **Crevichon** and the impressively crenelated Rosiére Steps. The gentle climb to the rocky southern plateau and Point Sauzebourge is rewarded by great views of the stunning seascapes of Sark and Brecqhou. Heading north along the eastern coast, the walk passes dramatic cliffs before reaching Caquorobert for the best views of the stunning white Shell Beach and the hidden gem of Belvoir Bay. The island's north is dominated by a flat, wild-flower-filled common with a few Neolithic tombs to explore. An obelisk is positioned about halfway along the north coast, which otherwise is covered by wind-blown sand

that hides an old wave-cut platform. The route turns down the west coast, passing **Rat's Island**, which can be bagged at low tide via the stone causeway, then returns to the harbour.
www.islandeering.com

Snorkelling from Shell Beach

The sands of this wonderful beach are framed by marram-fringed dunes and shallow turquoise waters making them feel like a tropical paradise. With reefs close to the shore, the snorkelling here is excellent. The small cafe is also well stocked for a family day out on the beach. It is also the jumping off point for the Puffin Patrol kayaking trip to see the most southerly puffin colony in Britain.
www.outdoorguernsey.gg

Camp under the stars

Herm gets busy in the day but if you stay overnight, you'll have it virtually to yourself. The Seagull Campsite is located in the middle of the island, just minutes from the cliff path leading to Belvoir Bay. Here you can wake up in the morning to an unforgettable view across the north end of Herm, Shell Beach and across to Alderney. A ten-minute walk from the harbour, there is also a free luggage transfer via a buggy.
www.herm.com/where-to-stay/camping

1

Other islands in the Bailiwick of Guernsey

There are around fifty-five islands in the Bailiwick, the majority of which are inaccessible or of little interest to the general traveller. One exception is **Brecqhou**, officially a tenement of Sark. Owned by the billionaire Sir Frederick Barclay, co-owner of *The Daily Telegraph* newspaper and *The Spectator* magazine, who, along with his brother who died in 2021, bought the island in 1993 for £2.3 million. The brothers undertook extensive landscaping works, feted as one of the most ambitious in Britain, where vast sections of cliffs were removed. Today, the once windswept island has an olive grove, vineyards, a carp pond, a football pitch and an organic market garden – none of which is open to the public. The brothers have had intermittent legal disputes with the government of Sark; they have expressed a desire to make Brecqhou politically independent and they drive cars and land helicopters on the island, both of which are banned under Sark law. Another private island, **Jethou**, is leased from the Crown and not open to the public. It is immediately south of Herm and has had a string of interesting residents,

including novelist Compton Mackenzie of *Whisky Galore* fame. It is now occupied by Sir Peter Ogden, one of the founders of Computacenter.

Alderney

ACCESS SMALL FERRY; PLANE

The closest Channel Island to both Britain and France, it is the least well known and hardest to get to but very much worth the effort. With its unhurried pace of life and strong community spirit this is a 'live and let live' sort of island with a distinct lack of stifling regulations. It is stacked with Victorian fortifications, reinforced by the German army during the occupation of World War II, that today make for some adventurous exploration in tunnels by torchlight. There is also plenty of great wildlife to see here too; the island has a high point of 90 metres. St Anne is a vibrant town with plenty going on and some great eateries as well as the main hub for a wide range of accommodation.

Walk the coast path

This dramatic eighteen-kilometre walk passes most of the military fortifications, sublime beaches, incredible views and astounding wildlife with an optional extra tidal island. Starting at Braye Harbour, the northern section of the route passes the secret rooms

1 Alderney, blue post box **2** Alderney, Braye **3** Alderney, window at Fort Tourgis
4 Alderney, Longis Bay **5** Alderney, wildlife bunker

and tunnels of the Cambridge Battery at Fort Tourgis and Clonque Bay. The route climbs to the cliffs of the island's western tip for the best views of Sark, Brecqhou, Guernsey and Herm. Close by, a plaque and concrete gates mark the entrance of the former Lager Sylt, the only German concentration camp built on British soil. The wilder, inaccessible south coast is framed by dramatic cliffs and bordered by woodland and fields of dairy cows. At the island's south-east tip the wide, sandy crescent of Longis Bay is bounded to the east by the tidal **Raz Island** and Fort Raz – an optional island to bag for the enthusiastic. Once back on the north coast the scenic Arch Bay, linked to neighbouring Corblets Bay at low tide, is connected to the island's campsite via a tunnel. At the western end of crescent-shaped Saye Bay the tunnels, bunkers and the armoured cupola of Bibette Head are great to explore by torchlight. Further along the coast, the impressive nineteenth-century Fort Albert sits above Braye Bay, which curves its way around to the restaurants and harbour of Braye itself. *www.islandeering.com*

Explore the rooms of Fort Tourgis

An extensive fortification and impressive structure at the northern end of Clonque Bay that is fun to poke around. Completed in 1855, it was designed to accommodate 346 men and was originally planned to be the largest of Alderney's Victorian forts before Fort Albert was built to accommodate a British fleet to defend against the French Navy. During the German occupation it was repurposed to protect the sea route from Cherbourg to St-Malo, and to resist potential British assault to recapture the islands. Today, part of the northern defences of Fort Tourgis is open to the public, who can explore the rooms and bunkers at their leisure and with their own torch. Cambridge Battery is an excellent example of how the original Victorian fortifications were adapted by German forces during World War II, when Alderney became one of the most heavily fortified sections of Hitler's Atlantic Wall.

Forage at Clonque Bay

Nestled in the island's north-west corner, this bay has a huge intertidal area with a wild, sandy beach and excellent rockpooling and foraging opportunities for samphire and shellfish at low tide; it is also home to over 100 species of seaweed. Facing west, it's a great place to watch a sunset across the Swinge, with the sun disappearing behind the adjacent island of Burhou. Fort Clonque, a nineteenth-century fortress accessed via a tidal causeway, sits on a rocky outcrop at the southern end of the bay. Owned by The Landmark Trust, it now provides comfortable self-catering accommodation spread across several different buildings.

Go underground in the Wildlife Bunker

The Wildlife Bunker on the island's south coast is a restored German-built structure that housed communication equipment during the occupation. The Alderney Wildlife Trust cleared and partially restored it to its original condition and have erected many information boards covering its history and the natural history of the island. The bunker is home to nesting swallows every spring. Perched on the clifftop it offers superb views to the other Channel Islands and the French coast.

Watch gannets diving in the Swinge

The pinnacles of **Les Etacs**, just 200 metres off Alderney's coastline, are home to nearly 6,000 pairs of gannets between March and the end of September. A walk to the Giffoine Headland offers fantastic views of the guano-whitened stacks. Bird cries fill the air and their bodies plunge into the swirling waters of the Swinge. Watching this spectacle can be combined with a walk through the steep sided, tranquil Vallée des Trois Vaux. The gannets can also be watched from boat trips run by the Alderney Wildlife Trust. *www.alderneywildlife.org*

Explore St Anne

This charming village, with a cobbled main street, pastel-coloured Georgian houses and colourful bunting criss-crossing the streets, is the island's main settlement. Full of quirky independent shops, bars that are always full of locals, an old-school cinema and one of the largest churches in the Channel Islands – it also has one of the best Indian restaurants of the archipelago, Nellie Grays. The village is also home to the Alderney Society Museum which tells the story of Alderney, from original Neolithic settlements through to the island's role in Roman trade, centuries of enmity with France and the resulting fort building in the Victorian era. It tells stories of the traumatic World War II period, when the vast majority of islanders were evacuated, and gives more information about the lives of the German invaders.

Camping next to the beach

Tucked away in the sand dunes that line the stunning white sands of Saye Bay and just two minutes from Corblets Bay and Arch Bay, Saye Beach Campsite makes a perfect base for a family holiday with plenty of adventure. The facilities of Braye and St Anne are within walking distance. The evenings are special here with the possibility of spotting blonde hedgehogs and amazingly clear night skies.
www.sayebeachcamping.co.uk

Blonde hedgehog night safari

These unique blonde hedgehogs were thought to have originated from the hedgehogs brought to the island as pets in the 1960s, where they either escaped or were released into the wild. With such low initial numbers the population is quite inbred, leading to their unusual blonde spines and pink noses, not the usual black ones. They are a common sight in gardens, verges and even wandering around town. The Alderney Wildlife Trust runs weekly bat and hedgehog walks, which almost guarantees a sighting.
www.alderneywildlife.org

Ride the Northern Line to the seaside

The only working railway in the Channel Islands opened in 1847 and runs for three kilometres between Braye Road and Mannez

Quarry. The current stock, drawn by a diesel engine, includes carriages from the London Underground. The railway was originally built to carry stone from the eastern end of the island to build a breakwater and Victorian-era forts. It was commandeered by the Germans during World War II and then the British Home Office. It is a fun way to travel around this part of the island.

Party at the Channel Islands' biggest festival

The annual Alderney Week in early August is a celebration incorporating over 100 events with live music, entertainment, parties, sports, carnivals and wacky family events including the Daft Raft Race and the Manpowered Flight. The carnival begins with the annual Cavalcade Day, where decorated carts and floats make their way through the town in this noisy, colourful parade and culminates in the famous Alderney Torchlight Procession, in which 2,000 torchbearers parade through St Anne.
www.alderneyweek.net

Burhou

ACCESS BOAT TRIP; RESTRICTIONS MARCH–APRIL
This small island, with a high point of twenty-six metres, lies 2.3 kilometres north-west of Alderney and is a bird sanctuary with a colony of around 100 pairs of puffins. It is quite a spectacle to observe these birds that mate for life reuniting here after nine months at sea. Each pair is completely loyal to each other, and they return to the same burrow every year where they will raise a single puffling. Landing on Burhou during the breeding period, 15 March to 1 August, is prohibited and a 'puffin friendly zone' was established here in 2018. Organised boat trips are available and you can also watch them online through a series of live webcams installed on the island. Storm petrels also breed on the island and there are many species of plant to be spotted including sea spurry, forget-me-nots, field bugloss and scarlet pimpernel.
www.alderneywildlife.org

Jersey

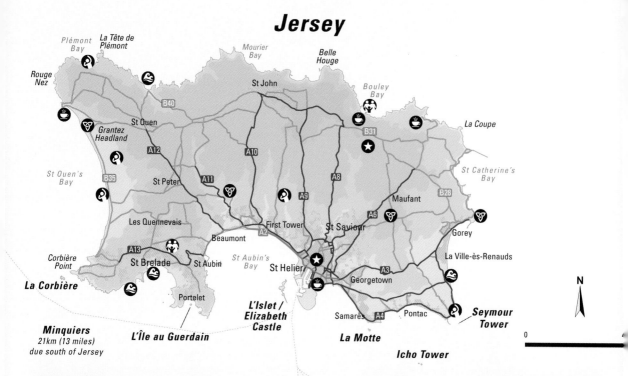

Plémont Bay
La Tête de Plémont
Rouge Nez
Mourier Bay
Belle Houge
St John
Bouley Bay
La Coupe
St Ouen
B40
Grantez Headland
A12
A10
B31
St Catherine's Bay
St Peter
A11
A8
St Ouen's Bay
B35
A9
Maufant
B28
Les Quennevais
A6
Beaumont
First Tower
A2
St Saviour
Gorey
Corbière Point
A13
St Brelade
St Aubin
St Aubin's Bay
St Helier
La Ville-ès-Renauds
Portelet
L'Islet / Elizabeth Castle
Georgetown
A3
La Corbière
Samarès
A4
Pontac
Seymour Tower

Minquiers
21km (13 miles)
due south of Jersey

L'Île au Guerdain

La Motte

Icho Tower

N

0

Jersey

ACCESS FERRY; PLANE

Jersey, just off the French coast, is the largest of the Channel Islands. It is an unusual multinational society with three languages – English, French and the local dialect, Jèrriais – and is a place of constant cultural and natural contrast. Its coast, much of it protected within the Jersey National Park, varies from steep cliffs and coves to vast stretches of golden sands. The island has a huge tidal range and at low tide there are plenty of special islets, rockpools and places of interest to discover. The island has a high point of 136 metres. The history of Britain's relations with the rest of Europe is evident everywhere, from the forts built to resist the French who wanted their island back (Jersey was part of Normandy until the whole of England became Norman after 1066), to the gun batteries and fortifications built under German occupation during World War II. At the same time it is at the cutting edge of the financial world and an offshore tax haven with the old potato warehouses now glass-fronted international banks. It has a cosmopolitan feel mixed with a very local vibe. The island is famous for its traditional produce: the Jersey Royal potato, the Jersey cow's creamy gold-top milk and the freshest of seafood with local oysters and lobsters aplenty. Liberation from the Nazis is a big thing here with the route along the seafront called La Route de la Libération towards Liberty Wharf and Liberation Square in St Helier, where you can catch the Liberty Bus from the Liberation Bus Station. The built legacy of the occupation now forms many of the tourist attractions, with other historic gems stretching back to Neolithic times. Jersey has a full range of accommodation and is served by ferries from Portsmouth, Guernsey and mainland France. Direct flights arrive from many European destinations.

Discover St Helier on foot

St Helier grew into a larger settlement in the nineteenth century with its harbours extended to become a commercial port. Although surrounded by a modern-day power station and high-rise blocks, the centre of the capital reveals a more charming side that is a wonderful blend of English and French history with its markets, pedestrianised streets and museums, including the Maritime Museum and Jersey Museum and Art Gallery. With a marina full of yachts and traffic thronging its streets, it's a busy, vibrant town. It also has a couple of good beaches including Havre des Pas, with its striking Art Deco-style lido, and West Park Beach, with safe swimming in the tidal Victoria Pool. A compact and very walkable city centre with plenty of places to eat, drink and people-watch, it is an excellent base for exploring the rest of the island. Built highlights include Liberation Square and the Royal Square with its gilded statue of George II at the centre, from which all distances in Jersey are measured. St Helier also has a historic, lively Central Market, with an ornamental fountain and fishpond, where you can find Jersey black butter, and the adjacent Beresford Street Market, which specialises in fish. The main Post Office in Broad Street sells Jersey stamps; nearby is the site of one of the first post boxes erected in the British Isles. Amongst the modern shops of New Street, the 16 New Street Georgian House Museum is an architectural jewel and a key reminder of the area's rich heritage.

Cycle the island

The island boasts 154 kilometres of waymarked cycle routes and seventy-seven kilometres of green lanes, which are country roads with a speed limit of fifteen miles per hour, where cyclists, horse riders and pedestrians have priority over cars. Despite the island's maximum altitude being only 136 metres, Jersey has plenty of hills. A seventy-five-kilometre cycle route around the whole island, using a variety

1 Jersey, St Helier **2** Jersey, cow **3** Jersey, quiet cycle routes

of small lanes, green lanes and main roads, climbs a total of 1,083 metres, with most of this from the numerous bays of the north coast. *www.islandeering.com*

Although the sea views are delightful and most of Jersey's ten official cycle routes do visit a beach at some point, steering clear of the coast offers a more relaxed and flatter cycling experience. In terms of dedicated cycling paths, there are traffic-free cycle paths along St Aubin's Bay linking the west of the island with St Helier, and a new off-road cycle path has been constructed that runs north to south up the lush St Peter's Valley. The original Railway Path, which turned Jersey's pre-war train track into a safe route for pedestrians and cyclists, is a further option.

Jersey Zoo

Jersey Zoo, previously known as Durrell Wildlife Park, is dedicated to conservation projects throughout the world. Established in 1959 by English writer and naturalist Gerald Durrell, the zoo's profits are invested back into global conservation projects. The zoo's residents are housed in four distinct habitats where exotic species such as the Mindanao bleeding-heart dove, hooded pitta, Andean bear and the Montserrat mountain chicken frog thrive. You can also stay at Jersey Zoo in a hostel or in glamping tents that recreate the feel of a luxury safari. *www.durrell.org*

Pick up a fresh seafood picnic for the beach

There are two great places to buy fresh seafood and fish for a beach picnic or barbecue. The famous Fresh Fish Company on Victoria Pier in St Helier is heaven for foodies with seasonal fresh spider crabs, local mackerel, turbot, Dover sole, John Dorey, monkfish and plump local scallops as well as freshly cooked lobster and crabs. They also cook dishes such as posh fish and chips, prawn cakes or freshly prepared king prawn and lobster Thai curries. Another spot for picking up fresh fish is Beresford Street Market, St Helier, with its fresh fish stalls intertwined with several eateries where you can try locally grown oysters, chancre crab and lobster. Just across the road is the central market selling a wide range of local fruit and vegetables and other produce in a beautiful glass domed building.

Chill out on the beaches or get wet and active

The Jersey coast is the major draw for many visitors from large family-friendly beaches full of great restaurants and cafes to hidden coves, low-tide islets and sea caves to explore. The south of the island is the destination for the wide expanse and golden sands of St Brelade's Bay, one of the most popular beaches with families, rockpoolers and water sports lovers. Backed by a promenade with shops and restaurants and the Fisherman's Chapel which sits at the western end of the beach, there is enough here for a full day out. Slightly further west, sheltered and uncommercialised Beauport Beach is a picturesque sunseeker's paradise backed by a nature reserve. Access is via a short climb down from the car park, or by kayak or boat. Another quiet bay on the south coast is Portelet Bay, accessible only by a steep climb, with high cliffs sheltering the beach. There are golden sands, rockpools and a tidal crossing or swim to the islet of **L'Île au Guerdain**, home to Janvrin's Tomb. This circular tower dates back to the 1720s when local sea captain Philippe Janvrin returned on his ship carrying the plague and died after being forbidden to land. Nearby, the clear, sheltered waters of secluded Belcroute Bay are good for snorkelling and swimming at high tide, and paddleboarding and sea kayaking on calmer days. On the southernmost point of Jersey, the three-kilometre stretch of white sand along Green Island Beach is one of the most popular on the island, with a full set of amenities making it a sunbather's paradise. The rockpools, gullies and crystalline clear waters here are also a major draw, offering a whole world of underwater life to explore. The grassy islet, **La Motte**, sits 250 metres off the beach and is also a wonderful place to explore at low tide. A Neolithic cairn, middens and cists have been found on the islet as well as other signs of early civilisation.

Jersey's north coast is rockier with steep cliffs down to hidden bays. Sweeping, pebbly Bouley Bay sits next to the highest cliffs on the island and is a great place for rockpooling. The deep harbour is good for swimming and very popular for scuba diving. Mad Mary's Beach Cafe is famous for its crab sandwiches. Bouley Bay is also the home of the Bouley Bay Hill Climb, a motorsports event which takes place in the winding roads around the harbour bringing competitors from all over the world. In the

north-west of the island, the sandy sheltered beach of Grève de Lecq is the most popular on Jersey's northern shore. With high cliffs to either side, it is sheltered from the wind most of the time. There is a large cave that runs all the way through the headland on the eastern side of the beach. At the other end are the foundations of an abandoned harbour wall. At the island's north-west tip, Plémont Bay is a beautiful, secluded cove with a great network of caves to explore with a sandy beach and scattering of large rocks. The beach is an excellent location for sunbathing with plenty of rockpools and excellent swimming or surfing in the right conditions. In the island's north-east corner, the small fishing port of Rozel is well known for its selection of superb eateries, including The Hungry Man for its legendary breakfast. However, when the tide drops it reveals a lovely beach of particularly soft, white sand.

On the east coast of Jersey, Grouville is an attractive, wide, sandy beach popular with swimmers as the shallow waters are warmed by the sun and the currents are not too strong, allowing for the wide variety of water sports on offer at the beach. Extremely low tides expose the rows of oyster beds – they're the largest oyster beds in the British Isles and you can take a guided low-tide walk out to the oyster fishery and mussel beds with a local expert. St Ouen's Bay runs the length of the west coast and is one of the best spots for surfing in the Channel Islands as it picks up plenty of Atlantic swell and is long enough never to get too crowded. It is also the home of Europe's oldest surf club. *www.jerseywalkadventures.co.uk*

Find the fairies on the Grantez Headland

Overlooking the long stretch of St Ouen's Bay, this peaceful area of open space consists of six National Trust Jersey sites and is criss-crossed by numerous paths. It is a haven for wildlife, including green lizards, kestrels and sparrowhawks. Explore the megalithic passage-grave known as Lé Cuex ès Faît'tchieaux, or 'place of the fairies', based on the old belief it was built by fairies or dwarfs. The grave dates back to 4000–3250 BC and is made from local granite. It was excavated in 1912, when

1

human and animal bones were found amongst piles of brightly coloured pebbles. The trust holds Sunset Concerts at Grantez annually on the first weekend of July and revellers can enjoy the harmonic sounds of a variety of bands performing in the beautiful natural amphitheatre whilst the sun sets into the sea.

Walk Jersey's coast path

This seventy-seven-kilometre circuit of the island starts in St Helier and is the best way to experience the variety of spectacular beaches and hidden coves that Jersey has to offer. The route passes many top attractions including the famous Mont Orgueil Castle and Seymour Tower, relics of the German occupation, as well as many natural wonders such as the moonscape of La Rocque and St Clement's Bay and the sea caves of Plémont. It passes through pretty fishing villages with plenty of excellent pit stops on the way. It can be completed over a number of days using St Helier as a base with its excellent bus service, or for those looking for a challenge it can be walked in a day at the annual charity event, the Island Walk.
www.islandwalk.je

Reg's Fairy Garden

This little garden in St Brelade is owned and maintained by Reg, who first created the garden in 1985, and is the perfect place to take children as their imagination can run wild. In the garden, miniature houses and toadstools are surrounded by hundreds of fairies. There are all sorts of dolls dressed up with angel wings or colourful butterfly wings amongst the grass and perched on tree stumps, playing out various fairy tales. Great for the kids.

Enjoy the view from Mont Orgueil Castle

Mont Orgueil Castle is an enchanting medieval stone castle perched above one of Jersey's prettiest villages, Gorey. It was built in the early thirteenth century after Normandy, tied to the English Crown from 1066, was seized by France, thus turning it from friend to foe. Mont Orgueil

Castle was England's first line of defence against French invasion until its position on a hill made it obsolete in the fifteenth century due to its vulnerability to cannon fire. It was replaced by Elizabeth Castle in the sixteenth century. Thereafter, it was converted into a prison during the English Civil War when it held men who had signed the death warrant of Charles I, including Thomas Waite and Henry Smith. It was occupied by German forces during World War II, with the invaders building concrete look-out posts into its masonry that can still be seen today. From its battlements, there are breathtaking views of the French coast and amongst the steep staircases, towers, and hidden passages there are plenty of gruesome tales and discoveries to make including the dance of death statue, the witches in hell in the dungeons, the wheel of urine in the turrets and the prayer nuts in one of the castle's rooms.

Visit one of the oldest buildings in the world

The tranquil and spiritual complex of La Hougue Bie, meaning 'mound of uncertain origin', housed in St Helier, contains one of the ten oldest buildings in the world. Older than the pyramids, it dates from the Neolithic period and is one of the largest and best-preserved passage graves in Western Europe. The site comprises a nineteen-metre passage chamber (or dolmen), the burial site of at least eight individuals, above which is found a twelve-metre-high earth mound crowned by two medieval chapels dating from the twelfth and sixteenth centuries. The burial chamber is aligned so as to allow sunlight to reach the back wall of its 'terminal cell' on the spring and autumn equinox. The on-site museum's collections of coin hoards, axes, swords, spears and even a rhinoceros skull and the adjacent command bunker built during the German occupation add further interest to this mind-blowing site.
www.jerseyheritage.org/places-to-visit/la-hougue-bie-museum

Grilled oysters in a World War II bunker

Faulkner Fisheries operate a quirky and excellent fish restaurant in a converted German bunker in L'Etacq at the northern tip of St Ouen's Bay. The famous summer barbecue is a unique experience with local fish and shellfish prepared from live stock within the bunker, and eaten al fresco while enjoying simply stunning views.

Discover occupation history

Jersey was occupied by the Germans from 1940 until it was liberated in 1945. The occupation was characterised by the introduction of numerous penal laws, severe food shortages, widespread fear and suspicion and the use of forced labour. The Channel Islands Military Museum is located in a German-built bunker near St Ouen's Bay and contains lots of military and civilian exhibits that tell this story. Similarly, the Jersey War Tunnels located in St Lawrence, were built by slave workers and civilian prisoners controlled by the paramilitary Organisation Todt. They stretch to over one kilometre in length and were large enough to hold tanks. Designed originally to help German infantry resist air raids and artillery bombardment, they were later equipped as a wartime emergency hospital and casualty clearing station, complete with 500 beds, air conditioning and heating systems and gas-proof doors. The tunnels

have now been turned into a substantial exhibition space, teaching visitors about the history of World War II, the occupation and the difficulties and dangers faced by local people.

Bioluminescence beach walk

This ecological wonder happens almost every night year-round on some of the island's beaches. At low tide on La Rocque Harbour, at the south-east tip of the island, small brown worms light up with a yellow-green colour when they are disturbed and the otherwise brown seabed become speckled with their tiny lights. Best seen when the moon isn't full, there are organised walks if you are unsure of tides or walking at night. *www.jerseywalkadventures.co.uk*

Walk in the enchanting Fern Valley

There are two main valleys in this area, with a stream running through the centre of each and a large meadow in the centre surrounded by a deciduous, fern-covered woodland. It makes for a wonderful and easy inland walk at any time of the year. There is an abundance of wild flowers which in the summer attract all sorts of insects including the day-flying Jersey tiger moth and the golden-ringed dragonfly. Red squirrels can be spotted here, along with great spotted woodpeckers and kestrels. *www.nationaltrust.je/project/fern-valley-2*

L'Islet / Elizabeth Castle

ACCESS TIDAL CROSSING; FERRY; NO DOGS
Constructed in the sixteenth century when the introduction of ships armed with cannon meant that the existing stronghold at Mont Orgueil was insufficient to defend Jersey, Elizabeth Castle makes for a fascinating trip from nearby St Helier. Today you can explore its hidden rooms, passageways, battlements and bunkers that date back to when Sir Walter Raleigh was Governor of Jersey. You can also discover its role in giving refuge to Charles II during the English Civil War and find the bunkers which were re-fortified to command the sea approaches to Jersey during the German occupation. The views from the high point of nine metres around the bay and the south coast of Jersey are incredible and you can walk to St Helier Hermitage and the end of the breakwater, which extends over two kilometres out to sea. Accessible via a low-tide causeway or ferry from St Helier.

Icho Tower and Seymour Tower

ACCESS TIDAL CROSSING
These islets are a great way to experience Jersey's impressive tides – the difference here between high and low tide is so vast that at low tide Jersey almost doubles in size, as the sea retreats up to 2.4 kilometres from the shore. Icho and Seymour towers, two coastal defence towers erected in the eighteenth century following France's attempt to invade Jersey, are located on islets (which have high points of under ten metres) off the south-east corner of Jersey. They can only be reached for a few hours every day, when the tide is low enough. Walking on the seabed is an eerie, unique experience. Seymour Tower is accessible almost every day, but Icho Tower can be reached only a few days per month as it's further away and spring tide conditions are needed to complete the journey safely. There are organised walks available to both towers.
www.jerseywalkadventures.co.uk

La Corbière

ACCESS TIDAL CROSSING

The world's first concrete lighthouse on La Corbière draws visitors as much for its striking architecture as for its dramatic location. The light stands at thirty-six metres above high water on a tidal island (with a high point of eighteen metres) surrounded by rocks on Jersey's south-west corner. It can be reached at low tide by a causeway, flanked by rockpools and small beaches. On the walk across peer into the rockpools and you might see the rare brittle star. A wonderfully atmospheric location, it is a fabulous place to watch Jersey sunsets and rolling Atlantic storms.

Écréhous

ACCESS BOAT TRIP; NO DOGS

This tiny archipelago, part of Jersey National Park, is one of the Channel Islands' best kept secrets. You feel like you are the middle of the ocean but you are only ten kilometres north-east of Jersey. The main islets in the group that remain above water at high tide are **Maîtr'Île**, which is the largest at 300 metres long, **La Marmotchiéthe** and **Lé Bliantch'Île**. The group has a high point of thirteen metres. At low tide the archipelago's landmass triples in size and the landscape becomes more like a moonscape with the rocky islets linked by sandbanks. There is plenty to do with rockpools to explore and shallow waters perfect for paddleboarding, swimming and fishing for seabass from the shore. Sea kayaking around the islets is also an incredible experience. Advanced paddlers can get to the islands under their own steam from Jersey, while the less experienced can rent kayaks taken out to the islands on larger boats. The islets have an interesting history starting in the thirteenth century when a small chapel existed with priory accommodation for a monk and servant who lit a navigation light every night. In the seventeenth century, smugglers used the island to transfer lead and gunpowder to St-Malo and thereafter came a succession of self-styled kings, fugitives and fishermen. Today none of the islets have permanent residents; there are a few fishermen's huts dotted around, some of which are used as holiday homes, and there is a customs house

1

on La Marmotchiéthe. The short boat trip that leaves from St Catherine's Breakwater in the north-east of Jersey is an exhilarating trip with plenty of wildlife to spot on the way, including Atlantic grey seals, basking sharks and bottlenose dolphins. There is a recommended code of conduct for visitors to allow the bird breeding season to go on without disruption.

Minquiers

ACCESS BOAT TRIP; NO DOGS
Roughly halfway between Jersey and Brittany and part of Jersey National Park, Minquiers is the southernmost part of the British Isles with just a cluster of fishermen's cabins clinging to the rocks. At low tide, the rock shelf around Minquiers has a larger surface area than Jersey itself, but at high tide only a few islets remain above water. **Maîtresse**, at fifty metres long and twenty metres wide and with a high point of fifteen metres, is the largest of these and supports a few stone cottages originally built by fishermen and quarrymen, a helicopter landing pad and a small hut that is home to

the most southerly toilet in the British Isles. It is a great place for swimming, paddleboarding or picnicking, especially from the large sandbank. Sea kayaking around the huge sandbars and rugged rocky outcrops is also an incredible experience and trips can be booked with local guides. The archipelago has had various claims over its sovereignty throughout history; perhaps the most bizarre came in 1998 when a small group of French citizens 'invaded' on behalf of the 'King of Patagonia' in 'retaliation' for the British occupation of the Falkland Islands. In 2019, history repeated itself as more people attempted to reclaim the island in the name of the king, but this time they also reclaimed the toilet, painting the door of the southerly shack blue, white and green. The invaders also placed a new plaque on the toilet, declaring it the most 'northerly building in the Kingdom of Patagonia'. Today there are no permanent inhabitants, though it gets plenty of passing yachtsmen, fishermen and day trippers in the summer. Boat trips leave from St Catherine's Breakwater in the north-east of Jersey. Dolphins are often spotted on the journey to the islands.

This Crown Dependency with its dramatic coastline, mountains and eighteen national glens offers a fantastic mix of outdoor pursuits, stunning beaches and unique natural beauty. With a diverse variety of family attractions, an eclectic mix of sporting and cultural events and delicious local food there is plenty here for everyone, including a handful of smaller islands to explore for the serious island bagger.

ISLE OF MAN

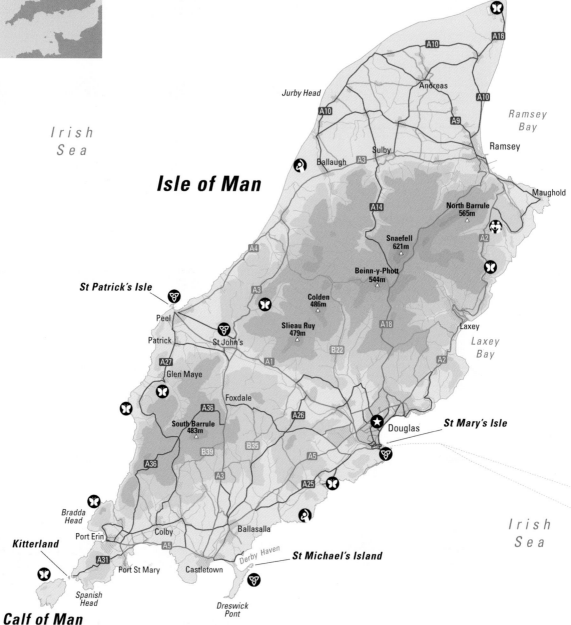

Point of Ayre

Ramsey Bay

A16

A10

A10

Andreas

Jurby Head

A10

A9

Ramsey

Sulby

Maughold

Ballaugh

A3

Isle of Man

A14

North Barrule
565m

Snaefell
621m

A2

Beinn-y-Phott
544m

*I r i s h
S e a*

St Patrick's Isle

A4

Colden
486m

Peel

A3

Slieau Ruy
479m

A18

Laxey

Patrick

St John's

*Laxey
Bay*

A27

Glen Maye

A1

B22

A2

Foxdale

A36

A26

South Barrule
483m

★ Douglas

St Mary's Isle

B39

B35

A5

A36

A3

A25

*I r i s h
S e a*

*Bradda
Head*

Port Erin

Colby

Ballasalla

Kitterland

A31

Port St Mary

Castletown

Derby Haven

St Michael's Island

*Spanish
Head*

*Dreswick
Pont*

Calf of Man

N

0   10km

Isle of Man

ACCESS FERRY; PLANE

Situated in the Irish Sea, midway between England, Northern Ireland and Scotland, the Isle of Man benefits from a mild climate and boasts more than 160 kilometres of beautiful coastline, with sweeping sandy beaches and steep, rugged cliffs. Inland, most of the island is undulating, with a mix of moorland, woodland and heath, rolling uplands and narrow glens with spectacular waterfalls. Snaefell, the high point of the island, reaches 621 metres. As a Crown Dependency it has its own parliament, Tynwald, which is the oldest continuous parliament in the world. It has many unique features including the Manx language, Manx cats (a rare breed of tailless cat that originated on the island) and its own currency called the Manx pound (Sterling is also accepted). There is plenty on offer to tourists, outdoor enthusiasts and nature lovers and many fascinating points of interest, including its capital, Douglas. For many it is known as the motorcycle capital of the world because of its famous TT motorcycle race. Douglas is easily accessible by ferry from Liverpool, Heysham, Dublin and Belfast; there are great air links with many major UK airports.
www.steam-packet.com

Walk a complete nation

The Raad ny Foillan, Manx for 'The Way of the Gull', is a 157-kilometre coastal path around the whole island. Starting in Douglas, the southern section runs along clifftop paths lined with heather and dwarf gorse, past the tidal races of Calf Sound, which separates the Calf of Man from the main island. North of Port Erin the route heads along the high cliffs, including The Stacks, and climbs three summits, the highest of which, at 437 metres, is Cronk ny Arrey Laa. The route continues through Peel with its castle, moves slightly inland to follow an old railway track, then returns to the coast again to reach the shingle beaches and lighthouse at Point of Ayre in the north. From here the trail heads

south along the more populated east coast, exploring some beautiful glens and coastal villages including Laxey, before reaching the promenades of Douglas. In addition to the Raad ny Foillan, there are two further long-distance paths across the hills and moors of the island's interior: the Millennium Way stretches for thirty-six kilometres from Ramsey to Castletown while the Herring Road runs for twenty-four kilometres from Peel to Castletown.

Walk all the island's parishes

The Parish Walk is a 137-kilometre competitive walk that challenges participants to walk around all seventeen of the Isle of Man's parishes in just twenty-four hours, ending on Douglas Promenade. It's not for the faint-hearted and many don't make it round the full course, stopping at one of the many checkpoints along the way. It's a unique sporting event to add to your bucket list.
www.parishwalk.com

Spectacular glens and waterfalls

There are eighteen mountain and coastal glens spread around the island. These havens of natural beauty and tranquillity are characterised by tumbling waterfalls, deep river pools and lush vegetation. Glen Maye, noted for its picturesque waterfall and fern-filled woodland, is one of the most beautiful. Located in the village of the same name about five kilometres south of Peel, it can also be reached via the Raad ny Foillan. One of the island's most popular natural wonders is Spooyt Vane, a waterfall at the end of a gently babbling stream through Glen Mooar. Surrounded by ferns, moss and tall, old trees creating a leafy canopy above with ruins of an ancient chapel to explore, it can be found just south of Kirk Michael. Glen Helen, one of the island's best-known glens, is on the western side of the Island, north of Ballacraine on the famous TT Course. It is a long, wooded valley with two waterfalls, the most dramatic is the Rhenass Waterfall, surrounded by sequoia, spruce, fir, oak, sycamore and beech trees. There are plenty of paths and footbridges around the glen, making it an easy one to explore. One of the largest waterfalls on the island, Dhoon Glen's 'Big Girl', is forty metres high and set over two levels in a secluded cove at the end of a steep valley. It is popular for its amazing rugged beauty, which also makes it one of the tougher glens to explore as some of the paths are rough or involve steep climbs. There is only one glen in the mountainous centre of the island, Tholt-e-Will Glen, nestled between Snaefell and Sulby Reservoir; its steep-sided valley follows the meanders of a mountain stream. On the east coast, Ballaglass Glen, just to the north of Laxey, is a good one for children. A sculpture depicting a wise old man, who is known as the Wizard of Mann, as well as the miniature fairy house and access to the glen on the Manx Electric Railway, make for a fun visit. In the same vein, just north of Douglas and the first stop on the Manx Electric Railway, Groudle Glen is charming and the miniature Groudle Glen Railway is fun to ride. For something completely different, The Chasms are a striking series of huge fissures cut deep into the cliffs along the island's south-east coast near the village of Cregneash and can be reached via the Raad ny Foillan from near Port St Mary. For the adventurous, local companies offer gorge scrambling to get more of an adrenaline fix from these natural wonders.

www.gov.im/categories/leisure-and-entertainment/walking/national-glens

Ayres National Nature Reserve

This vast expanse of shingle beach and sand dunes on the north-west coast from Smeale Beach to the Point of Ayre Lighthouse, the most northerly point of the Isle of Man, is a wonderful place to walk and watch gannets, seals and porpoises. There's a small visitor centre with a car park in the middle of the reserve with three marked nature trails that wind through the marram dunes and on to the heath with its extensive lichen flora to discover.

www.mwt.im/nature-reserves/ayres-visitor-centre-and-nature-trail

Stand astride two tectonic plates

The Niarbyl Fault is an exposed section of the Iapetus Suture, a fault caused by the collision of two ancient tectonic plates – Avalonia, on which present-day England is located, and Laurentia, which contains North America and parts of Scotland – that extends across the Irish Sea. The fault is visible close to the shoreline downhill from the Niarbyl Cafe and Visitor Centre in Niarbyl; you can place each foot on different rocks derived from two separate continents. The area also offers a hidden bay and dramatic coastal path with views across to the Mountains of Mourne in Ireland on a clear day and along the Manx coastline to the Calf of Man. One of the fishermen's cottages here was used as Ned Devine's cottage in the 1998 film *Waking Ned*.

Discover Douglas

The pretty capital of this tiny island nation sits on the shore of a beautiful bay into which the River Douglas flows. It is an easy town to walk around, including a three-kilometre promenade with excellent views of the harbour, bay and the Tower of Refuge on its tiny island. Attractive buildings line the streets, such as the Legislative Building, home of the Manx parliament, and the Villa Marina and Gardens, which hosts regular outdoor concerts. The Royal Hall and the excellent Gaiety Theatre are great venues for operas, shows and music. Some of the very best views on the Isle of Man can be enjoyed from Douglas Head, a rocky outcrop overlooking Douglas Harbour and accessible through the ornate gate of historic Marine Drive. Here you'll also find the famous Great Union Camera Obscura, which uses natural light and a series of mirrors to project images of the surrounding area on to the darkened building's walls to stunning effect. The Douglas Head Lighthouse, built in 1857, is a significant landmark on this headland and easily accessible by a public footpath. Other notable landmarks include the William Hillary Statue, a tribute to the founder of the RNLI and a long-time resident of the island. There is a wide range of other

1 **Isle of Man,** Fenella Beach © Peter Mason   2 **Isle of Man,** Peel Harbour © Peter Mason
3 **Isle of Man,** Manx queenies   4 **Isle of Man,** Bradda Head from Port Erin © Peter Mason

tourist attractions from horse-drawn trams and Victorian steam train journeys between Douglas and Port Erin, to great pubs, restaurants and cafes to sample the local food.

Port Erin

The picturesque resort town of Port Erin lies at the head of a deep bay in the shadow of 116-metre-tall Bradda Head. It's the terminus of the Isle of Man Railway from Douglas. The coast here is a great place to walk with some of the island's wildest scenery; watching the spectacular sunsets over Port Erin Bay make it a popular destination with locals and visitors alike. The town has a sandy beach within the harbour, lovely parks and gardens and plenty of cafes and restaurants. Look out for the commemorative plaque to Fletcher Christian, who instigated the famous mutiny on the *Bounty*. To the north of the bay, there are walks from Bradda Glen along the coast path to Milner's Tower, atop of Bradda Head, for incredible panoramic views across to the Calf of Man.

Snaefell and the mountain railway

Snaefell is the island's highest mountain at 621 metres above sea level. On a clear day from its summit you can see the so-called 'Seven Kingdoms of Man' – the Isle of Man, England, Ireland, Scotland, Wales, Heaven and Manannán (the sea). Using the clear footpath from the A18 Snaefell Mountain Road, the summit can be reached in around forty-five minutes. The seasonal Snaefell Mountain Railway offers an easier route. This Victorian-era electric train departs from Laxey and reaches the summit in about thirty minutes. The Snaefell Summit Restaurant offers stunning views at the top.
www.manxelectricrailway.co.uk/snaefell

Watch the world's best motorbike race

The Isle of Man TT Races are the reason this island is famous worldwide. The annual motorcycle festival is often called one of the most dangerous racing events in the world, with over 250 rider fatalities since the early twentieth century. It brings many spectators to the island for two weeks in May and June every year along with funfairs, beer tents and an electric atmosphere. The race is run on a time-trial format on public roads and consists of one week of practice sessions followed by one week of racing. It has been a tradition for spectators to tour the sixty-one-kilometre TT Course which climbs to a height of over

400 metres and traverses over 200 bends on motorcycles during 'Mad Sunday', an informal and unofficial sanctioned event held on the Sunday between practice week and race week. The current lap record has an average speed of 217.989 kilometres per hour.
www.iomtt.com

World Tin Bath Championships

Every July in the World Tin Bath Championships, over 100 competitors race around a 400-metre course in Castletown's Middle Harbour in 'strictly regulated' and sometimes less than seaworthy old tin baths. Competitors come from as far away as New Zealand, Australia, South Africa and the USA to compete, often in fancy dress ranging from pirates, captains, ducks, gorillas and Vikings to nuns and American presidents. Organised by the Castletown Real Ale Drinkers Society, the race was started in 1971 and all the money raised by the event goes to local charities. There are plenty of activities for spectators to have a good time too.
www.facebook.com/ WorldTinBathsChampionships

Crab sandwiches, ice cream and beaches of Peel

Peel's golden and gently sloping sandy beach is set in a beautiful bay, bounded by Peel Castle and Peel Harbour on one side and red sandstone cliffs on the other. This north-west-facing beach has some spectacular sunsets over Ireland's Mountains of Mourne. The hidden gem of the beautiful, pebbly Fenella Beach is just west of the road across to Peel Castle. Going to Peel isn't just about beaches though, and enjoying a crab sandwich or ice cream here epitomises summer on the Isle of Man for many locals. Peel is the island's main fishing port, so the crab here doesn't get much fresher. The ice cream from Davison's Ice Cream Parlour includes all the usual delicious flavours along with the weird and wonderful. From iron brew and smarty pants to jellybean and blackcurrant and liquorice, they have thought of everything and are always experimenting with new flavours.

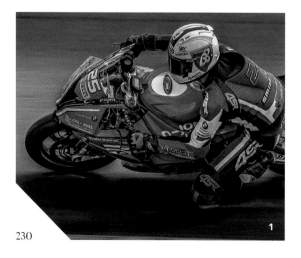

Immerse yourself in the stars

Home to twenty-six UK Dark Sky Discovery Sites, the spectacularly starry skies of the Isle of Man are some of the darkest in Europe. One of the best places to stargaze is the small pebble beach at Port Soderick, south-west of Douglas. Another good spot is The Ayres at the northern tip of the island where, under the right conditions, it is also possible to see the northern lights. If the weather isn't great, an alternative is the planetarium in The Dome, Douglas. Now with state-of-the-art immersive digital media technology, it was originally launched as a secret cinema and is located in the Nunnery Estate's stables block.

Spot basking sharks and dolphins

The Isle of Man is one of the best places in the British Isles to see basking sharks. From May until August, these incredible marine animals can be seen feeding within one kilometre of the south and south-west coasts and can be spotted from many points on the island's coast path. Also, keep an eye out for Risso's dolphins with their distinctive blunt heads and white skin.
www.manxbaskingsharkwatch.org
https://uk.whales.org

Debate in the world's oldest continuously running parliament

The Isle of Man has its own independent parliament; its members are elected to the House of Keys instead of the UK's House of Commons. Their former meeting place, at Tynwald Hill, is on a hill thought to be made with soil from all of the Island's seventeen ancient parishes. At the Old House of Keys in Castletown visitors can participate in a debate on the hot topics of the day. On Tynwald Day, the national day of the Isle of Man which falls sometime in early July, you can watch the formal ceremony on Tynwald Hill. The sitting includes the reading of the island's new laws in both English and Manx and proceedings also include the chance for protesters to present petitions to the Lieutenant Governor. Based on Norse traditions, the event has been marked on the island for over 1,000 years.
www.manxnationalheritage.im/our-sites/old-house-of-keys

Sample the national dish

In 2018, Manx queenies were crowned as the Isle of Man's new national dish following a public vote. The juicy, delicious queen scallop was a clear leader. In second place was chips, Manx cheese and gravy; then Manx kippers. Previously the traditional national dish was *priddhas an' herrin* – a meal of

boiled potatoes and steamed herring. There is plenty of other great local food and drink to try including Isle of Man Creamery cheese and butter, Ramsey Bakery bread and the local Bushey's ales – probably best supped in the Rover's Return, an authentic Manx boozer in Douglas.

St Michael's Island

ACCESS ROAD CAUSEWAY

St Michael's Island, or Fort Island, is worth the trip for its remote beauty and wildlife and to see one of the best viewpoints in the Isle of Man; the views extend across the bay to Derbyhaven, along the coastline to Santon Head and west across the island to Bradda Head. The ruins of two ancient buildings here are also fascinating to observe. The older building is a stone-built, Norse-Celtic chapel, dedicated to St Michael and dating from around the twelfth century. It is now roofless and consists of just four walls and a bell turret. The other building is a fort that dates from 1645 and was built during the English Civil War to defend Derbyhaven, which was then a major port, from the forces of the Parliamentarians. Towards the end of

the eighteenth century the fort served as a lighthouse. The island is the site of two great battles in 1250 and 1275, when England, Scotland and the Manx were fighting for control of the island. The Manx won the first battle, but they lost control to Scotland in the second. Today the island, which has a high point of less than five metres, is a sanctuary for birds and other wildlife, including seals. The buildings are closed to the public, although there are a number of walks which allow visitors to explore the surroundings. The island lies to the east of Derby Haven Bay and is approached by road via Langness and accessed by an extremely narrow road along a causeway.

St Mary's Isle

ACCESS TIDAL CROSSING; KAYAK

At high tide you'll see the fortress-like building known as the Tower of Refuge rising directly out of the sea across Douglas Bay; at low tide you'll also see the long, menacing reef of rock, known as St Mary's Isle, or Conister Rock, on which this structure is built. The tower had no military or defensive function and was built to indicate the presence of the dangerous reef below and to provide shelter to the crews of the many vessels that were wrecked nearby.

1

The best-known wreck was that of the *St George* in 1830 when the Douglas lifeboat rescued all on board. William Hillary, who lived in Douglas and was the founder of the RNLI, was a member of the lifeboat crew that rescued the crew of the *St George*. Afterwards, he had the idea of building a refuge on Conister Rock. Today the tower is owned by the RNLI, and proudly flies their flag. It is possible to walk to the island, which has a high point of less than five metres, from Douglas on low spring tides.

St Patrick's Isle

ACCESS ROAD BRIDGE

Outside Peel Harbour and linked to the mainland by a narrow causeway, the rocky St Patrick's Isle, which has a high point of twenty-four metres, is home to Peel Castle. The island has sheltered Christian missionaries, Viking warriors and kings, while the castle has been a royal residence, centre of government and military stronghold. Constructed originally by the Vikings in the eleventh century, the castle is an impressive feature and its extensive grounds and ancient ruins are fascinating to explore. Listen out for 'Moddey Dhoo', a black dog with fire-red eyes that is said to roam the halls, and for the old tales of the site being a possible location of the Arthurian Avalon. Seals and basking sharks are often spotted along the coast nearby.
www.manxnationalheritage.im/our-sites/peel-castle

Calf of Man

ACCESS BOAT TRIP; NO DOGS

Located off the south-west tip of the Isle of Man, the Calf of Man is an island famed for its rugged wild beauty and birdlife. Owned by Manx National Heritage and managed by the Manx Wildlife Trust, the island has been a bird observatory since 1959 with wardens resident from spring to late autumn. Around thirty-three species of bird breed here annually and it is located on one of western Britain's major migration routes. Breeding seabirds include Manx shearwater, kittiwake, razorbill and shag. Other species normally observed on the island include peregrine falcon, hen harrier, chough and raven. The island has a high point of 128 metres. The Calf has an interesting history and evidence of the once thriving community includes the two lighthouses built in 1818, a recently decommissioned modern lighthouse building built in 1968, a mill and a smithy. Signs of earlier habitation of the island range from prehistoric worked flints and early Christian graves, through to defences dating from 1651 until 1713, such as the gun emplacement on the Burroo. The bird observatory has space for up to eight visitors in basic self-catering accommodation which can be booked through Manx National Heritage. Boat trips to the island leave from Port St Mary and Port Erin.
www.mwt.im

Kitterland

ACCESS NOT PERMITTED; VIEW FROM MAINLAND PATH

Sitting between the Isle of Man and the Calf of Man in Calf Sound, this Manx National Heritage-owned islet is full of bird and marine life. There are several stories linking the island with Celtic mythology, and with the Vikings, including the death of the Norwegian Baron Kitter, but today it is best known as a hotspot for seal spotting on the wildlife watching boat trips from Port Erin.

The Islands: top tens

Top 10 islands for natural features
1. Flory Island and Zacry's Islands *p27*
2. Bedruthan Steps *p28*
3. Old Harry Rocks *p53*
4. Spurn Head *p118*
5. Black Nab and Saltwick Nab *p120*
6. Ynys Lochtyn *p158*
7. Pen Pyrod / Worms Head *p176*
8. Alney Island *p186*
9. Sark *p202*
10. Isle of Man *p227*

Top 10 islands for beaches
1. St Martin's *p18*
2. Bedruthan Steps *p28*
3. Asparagus Island *p32*
4. Isle of Wight *p44*
5. Scolt Head Island *p111*
6. Black Nab and Saltwick Nab *p120*
7. Lindisfarne / Holy Island *p124*
8. Ynys Môn / Anglesey *p140*
9. Jersey *p215*
10. Isle of Man *p227*

Top 10 tidal crossings
1. Bryher to Tresco *p17*
2. Bedruthan Steps *p28*
3. Scolt Head Island *p110*
4. Lindisfarne / Holy Island *p124*
5. Piel Island *p130*
6. Hilbre Island *p130*
7. Ynys Llanddwyn / Llanddwyn Island *p144*
8. Pen Pyrod / Worms Head *p176*
9. Lihou *p201*
10. Seymour Tower *p219*

Top 10 islands for stargazing
1. St Martin's *p18*
2. Bedruthan Steps *p28*
3. Lundy *p37*
4. Isle of Wight *p49*
5. Ynys Môn / Anglesey *p137*
6. Ynys Enlli / Bardsey Island *p154*
7. Ynys Sgomer / Skomer Island *p167*
8. Ynys Sgogwm / Skokholm Island *p169*
9. Sark *p204*
10. Isle of Man *p231*

Top 10 islands for walking
1. St Mary's *p5*
2. Isle of Wight *p44*
3. Isle of Dogs *p83*
4. Ynys Môn / Anglesey *p137*
5. Ynys Gybi / Holy Island *p150*
6. Guernsey *p198*
7. Sark *p203*
8. Alderney *p207*
9. Jersey *p217*
10. Isle of Man *p227*

Top 10 walks around a whole island
1. Bryher *p14*
2. Lundy *p39*
3. Isle of Dogs *p83*
4. Mersea Island *p103*
5. Ynys Môn / Anglesey *p137*
6. Ynys Dewi / Ramsey Island *p166*
7. Sark *p203*
8. Herm *p206*
9. Alderney *p207*
10. Isle of Man *p227*

Top 10 islands for cycling
1. Isle of Wight *p45*
2. Portsea Island *p56*
3. Hayling Island *p59*
4. Foulness Island *p95*
5. Spurn Head *p118*
6. Ynys Môn / Anglesey *p137*
7. Ynys Gybi / Holy Island *p149*
8. Guernsey *p200*
9. Jersey *p213*
10. Isle of Man *p227*

Top 10 islands for paddleboarding
1. Tresco *p16*
2. St Clement's Isle *p30*
3. Burgh Island *p35*
4. Hayling Island *p58*
5. Oliver's Eyot *p87*
6. Packing Shed Island *p104*
7. Spike Island *p186*
8. Guernsey *p195*
9. Herm *p205*
10. Jersey *p213*

Top 10 islands for wild swimming
1. St Mary's *p7*
2. St Clement's Isle *p30*
3. Asparagus Island *p32*
4. Scolt Head Island *p110*
5. Ynys Llanddwyn / Llanddwyn Island *p146*
6. Ynys Gifftan *p158*
7. Gateholm Island *p170*
8. Lihou *p201*
9. Sark *p204*
10. Minquiers *p221*

Top 10 islands for birdwatching

1. Annet *p10*
2. Lundy *p37*
3. Brownsea Island *p50*
4. Isle of Sheppey *p69*
5. Havergate Island *p110*
6. Spurn Head *p118*
7. Farne Islands *p121*
8. Ynys Môn / Anglesey *p142*
9. Ynys Dewi / Ramsey Island *p166*
10. Ynys Sgomer / Skomer Island *p168*

Top 10 islands for wildlife boat trips

1. Western Rocks *p10*
2. Godrevy Island *p27*
3. Havergate Island *p110*
4. Coquet Island *p121*
5. Farne Islands *p121*
6. Ynysoedd y Moelrhoniaid / The Skerries *p149*
7. Ynys Aberteifi / Cardigan Island *p158*
8. Ynys Gwales / Grassholm Island *p168*
9. Écréhous *p220*
10. Calf of Man *p233*

Top 10 islands for families

1. St Martin's *p18*
2. Isle of Wight *p44*
3. Brownsea Island *p50*
4. Hayling Island *p58*
5. Isle of Dogs *p83*
6. Mersea Island *p102*
7. Scolt Head Island *p110*
8. Ynys Môn / Anglesey *p137*
9. Herm *p205*
10. Isle of Man *p227*

Top 10 islands for campsites

1. St Agnes *p11*
2. Looe Island *p32*
3. Lundy *p37*
4. Brownsea Island *p50*
5. Piel Island *p130*
6. Ynys Môn / Anglesey *p137*
7. Ynys Gybi / Holy Island *p149*
8. Sark *p202*
9. Herm *p206*
10. Alderney *p210*

Top 10 islands for local food and cafes

1. St Martin's *p18*
2. Isle of Wight *p44*
3. Hayling Island *p58*
4. Mersea Island *p102*
5. Ynys Môn / Anglesey *p137*
6. Ynys Enlli / Bardsey Island *p154*
7. Sark *p202*
8. Alderney *p207*
9. Jersey *p213*
10. Isle of Man *p227*

Top 10 islands for pubs

1. St Agnes *p12*
2. St Martin's *p19*
3. Lundy *p38*
4. Portsea Island *p55*
5. Isle of Dogs *p84*
6. Walney Island *p126*
7. Piel Island *p130*
8. Ynys Echni / Flat Holm *p184*
9. Spike Island *p186*
10. Alderney *p207*

Top 10 islands for wellness and retreat

1. St Mary's *p5*
2. Tresco *p16*
3. St Michael's Mount *p30*
4. Osea Island *p101*
5. Lindisfarne / Holy Island *p123*
6. Ynys Llanddwyn / Llanddwyn Island *p144*
7. Ynys Enlli / Bardsey Island *p154*
8. Ynys Gybi / Holy Island *p149*
9. Ynys Bŷr / Caldey Island *p171*
10. Ynys Echni / Flat Holm *p185*

Top 10 islands for ancient history

1. St Mary's *p5*
2. St Michael's Mount *p30*
3. Lindisfarne / Holy Island *p123*
4. Ynys Môn / Anglesey *p137*
5. Ynys Llanddwyn / Llanddwyn Island *p144*
6. Ynys Gybi / Holy Island *p149*
7. Ynys Enlli / Bardsey Island *p154*
8. Guernsey *p195*
9. Jersey *p213*
10. Isle of Man *p227*

Top 10 islands for modern history

1. Drake's Island *p34*
2. Portsea Island *p55*
3. Isle of Sheppey *p69*
4. Isle of Dogs *p83*
5. Eel Pie Island *p88*
6. Foulness Island *p95*
7. Cei Ballast *p157*
8. Spike Island *p186*
9. Steep Holm *p188*
10. Guernsey *p195*

Index